Chiasmus and Culture

Studies in Rhetoric and Culture

Edited by **Ivo Strecker,** Johannes Gutenberg University Mainz and Addis Ababa University, **Stephen Tyler,** Rice University, and **Robert Hariman,** Northwestern University.

Our minds are filled with images and ideas, but these remain unstable and incomplete as long as we do not manage to persuade both ourselves and others of their meanings. It is this inward and outward rhetoric which allows us to give some kind of shape and structure to our understanding of the world and which becomes central to the formation of individual and collective consciousness. This series is dedicated to the study of the interaction of rhetoric and culture, and focuses on the concrete practices of discourse in which and through which the diverse and often also fantastic patterns of culture – including our own – are created, maintained and contested.

CHIASMUS AND CULTURE

∎ ∎ ∎

Edited by
BORIS WISEMAN AND ANTHONY PAUL

berghahn
NEW YORK · OXFORD
www.berghahnbooks.com

First published in 2014 by
Berghahn Books
www.berghahnbooks.com

©2014 Boris Wiseman and Anthony Paul

Library of Congress Cataloging-in-Publication Data

Chiasmus and Culture / edited by Boris Wiseman and Anthony Paul.
    pages cm. -- (Studies in Rhetoric and Culture; 6)
    ISBN 978-0-85745-960-2 (hardback) -- ISBN 978-0-85745-961-9 (ebook)
    1. Rhetoric--Social aspects. 2. Chiasmus. 3. Interpersonal relations and culture. I.
Wiseman, Boris, editor of compilation. II. Paul, Anthony, 1941, editor of compilation.
    P301.5.S63C48 2014
    808--dc23

                                                                    2013022494

British Library Cataloguing in Publication Data

A catalogue record for this book is available from the British Library

Printed on acid-free paper.

ISBN: 978-0-85745-960-2 hardback
ISBN: 978-0-85745-961-9 ebook

Contents

■ ■ ■ ■ ■ ■ ■

Part III ■ Sensuous Experience Mediated by Chiasmus

Part IV ■ Chiastic Structures in Ritual and Mytho-Poetic Texts

Figures

■ ■ ■ ■ ■ ■

CHIASMUS IN THE DRAMA OF LIFE

Anthony Paul and Boris Wiseman

■ ■ ■ ■ ■ ■ ■

The essays in this volume are concerned with chiastic inversion, and its place in social interactions, cultural creation and, more generally, human thought and experience. They explore from a variety of angles what the unsettling logic of chiasmus has to tell us about the world, human relations, cultural patterns, psychology, and artistic and poetic creation. They treat chiasmus not only as a figure of speech, but as a generative principle, an aesthetic idea, a method of composition, a tool of ideological manipulation, a matrix of social interaction, a philosophical problem, a metaphor, an elemental image or sign. At many points they engage in dialogue with one another as well as with key thinkers and authors who have written about or under the inspiration of chiastic logic.

The claims we are making for chiasmus may seem surprising in the light of the somewhat shadowy and far from distinguished status of this figure within traditional rhetoric. As Anthony Paul remarks in his essay in this volume, the history of chiasmus is easily told, since it was only in the late nineteenth century that some scholars began to think it could be anything more than a local decorative literary effect. Even today, anyone who has heard of chiasmus is likely to think of it as no more than a piece of rhetorical playfulness, a lively figure, at times challenging, useful for supplying a memorable sententious note or for performing a terpsichorean pirouette of syntax and thought.

It is the aspect most emphasized in handbooks of style and rhetoric. Surveying the figures of rhetoric in *The Arte of English Poesie* (1589), George Puttenham says of chiasmus (without naming it): 'Ye haue a figure which takes a couple of words to play with in a verse, and by making them to chaunge and shift one into others place they do very pretily exchange and shift the sence.' Chiastic patterning was indeed frequently and at times almost obsessively employed in this spirit in the courtly and ornamental poetry and prose of the English Elizabethan period, so it is entirely natural that Puttenham should have thus emphasized the playful and ornamental possibilities of the figure. But precisely four hundred years after the publication of his book, Katie Wales (*A Dictionary of Stylistics* 1989) defines chiasmus in essentially similar terms:

> From Gk meaning 'cross-wise', **chiasmus** is a rhetorical term to describe a construction involving the repetition of words or elements in reverse order (ab : ba); also known as **antimetabole**. It is often used for witty or aphoristic effect: so Michelangelo is reputed to have said: *Trifles make perfection, and perfection is no trifle.* Syntactic inversion is common in the couplets of eighteenth-century [poets] *Renown'd / for conquest, and in council / skilled* (Addison: *The Campaign*).

The persistently restricted perception of chiasmus has meant that such attention the figure has received within literary and rhetorical studies has been narrowly focused, failing, one might say, to participate in the spirit of chiastic inversion and allow the questioner to be questioned by his own object of attention.

However, one area in which chiasmus has demanded and received a good deal of attention is that of biblical studies. The large-scale chiastic or concentric structuring of biblical and other ancient and pre-modern texts (Homer, Beowulf) is well known (these texts make much use of sequences of the type: a,b,c,d,e → e,d,c,b,a usually termed 'extended chiasmus'). Here, chiasmus is indeed linked to broader cultural, historical and anthropological considerations. In particular, the literature in this area raises the key question of the uses of chiasmus as a mnemonic device. The challenge here is to understand the place of chiasmus in forms of recollection that are different to our own, in the constitution of another kind of memory, principally an oral memory, which has its own supports and modes of functioning. Edwina Palmer has identified chiastic features in a Japanese poem-song dating from around AD 714, belonging to the Fudoki genre of eulogistic provincial descriptions – features that she suggests are a vestige of Japan's pre-literate oral heritage. Through a sophisticated form of punning based on symbolic substitution and chiastic reversal (Palmer 2000: 81) the place name of the Womë-no moor is transformed into a cryptic reference to a song for omi purification rites. Chiasmus, here, has a quite different status than in the Western rhetorical tradition evoked above. It is an integral feature of an ancient poetics, albeit one unfamiliar to the vast majority of Western readers. One is reminded here of Saussure's hypothesis (which he was never able to prove) that Saturnian poetry, one of the oldest forms of Latin verse, concealed anagrams which designated keywords for the poet – that of a central theme, of an important object, or the name of a god, for example.

John A. Bengel, arguably the founder of the study of chiasmus in exegesis, had already noted how chiasmus, beyond its ornamental value, shaped reading practices and oriented interpretation. In the fifth volume of his *Gnomon Novi Testamenti*, or *Exegetical Annotations on the New Testament* (1742) (p. 399), Bengel wrote: 'Often there is the greatest use in the employment of this figure, and it is never without some use, viz, in perceiving the ornament, in observing the force of the language; in understanding the true and full sense; in making clear the sound exegesis; and in demonstrating the true and neat analysis of the sacred text.' Recently, biblical scholars have gone further along the path indicated by Bengel. One other book-length work on the topic is Ian Thomson's *Chiasmus in the Pauline Letters* (1995). One of Thomson's thought-provoking arguments is that Paul's audience would have been more aware of chiastic patterns in the *Letters* because of the ancient education system they received, which was steeped in classical rhetoric. As a result, in biblical times, reading from left to write was not a naturally enshrined phenomenon. The Greek texts that schoolchildren studied sometimes switched from left to right to the opposite in a matter of lines. Children were often taught to recite the alphabet from alpha to omega and omega to alpha. These same children may well have been brought up by parents who used scripts that were read in different directions, as was the case with the Greek-speaking Hebrews or the Hebrew- or Aramaic-speaking Greeks, Thomson points out. The readers – or listeners – for whom Paul wrote his letters, seem to have had a more ambilateral view of language and perhaps by extension of the world in general (mirror writing, apparently, was quite common). They pose, in this respect, an anthropological question: to what extent and in what ways do the institutions, technologies and practices of a given culture determine what one might think of as its 'style' – for there do seem to be cultures that are more chiastically minded than others (the Brazilian Caduveo, for example), just as there are more chiastically minded authors or thinkers.

The power of chiasmus as an instrument to shape and embody meaning, acting as a dialectical tool, is exemplified by Karl Marx, who in *Die Deutsche Ideologie* (The German Ideology) refigures the relations between socio-economic infrastructures and ideology in terms that are essentially chiastic. As he puts it:

> Consciousness can never be anything else than conscious existence, and the existence of men is their actual life-process. If in all ideology men and

their circumstances appear upside-down as in a *camera obscura*, this phenomenon arises just as much from their historical life-process as the inversion of objects on the retina does from their physical life-process. In direct contrast to German philosophy which descends from heaven to earth, here we ascend from earth to heaven.

The principle of chiastic inversion applies not only to the relations between 'the phantoms formed in the human brain' (ideology) and the 'material life-process' of which these phantoms are sublimates, but to Marx's own method of approach: 'we do not set out from what men say, imagine, conceive, nor from men as narrated, thought of, imagined, conceived, in order to arrive at men in the flesh. We set out from real, active men, and on the basis of their real life-process we demonstrate the development of the ideological reflexes and echoes of this life-process.' Philosopher Sarah Kofman in her classic study *Camera Obscura: Of Ideology* (1998) has shown to what extent the texts of Freud and Nietzsche, like those of Marx, have also displaced traditional oppositions by means of mechanisms of inversion which are given form by the metaphor of the camera obscura common to all three. One might have cited other thinkers who proceed similarly. Lévi-Strauss, for example, uses an optical model to try to understand what happens at the limits of narrative transformations. In the final section of his famous essay 'La geste d'Asdiwal' he argues that as myths cross thresholds between linguistic and social groups, their structural features are initially weakened. However, as this weakening reaches a certain threshold, the same myths may regain precision and coherence by inverting.[1] Chiastic inversion is mobilized here to understand the limits of communication. The model clearly has applications beyond mythical narratives.

There is doubtless a chiastic dimension to Marcel Mauss's refiguring of social relations through gift theory, although it is not expressed through an optical analogy. He roots the obligation to reciprocate in a certain assimilation of the gift to the giver and the giver to the gift (for example in his analyses of the turtle- and pig-eating ceremonies celebrated by the Andaman islanders). Furthermore, if the principle of reciprocity is not respected, the good social relations created through gift giving may be inverted: friendship becomes hostility. The possibility of reversal, in other words, is what guarantees that gifts continue to circulate.

In each of these cases, chiasmus provides a powerful explanatory principle. Its dynamism is no doubt to be found, in part, in a contradictory feature of the rhetorical figure. In one sense, one may see it as a pattern or structure, one that is commonly expressed as 'ABBA'. But the reversal this formula describes occurs in time. In other words it is also a process and a process of change. The models outlined above share and make use of this contradiction which is also a productive tension that may be mapped onto the world and used to explore phenomena that lie somewhere between diagram and force, system and movement.

A step in this direction was taken by a pioneering account of chiasticism or chiasticity as a psychological condition, Ralf Norrman's study of the obsessively chiastic late-Victorian writer Samuel Butler (Norrman 1986). Norrman sees Butler as a 'chiastic personality', that is to say a psychological, indeed psychopathological case. In his anatomizing of Butler, as in his comments on Henry James, Norrman understands the chiastic personality as one who will be blocked and frustrated at every turn by his fatal insistence on balancing every statement or argument with its opposite. Butler was a compulsive reverser rather than a systematic sceptic, a term that might be applied to Montaigne, for whom, as for the ancient sceptics, the chiastic aporia was not paralysing but, as Phillip John Usher shows us in this volume, a powerful instrument for opposing dogmatism and time-honoured nonsense. Yet another distinctly different kind of 'chiastic personality' was the Argentine poet-anthropologist Néstor Perlongher, whose interwoven life and work are discussed here by Ben Bollig.

Chiasmus is a thread, generally hidden from view but at moments emerging as an explicit conceptualization. This is the case for a number of twentieth-century thinkers, notably Freud, Heidegger, Merleau-Ponty, Lévi-Strauss and Lacan, all of whom are present in this volume. The thinking of Heidegger – and of Hegel – underpins Stephen Tyler's 'thought pictures'; Merleau-Ponty's analogy of chiasmus is scrutinized by Isabelle Thomas-Fogiel; Boris Wiseman identifies and explicates the chiastic equation that is central to Lévi-Strauss's understanding of mythical thinking, and uses it to uncover a mythical dimension to a story by Hans Christian Andersen; and Alain Vanier's very compact account of 'Chiasm in Suspense in Psychoanalysis' brings together Merleau-Ponty, Lévi-Strauss, Freud and Lacan, setting up resonances with the contributions of Thomas-Fogiel and Wiseman, while taking the discussion into an important new area.

■ ■ ■

The present volume forms part of the ongoing International Rhetoric Culture Project (www.rhetoricculture.org), whose genesis and history is outlined in the Preface by Ivo Strecker and Stephen Tyler to the first volume of the series, *Culture and Rhetoric*. The stated aim of the project is 'to rethink the concept [of culture] and locate culture in the domain where it ultimately belongs – that is, rhetoric' (Strecker and Tyler 2009). Since its beginnings in the late

1990s the project has grown into a large and highly dialogical collaboration of scholars from a wide range of countries and disciplines in which rhetoric, anthropology, literary studies and philosophy interweave and interact. It is an ambitious project, and this volume is not the least ambitious part of it: its aim is to claim for chiasmus a prominent place on the map of discourse and culture as a figure and concept that plays a defining or shaping role in many areas of human experience, and is endowed with meaning-making potentialities comparable to those of metaphor.

The contributors to this volume share an integrative, anti-dualistic and anti-mechanistic view of human culture, recognizing how linguistic expression is bound up with experience, constitutive of experiential reality as well as responsive to it, and essentially rhetorical. In the words of the influential anthropologist Stephen Tyler, language is to be seen as 'neither an objective form nor a formal object, but as … a rhetorical instrument which makes use of objective forms and formal objects only in the interest of getting the work of the world done' (Tyler 1978: xi). So the bringing together of rhetoric and culture is a natural development. The participants in this project, while each being a specialist in his or her own field of research – be it literature, philosophy, ethnography, psychoanalysis or rhetoric – have all agreed for the period of this collaboration to explore, not so much the research questions ahead of them, but those that laterally connect one discipline to the next, cutting across ordinary disciplinary boundaries. 'Rhetoric culture' is best understood not as a restrictive category but a liberating one, the two terms more dynamically related than they would be in 'rhetorical culture', which would be pleonastically redundant in the same way as 'bodily dance' would be. 'Rhetoric culture' is more like 'body dance': instead of the two components of the term folding together easily with one subordinate to the other, a new and possibly awkward whole is formed of two equal halves that rub together, generating a creative friction. The body is what dances and the dance is what happens through the body. Each term enables the other, and just as we cannot easily tell the dancer from the dance, the medium from the performance, so we cannot easily tell the rhetoric from the culture.

The perception of the place of rhetoric in the panorama of the human and social sciences has undergone a significant transformation in recent years; the present volume represents both a response to this and a contribution to the ongoing process. A particular understanding of rhetoric has been central to modern critical theory and modern readings of literature. Marc Fumaroli in France and Paul de Man in America, although working in very different traditions, both illustrate well the shift that occurred in the early 1980s. It put rhetoric at the core of interpretative processes.[2] The 'linguistic' and 'metaphoric turn' of the later twentieth century paved the way for a new awareness of the foundational role of tropes in culture, for the emergence of figuration to the forefront in anthropology, and for broader and more powerful notions of rhetoric than had previously existed. Rhetoric has always, since Antiquity, been defined as the power of persuasion that, linked with speech (*logos*), distinguishes man from the animals and as a skilful refinement of speech most successfully deployed by an educated elite, boldly defined as 'the most intelligent people' by Isocrates, fourth century BC (quoted by Meyer 2009: 33).[3] Modern thought about language and discourse – one striking and influential, if still controversial, instance being Derrida's reversal of the priority of speech over writing, made possible by the introduction of a new notion of 'writing' or 'arche-writing' – has helped open the way to understanding rhetoric (considered as a form of 'writing' in Derrida's sense), not as an advanced human skill found in highly evolved communities but as a condition of the possibility of meaning. We can now see the ancient Greeks as having appropriated and professionalized rhetorical practices that are inherent in language behaviour, whatever its forms, codifying them into a science and thereby reserving for the powerful, or at any rate those who had received a specialist education, what properly belonged to everyone.

Another way of stating the aim of the Rhetoric Culture Project might then be 'to return rhetoric to daily life and relocate it at the basis of human culture'; in rethinking culture, that is to say, we are also necessarily rethinking rhetoric. Chiasmus occupied from the first a privileged position within the whole Rhetoric Culture Project, Ivo Strecker and Stephen Tyler having long been aware of the way rhetoric and culture themselves stand in chiastic relation to one another.[4] For this reason, Part One of the first volume in the series bears the title 'The Chiasm of Rhetoric and Culture'. It was because of this realization of the importance of chiasmus that Ivo Strecker sought out our own investigations (Paul 1992; Wiseman 2001) into ways chiasmus can operate within texts and systems of thought structurally and as a figure constitutive of meaning, something far more significant than a local stylistic effect, and we became involved in the budding project. Dialogue and correspondence ensued, some of which is recalled in Ivo Strecker's contribution to this volume. Chiasmus is indeed strongly present in the first volume of the series, *Culture and Rhetoric*, as it was prominently represented at the conference in Mainz in February 2005, soon after which it became clear that the creative and hermeneutic powers of this figure and, as was gradually becoming apparent, its ubiquity in all areas of culture, demanded further investigation, and that it would be a logical step to devote a whole volume to 'chiasmus in the drama of life'. Our plan, which we have since followed, was to open up existing research on the figure to broader cross-cultural and cross-disciplinary considerations, and in the process explore not only what we can say about chiasmus but what chiasmus can say about us.

▪ ▪ ▪

The four-stage structure of this book corresponds roughly to the stages of the collective project that began with a growing awareness that chiasmus was a figure whose power and possibilities had not been recognized, went on to chart this new and interesting terrain, and then developed a sense of the timeliness of chiasmus, and of its relevance and usefulness as a key to questions that are of particular concern to our own time, in such fundamental areas as epistemology, psychology and the understanding of the nature of lived experience.

The four sections into which this collection is divided represent general differences of perspective but in many ways overlap and are very much in communication with one another. The more theoretically oriented studies in the first two sections also at many points apply the figure to life, literary texts or ethnographic examples from the field. The essays in the third and fourth sections, concerned with the possibility of using the figure of chiasmus to model a broad array of phenomena from human relations to artistic creation, in doing so also investigate the nature of chiastic thought.

The three essays in Part I, 'The Pathos of Chiasmus', investigate the mental and emotional impact that characterizes chiasmus, the 'vital, arrogant, fatal, dominant X' in the words of the American poet Wallace Stevens, quoted and dissected by Robert Hariman. They are concerned with defining and map-ping chiasmus, and they explore how we try to cope with, and sometimes even manage to overcome the frustrations and constraints of human exis-tence. Chiasmus emerges from these three studies as a figure whose various facets and applications include the philosophical, the social and the magical.

Anthony Paul's 'From Stasis to Ékstasis: Four Types of Chiasmus' pro-vides a functional typology of the figure, identifying four basic modes of operation, represented as simple imagined shapes that correspond to the ways in which chiasmus is variously figured: as an X, as a mirroring, as a circle and as a spiral. Paul imagines the X as a sturdy piece of furniture as it were, standing firmly on its two feet: the chiasmus that asserts the balance and symmetry valued by, for instance, the Romans Quintilian and Cicero, and by eighteenth-century English neoclassical poets, the chiasmus that asserts a proper, ordered reciprocity. The mirror is seen as the chiasmus that confronts us with a baffling reversal, inducing various sorts of negative experience: the frustration of action, blockage of the will, the aporia found in the poetry of Rilke by Paul de Man in an influential study. The third type is the circle, in which there is movement but no escape, exemplified in Paul's account by a sentence of Proust's and one of Petrarch's sonnets, both finding a formal equivalent for one of the most persistent obsessions of European culture, the inescapable and impossible nature of desire. The fourth type, the spiral, represents the power of chiasmus to embrace paradox and contradiction in an enlarging and possibly unending process which opens possibilities of transcending the ordinary constraints of our understanding of reality.

In 'What is a Chiasmus? Or, Why the Abyss Stares Back', Robert Hariman investigates the nature of chiasmus at a deeper philosophical level; his answer to his own question involves him in reflections on the nature of language and the gap between language and reality represented by chiasmus, which by the end of the essay is seen as 'an emblem of the pathos of human communication'. Hariman sees chiasmus as a figure that creates an absence at its centre, subscribing to the view advanced by de Man that 'chiasmus ... can only come into being as the result of a void, of a lack that allows for the rotating motion of the polarities'. Hariman puts forward two new ideas about chiasmus: that the figure involves the generation of a third term, which 'grounds an ontological claim', and 'that it involves a guarded relation between self and other that nevertheless reflects the profoundly social character of human communication'. In arguing and illustrating these two theses, a subtle reading of a poem by the famously elusive and philosophically complex Wallace Stevens forms a substantial centrepiece. Hariman's analysis of Stevens' poem, discovering in it chiastic patterns and thoughts that are far from easily apparent or accessible, works, like the whole of his essay, to enlarge and extend our whole sense of what chiasmus might be, what makes it a philosophical figure, and one that is 'profoundly social but perhaps disturbingly so'.

Ivo Strecker's 'Chiasmus and Metaphor' is a wide-ranging essay concerned with the dramatic nature of both metaphor and chiasmus, and is itself given a dramatic liveliness by its generous dialogic engagement with a number of the other contributors to this volume. Strecker cites past exchanges, and engages in new dialogue with Anthony Paul, Robert Hariman and Stephen Tyler, in particular. After a prelude describing the growth of the chiasmus project as part of the Rhetoric Culture Project, Strecker compares chiasmus and metaphor as essentially dramatic figures, both of which involve the 'reverberation' identified in metaphor by I.A. Richards, 'and a concomitant state of mental and emotional "confusion"'. Strecker shows how metaphor and chiasmus are alike in that 'the internal organisation of tropes is dramatic', but unlike in their internal dynamics, chiasmus being destabilizing while metaphor is stabilizing. The second part of the essay looks at what Strecker sees as the magical dimension of chiasmus, taking as an example the line in Shakespeare's *Macbeth* 'Fair is foul and foul is fair', and differing from both Paul (in *Culture and Rhetoric*, 2009) and Hariman (in the present volume) by seeing the line as neither inducing stasis (Paul) or making any ontological claim (Hariman), but operating as a magical spell. Strecker then looks further into the ways in which 'all well-formed tropes are magical', drawing on his rich store of ethnological observations among the Hamar of southern Ethiopia.

Part II, 'Epistemological Reflections on Chiasmus', consists of the three contributions to this volume that are most directly concerned with philosophy *pur sang*, from the foundational Aristotle to twentieth-century thinkers such as Heidegger and Merleau-Ponty whose continuing contemporary relevance is shown to be variously involved with, as it is illuminated by, chiasmus as a metaphysical and epistemic instrument.

As a thinker who made prominent use of chiastic reversal both as a method of thinking and as a theoretical notion, it is appropriate that Maurice Merleau-Ponty should have a prominent place in this volume. After a long period of his being out of fashion, new readings have transformed our understanding of this key figure over the past twenty years or so, both within the linguistic turn of modern philosophy and beyond, in such various areas as art criticism, neuroscience and, of course, anthropology, disciplines in which his notion of embodied cognition has been and is still being put to fruitful use. Partly because he died before he could elaborate on the ideas adumbrated in his last (incomplete) work, *Le visible et l'invisible* (The Visible and the Invisible), whose last completed chapter is entitled 'The Intertwining and the Chiasm', there is no clear consensus as to the status of the concept in his thought. As Alain Vanier reminds us, it was the anatomical meaning of chiasm or *chiasma*, the inter-crossing of the optic nerves on the body of the sphenoid bone, that prompted Merleau-Ponty 'to turn chiasm into a concept ... but ... without specifying or developing it in any way' (Vanier, this volume). One may feel that this does Merleau-Ponty less than justice: his thoughts in that last chapter may not be fully worked out, yet it is still a richly suggestive reflection on the nature of the body–world relationship, the 'double and crossed situating of the visible in the tangible' and vice versa, and how the body's 'double belongingness to the order of the "object" and to the order of the "subject" reveals to us quite unexpected relations between the two orders' (The Visible and the Invisible, 134, 137).

Isabelle Thomas-Fogiel sets out to defend Merleau-Ponty against the commentators who, whether hostile or admiring, tend to regard him as a 'literary' thinker rather than a philosopher *pur sang* and his chiasm as merely a metaphor lacking in cognitive content and epistemic rigour. Thomas-Fogiel cogently puts the case both for the value and necessity of metaphor in all thinking, and for Merleau-Ponty as a thinker who uses chiasmus (and related concepts) 'to subvert all the classical oppositions of modern metaphysics', rejecting not only the Cartesian conception of space but 'the position of the subject in front of the world, introduced by perspective'. In the chiastic as opposed to the perspectival relation, the subject is not separate from, but intertwined with the world. Merleau-Ponty's purpose is to reconfigure the relation as identity of opposites – or the crossing and reversibility of opposites – rather than an interface between distinct and separate entities.

Thomas-Fogiel's eloquent account of Merleau-Ponty affirms the vital importance of the 'figure of encroachment' not only to the interweaving of various areas of thought, culture and science but to the very definition of philosophy, if, as Merleau-Ponty believed, all meditation aims at 'concrete universality'.

Stephen Tyler's essay is the only one not to have been specially commissioned but, in various ways, and despite its date (1998), it might be taken as a starting point of sorts, as an *entrée en matière*. It captures a critical moment in Tyler's thought that is as vital to the understanding of the productivity of the figure of chiasmus as it is for that of the anthropological endeavour.

In the space of a few short pages, and the six 'thought-pictures' that accompany them, Tyler grasps at once, in a series of conceptual schemas, some of the crucial stages in the history of Western thinking about difference, what is problematic with these approaches to difference and how one might overcome these problems.

Tyler's starting point is Hegel's dialectic, whose principal flaw is that it neutralizes the difference between thesis and antithesis in its unifying synthesis. Heidegger's model of a same that is not identity but made up of continuously joining and separating differences seems to provide an alternative to Hegel's false unity of differences. But the oscillation between differences that is central to Heidegger's model misses the valuable creativity of the dialectic, lost to repetition.

Chiasmus provides Tyler with a series of intriguing alterative models, which are elaborations of and departures from the above ways of figuring difference. These explore something like a transformational group. The familiar and basic form of the chiasm is related, here, to a series of cognate figures, including various interlocking spirals. The feature of chiasmus that holds the key to the metaphysical efficacy of this figure is one that retains the attention of several other authors in this volume, and which rhetoricians have also put at the heart of their definitions of chiasmus, namely the point where the bars of the X cross, which is also the turning point upon which chiastic reversal occurs – a point that is presented here as one of simultaneous joining and splitting.

Philippe-Joseph Salazar's essay exemplifies, itself, a chiastic toing and froing that belongs to a more general pattern in the movement of thought, which is constantly engaged in a work of construction and the critical examination of that work. His essay has its source in two 'scruples', stones in his rhetorician's shoes according to the Latin etymology of the word 'scruple', which require a return to a seemingly small number of lines, a fragment of text, one whose brevity belies its import: the opening section of Aristotle's *Rhetoric*. The significance of this text lies in its claim to be the foundational moment of the discipline of rhetoric. However, as Salazar shows, this foundational moment is highly problematic – no stable building ground is provided here. Aristotle's gesture of foundation, Salazar shows, is one that presents us with a series of problematic choices – forks in the road – as well as a problematic crossing out of all that rhetoric needs to exclude (random, careless, spontaneous speech) in order to become itself. The gesture of foundation, for Salazar, is eminently chiastic. And the chiasm it presents to us is one that simultaneously 'binds and halts'. Ultimately, the question posed by Aristotle's text is that of the 'tense bond' between method and theory, and it is by resorting first to Deleuze and then to an enigmatic sculpture, itself an X of sorts, Miró's *Fourche*, that Salazar will provide us, not so much with an answer to that question, but at least with a narrative about it. It takes the form of a new version of an old story, one pregnant with political resonances, that of Theseus's slaying of the Minotaur and of his escape from the labyrinth.

The essays gathered in Part III, 'Sensuous Experience Mediated by Chiasmus' and Part IV, 'Chiastic Structures in Ritual and Mytho-Poetic Texts' are, as the headings indicate, more concerned with applying chiasmus as a hermeneutic device, focusing on various texts – literary, philosophical, ritual, and so on – which they inspect and illuminate by looking at them through the prism of chiasmus. But the essays do not stop at an interpretation of the texts. These readings are the means of addressing a series of critical questions: aesthetic creation (via Lévi-Strauss and H.C. Andersen); the liberating potentialities of linguistic and conceptual reversal (as seen in Montaigne and in the work of the poet-anthropologist Néstor Perlongher); and the nature and power of sacred and ritual language.

An instance of Merleau-Ponty's fruitful 'encroachment' is the interaction between philosophy, anthropology and psychiatry, which is the subject of Alain Vanier's essay on 'Chiasm in Suspense in Psychoanalysis'. Although Freud never mentions chiasmus as such, the figure is, Vanier points out, of central relevance to psychoanalytic theory, which is to say the human condition as defined by Freud and his successors, with the central division of the figure corresponding to the division between conscious and subconscious. Vanier provides a compact and lucid account of the thinking of Lacan in this connection. For Lacan the chiastic turning point or division is also the point around which revolves our predicament as beings cut off from a primordial totality, selves separate from the Other. The importance of chiasmus to psychoanalysis seems indeed sufficient to justify Lacan's resonant declarations that the psychoanalyst is the sophist and the rhetor of our time.

Chiasmus as a philosophical instrument and concept is of course not a twentieth-century development; this is made clear by Phillip John Usher's 'Quotidian Chiasmus in Montaigne'. Montaigne's chiastic method and habit of mind is consistent with his admiration for Pyrrhonian scepticism, whose most fundamental principle is that of opposing to every proposition [λόγος] an equal proposition. In Montaigne's words: 'Il n'y a raison qui n'en aye une contraire'. Usher points out that chiastic reversal is a structural principle in those essays of Montaigne that earn him his reputation as 'the inventor of cultural relativism', and shows us how in considering 'quotidian' questions such as the possible causes of sexual impotence or the rights and wrongs of suicide, Montaigne uses chiasmus to apply rationality in place of the magical dogmas of demonology. A man's impotence may be cured, says Montaigne, by a reversal of his thinking; the condition is not, as his contemporaries would have it, one inflicted by demons but psychological. It is striking that the aporetic aspect of chiasmus, as of Scepticism, does not condemn Montaigne to the paralysis found in Rilke by Paul de Man and in Samuel Butler by Ralf Norrman: chiastic thinking is in the *Essais* a means of liberation from stifling certainty, and, as later for Merleau-Ponty, a condition not for finding truth to be a delusive mirage but for embracing its pluriformity and perceiving at least the possibility of a transcendent viewpoint. Usher's account leaves one with a renewed sense of Montaigne's perennial modernity and a clearer view of his status as one of the key figures within a long tradition of chiastically informed thinking.

Like Ivo Strecker's essay, mentioned above, that by the Hispanist Ben Bollig bridges the literary-philosophical and the ethnographic components of this volume. The title of Bollig's essay is '*Travestis, Michês* and Chiasmus: Crossing and Cross-Dressing in the Work of Néstor Perlongher'. Néstor Perlongher was an Argentine poet, anthropologist and gay activist, in all three capacities intensely involved in the sub-world of transvestites and homosexual prostitutes in Buenos Aires, where he was born in 1949, and Sao Paulo, where he died of AIDS in 1992. In Perlongher's border-crossing life and work, chiasmus and chiastic thought, combined in his poetry with '*travesti* aesthetics', were a central strategy, used to attack and destabilize received perceptions of sex, gender, the body and identity, and to articulate a radical sexual politics. Both the poetry and the anthropological work take us into a sensuously luxuriant world of orgiastic sexual practices, glittering with reflected reflection: the *travesti* is compounded of ambiguities and contradictions, and the transactions between *michê* and client involve many reversals and counter-reversals of the binary polarities by which conventional society lives. Perlongher celebrates and epitomizes this milieu as poet, while as anthropologist he analyses it and theorizes it in the destabilizing spirit of

Deleuze and Guattari. Bollig in turn evokes this Dionysiac world through his own sensuously alert response to 'a text that is almost sticky to read', inviting the reader to engage with his own text as much imaginatively as intellectually. The magical potentialities of rhetoric and language are central to Douglas Lewis's essay 'Parallelism and Chiasmus in Ritual Oration and Ostension in Tana Wai Brama, Eastern Indonesia'. Lewis takes two cases of inversion in rituals performed in Tana Wai Brama in east central Flores, eastern Indonesia – the first inadvertent, the second deliberate. The first case concerns the death of a ritual specialist as a result of an unintended chiasmus inserted into a ritual narration; the second, a topsy-turvy funeral meal. The unexpected death of the unfortunate chanter took place during the rare and solemn public invocation of their deity, and was ascribed by all informants to his having misrepresented the order of the world: to speak an untruth in the sacred language was to violate cosmological axioms.

Lewis draws a contrast between quotidian and ritual speech. The one is fragmentary, unpredictable, creative, the other fixed and bound to the unchanging and unchangeable order of the universe. The error in question was 'a verbal catastrophe that violated the order of the world'. The deity itself 'did not seem to mind. But language and the world did, and Rénu died'. The essay reflects on the power and danger that words may possess, and the fundamental nature of ritual language. One challenging suggestion Lewis reports is that made by various neurologists, that ordinary and ritual language come from different hemispheres of the brain, the latter being stored in the right hemisphere and perhaps linked to the limbic system.

The second account is of a funeral meal prepared for the deceased in which all culinary procedures are reversed, since the dead are taken to inhabit a mirror world. So there is a 'tension between the unchangeable oratory and the mutable ostension of Wai Brana ritual', which may be evidence for the chiastic interplay of rhetoric and culture – a notion that invites further investigation.

In the final contribution to this volume, 'Chiasmus, Mythical Creation and H.C. Andersen's 'The Shadow', Boris Wiseman looks at echoes of mythical thought in a literary tale. The essay draws, in part, on the understanding of morphodynamic processes provided by Lévi-Strauss's so-called 'canonical formula', $fx(a) : fy(b) : : fx(b) : fa\text{-}1(y)$, and by the discussions by anthropologists, philosophers and mathematicians to which it has given rise. The structure described by this formula, that of a chiasmus followed by a sort of 'double twist', provides a revealing way into a text and its inner logic or indeed, here, mytho-logic. Far from using the formula as a sort of automatic reading grid, Wiseman's aim throughout has been to seek out its echoes in a text whose flesh and bones in turn will hopefully give life to a series of symbols which may otherwise seem dauntingly austere. Avoiding formalism, the essay uses this mathematical description of a structure, a canonical structure when it comes to myth if we are to believe Lévi-Strauss, as a sort of translating device. Somewhat in the manner that French composer René Leibovitz (1913–1972) once translated a similar mythical structure identified by Lévi-Strauss into a musical composition (the score for piano still exists and has been played on French radio). The essay is followed by a response from anthropologist and mathematician Lucien Scubla, which reveals a further series of mythical sources to Andersen's tale, this time Classical, and traces what it owes to them.

■ ■ ■

The essays outlined above are the result of a broad cross-disciplinary collaboration, one that involves numerous researchers belonging to the human and social sciences. Perhaps one of the most remarkable attributes of the figure of chiasmus is its ability to traverse such a broad field, from one shore to the other as it were, while soliciting a multitude of responses, at once diverse and in relationship to one another. These responses in turn provide a thread linking up fields of thought seldom joined up in this way. Psychoanalysis is made to enter into dialogue with philosophy, and philosophy with anthropology and rhetorical studies – each of these with critical theory and more. Many permutations are possible.

In his account of his use of 'colour-sound' montage, the great film director Sergei Eisenstein (1898–1948) invokes the synaesthesia of Japanese *kabuki* theatre. As with *kabuki* his ambition, he explains, is to allow the spectator to 'perceive light vibrations as sound' and 'hear tremors of air as colours'. He wants us to hear light and see sound. This provides a fitting metaphor for the view of the world we would like to invite our readers to provisionally adopt. Our ambition is, in the manner of *kabuki* or Eisenstein's colour-sound montage, to provide you with an opportunity to see and to hear crosswise.

Notes

1. See also, 'Comment meurent les mythes' pp. 304–5 (*Anthropologie strucutrale deux*).
2. See Fumaroli 1980; Paul de Man 1979. Marc Fumaroli held a Chair in Rhetoric and Society in Europe (sixteenth and seventeenth century) at the Collège de France from 1986 to 2002, and Paul de Man was to become one of the leading figures of the Yale School of deconstruction.
3. Robert Hariman has pointed out to us that Isocrates' phrase must not be allowed to occlude 'the fact that philosophy and other arts partook of the same elite habitus,

and that rhetoric was at the same time valued by the middle classes as one of the very few means for social mobility upwards' (personal communication).

4. One might reasonably think it impossible for culture to belong in the domain of rhetoric (as mentioned earlier) while at the same time rhetoric and culture stand in chiastic relation to one another. In a statically conceived reality one would exclude the other; but contradictory relations can exist side by side within the dynamic and paradoxical reality of chiasmus: at one moment one focuses on 'how culture provides the tools for rhetorical practice, at another moment one focuses on how rhetoric provides the tools to create the institutions, values and aesthetics that we call culture' (Ivo Strecker, personal communication).

References

Fumaroli, Marc. 1980. *L'Âge de l'éloquence : rhétorique et "res literaria", de la Renaissance au seuil de l'époque classique*. Geneva: Droz; Paris: H. Champion.

Kofman, Sarah. 1998. *Camera Obscura: Of Ideology*. Translated by Will Straw. London: Athlone.

Man, Paul de. 1979. *Allegories of Reading: Figural Language in Rousseau, Nietzsche, Rilke, and Proust*. New Haven, CT: Yale University Press.

Meyer, Christian. 2009. 'Precursors of Rhetoric Culture Theory' in *Culture and Rhetoric*, eds Ivo Strecker and Stephen Tyler. New York and Oxford: Berghahn Books.

Norrman, Ralf. 1986. *Samuel Butler and the Meaning of Chiasmus*. Basingstoke: Macmillan.

Palmer, Edwina. 2000. 'The "Womë-No" Poem of "Harima Fudoki" and Residual Orality in Ancient Japan', *Bulletin of the School of Oriental and African Studies* 63(1).

Paul, Anthony. 1992. *The Torture of the Mind: Macbeth, Tragedy and Chiasmus*. Amsterdam: Thesis Publishers.

Strecker, Ivo, and Stephen Tyler (eds). 2009. *Culture and Rhetoric*. New York and Oxford: Berghahn Books.

Thomson, Ian. 1995. *Chiasmus in the Pauline Letters*. Sheffield: Sheffield Academic.

Tyler, Stephen. 1978. *The Said and the Unsaid*. London and New York: Academic Press.

Wiseman, Boris. 2001. 'Claude Lévi-Strauss, Chiasmus and the Ethnographic Journey' *Arachnofiles: A Journal of European Languages and Cultures* 2.

■ ■ ■ ■ ■ ■ ■

PART I

THE PATHOS OF CHIASMUS

CHAPTER 1

From Stasis to Ékstasis

Four Types of Chiasmus

Anthony Paul

■ ■ ■ ■ ■ ■ ■

The Slow Rise of Rhetoric

Mistrust of rhetoric is as old as rhetoric itself. It has been maligned as the stock-in-trade of power seekers, political and intellectual, the box of tricks of the professionally deceitful and the intimidating jargon of the professionally obscure. This double mistrust is voiced by Montaigne, who associates rhetoric with public disorder: 'It is a means invented for manipulating and stirring up the mob and a community fallen into lawlessness ... Rhetoric flourished in Rome when their affairs were in their worst state and when they were shattered by the storms of civil war' (Montaigne 1993: 342) – 'C'est un outil inventé pour manier et agiter une tourbe et une commune déréglée ... L'éloquence a fleuri le plus à Rome lorsque les affaires ont eté en plus mauvais état, et que l'orage des guerres civiles les agitait' (Montaigne 1965: 424). Montaigne also attacks the terminology of rhetoric as pretentious and unnecessary, a fancy way of talking about ordinary matters: 'When you hear grammatical terms such as metonymy, metaphor and allegory do they not seem to refer to some rare, exotic tongue? Yet they are categories which apply to the chatter of your chambermaid' (1993: 343) – 'Oyez dire métonymie, métaphore, allégorie et autres tels noms de la grammaire, semble-t-il pas qu'on signifie quelque forme de la langage rare et pellegrin? Ce sont titres qui touchent le babil de votre chambrière' (1965: 426).

Traditional views of rhetoric, whether negative or positive, long ignored its real nature and importance. It took more than two millennia for rhetoric to be seen and recognized as something much more than the art of persuasion and of eloquence; for men to realize that before it is a sophisticated deployment of language, rhetoric is an activity integrally embedded in all discourse and thus in human society and institutions. Montaigne was quite right in observing that rhetoric, like grammar, is essentially no more than a description of the language everybody uses; we all speak rhetorically, just as in Molière's *Le Bourgeois Gentilhomme* M. Jourdain finds he has been speaking prose for forty years without knowing it (one of Molière's many echoes of Montaigne). But in his mockery of the grandiosity of rhetorical terminology Montaigne is in fact only a hairsbreadth away from recognizing its true significance: metonymy, metaphor and so on are indeed the stuff of ordinary language; the figures of rhetoric are not something added to speech or writing to make them more effective, but are the property of everyone, educated and uneducated alike; not a latter-day product of civilization but fundamental productive principles of human discourse. They are the forms and categories we all think and speak with.

The central importance of what is called rhetoric in shaping human speech and thought was first recognized by Giambattista Vico in the early eighteenth century. After a brief account of how in all languages man's linguistic conceptual apparatus is constructed through metaphor, synecdoche, metonymy and, at a later stage, irony, Vico states that 'all the tropes (for all can be reduced to these four), which have until now been believed to be the ingenious discoveries of writers, were necessary modes of expression of all early poetic nations' ('tutti i tropi (che tutti si riducono a questi quattro), i quali sono finora creduti ignegnosi ritruovati degli scrittori, sono stati necessari modi di spiegarsi [di] tutte le prime nazioni poetiche') (Vico [1744] 1977: 287). He goes on to say that two common errors of grammarians are to suppose that the speech of prose writers is 'proper' (*propio*), that of poets 'improper' (*impropio*), and that prose preceded verse. Vico's original and important central thesis is that human thinking, and thus the development of the forms of human life, is a process driven by the poetic impulse. Vico was the first to perceive that human nature is not permanent and unchanging but should be perceived in the flux of experience: it is a process (*nascimento*) and a social activity. He thus provides the foundation for a vitalist, humanist sociology. Vico's revolutionary insights into the nature of human history and culture were slow in making any impact. His vast, rambling, famously unreadable *La Scienza Nuova* (first published in 1725) was ignored in its time, and when his ideas achieved some currency during the nineteenth century, thanks mainly to the enthusiastic advocacy of the historian Jules Michelet, his idea of history, in which he had anticipated

Herder and Hegel, attracted more attention than his views on language, the figures of rhetoric, or the centrality of the shaping poetic impulse to all forms of social organization.[1] The central importance of the tropes, at any rate of metaphor, to the ways humans construct their reality did not become common intellectual currency until well into the twentieth century.

It has taken still longer for it to be understood that rhetorical *schemes* too may be structurally and even thematically significant in the construction of textual meaning, and in the ordering and understanding of life. Tropes, such as metaphor, metonymy, oxymoron, litotes and irony, involve lexical or semantic deviation, and have always been recognized as ways of shaping or distorting truth. Schemes, on the other hand, which include phonetic arrangements like assonance and alliteration as well as forms of parallelism, repetition and inversion such as anaphora, antithesis and chiasmus, have until well into the twentieth century been generally perceived as no more than formal features of a text whose function is confined to ornament, to adding emphasis, or to packaging a message more effectively. It is a fairly recent discovery that they may also be integral to the thematic content and meanings of a text. Still more recent is the perception that such rhetorical figures are not confined to language and literature but represent structures present in many areas of life, as organizing principles of all kinds of events, relationships, patterns of behaviour and experience.

The history of chiasmus from Antiquity to the present is swiftly told. This is because chiasmus was not regarded as a subject worth discussing until about thirty years ago. The standard textbook example, 'Non ut edam vivo sed ut vivam edo' (I do not live to eat but eat to live), provided by Quintilian (AD 35–100), was by him called antimetabole; the word 'chiasmus' was not coined until the second century, by Hermodorus of Tarsus. The distinction between the two terms is that antimetabole involves repetition of the same words in reverse order, chiasmus an inverted repetition of grammatical structure. Hermodorus' coinage made slow headway: the word 'chiasmus' did not enter the English language until 1871, according to the OED, although the dictionary provides a quotation from 1870 for the Anglicized form 'chiasm', and one from 1868 for 'chiastic'. It is reasonable to assume that the story is not very different for other European languages. Over the centuries 'antimetabole' too remains almost as much of an exotic rarity – the word, that is, not the figure itself. So we shall make no further distinction between antimetabole and chiasmus.

Of course rhetorical figures do not need to be named in order to be applied. Shakespeare makes dazzling uses of chiasmus (as well as antimetabole) without using these or other rhetorical terms. He uses the word 'rhetoric' eight times in his work, and 'figure' in the rhetorical sense rather more often. But the only names of rhetorical figures he uses are 'metaphor' (four times), 'hyperboles' and 'hyperbolical' (each occurring twice). In order to discuss rhetoric rather than practise it, the terms are, however, necessary; and chiasmus, and chiastic structure, although much employed by English writers from the sixteenth century on, not to mention the authors of the Hebrew and Greek Bible, as well as their English translators, was not discussed until the late nineteenth century.

The first study of chiasmus as a figure running through a writer's work and integral to both thematic content and macrostructure is Paul de Man's chapter on Rilke in *Allegories of Reading* (de Man 1979).[2] The psychological notions of 'chiasticism' and 'chiasticity' were first defined and named by Ralf Norrman in *Samuel Butler and the Meaning of Chiasmus* (1986),[3] the first and up to the present only book-length study of chiasmus as a central feature of a writer's work and personality. Norrman's pioneering work might have had its successors had he taken as his subject a more illustrious and more widely read author than Butler (author of *Erewhon* and *The Way of All Flesh*, 1835–1902). As Norrman disarmingly admits in his preface, by choosing Butler he created for himself 'what one might call a marketing problem'. We are still waiting for large-scale accounts of the place of chiasmus in the work (and the lives) of the more 'marketable' but no less obsessively chiastic James Joyce, T.S. Eliot and Samuel Beckett.

The long indifference to chiasmus as a feature of thought, experience and the cosmos may seem remarkable in view of the antiquity and ubiquity of chiastic patterning in, for instance, both Biblical texts and some of the earliest Greek attempts to understand the physical world. Heraclitus tells us that 'Fire lives the death of air and air lives the death of fire; water lives the death of earth, earth that of water' (fragment 20, quoted in Frankfort et al. 1949: 257); and according to Ovid, Pythagoras saw the operations of Nature and the elements as a cyclical toing and froing (or 'hithering and thithering' to borrow Joyce's words), earth changing to water, water to air, air to fire, then fire back to air, air back to water and water back to earth again (as reported by Ovid in *Metamorphoses*, Book XV). In these accounts of the workings of the elements, chiasmus is not merely employed as a stylistic device but is perceived to be an ordering principle of the physical world. Yet for well over two thousand years rhetorical categories were seen as nothing more than ways of organizing language; it was never thought that they might represent structures that apply beyond the boundaries of verbal discourse. It is somewhat as if for centuries mathematics was used only as a tool in building and manufacture. The realization that rhetorical figures correspond to patterns and structures that are deeply inscribed in human thought and experience, and in the physical world, has still barely begun to reveal its implications for our understanding of every aspect of existence.

FOUR TYPES OF CHIASMUS

The reverse parallelism of chiasmus can symbolize a wide range of relationships and situations. These various functions correspond to different ways in which the figure is used and different ways in which it may be schematized, that is to say different shapes it may be imagined as having. In the present preliminary attempt at a typology of chiasmus I shall distinguish four basic schematizations: the cross, the mirror, the circle and the spiral.

The word 'chiasmus' means 'a placing crosswise', and any chiasmus is, formally and visually, a crosswise arrangement. My concern here however is not with form but with semantic content and with the way the figure lends itself to being perceived or conceptualized in distinctly different ways.

Before going into a more detailed discussion of each type, here is a preliminary outline of their respective characters:

(1) Chiasmus is experienced as 'cross-shaped' when it is a single coherent statement with no inner contradiction; the cross-chiasmus is associated with such qualities as reciprocation, balance and the orderly relation of things. For example:

> If a gift is given it can be received; when it is received it can be given.
> Man is made for woman and woman for man.

No contradiction or clash of meanings is involved here, and the effect is mind-balancing. So, probably, is that of John Keats's line 'Beauty is truth, truth beauty' (in 'Ode to a Grecian Urn'). I say 'probably' because individual sense of such 'soft' and porous categories as beauty and truth will vary, and this will affect the way one experiences the line: one might take it as uncontroversially pleonastic, as questionable or even nonsensical, or as opening up new possibilities. If it is taken as saying that beauty and truth are synonymous, then it is an unambiguous and pleonastic cross-chiasmus, whether or not one agrees with the statement; if it is taken as saying that beauty is a form of truth and truth a form of beauty, it becomes more complex, and possibly spiral – see (4) below.

(2) Chiasmus is experienced as a 'mirroring' (or reversal) when it combines formal symmetry with paradox or contradiction; mirror-chiasmus is characteristically associated with mental blockage, stasis or paralysis. For example:

> Fair is foul and foul is fair. (Shakespeare, *Macbeth*, 1, 1, 11)

In this extreme case of the mirror-type, cognitive dissonance is induced: there are various things we can do with the witches' line, but using it to reason with is not one of them.

(3) Chiasmus is experienced as a 'circling' when it invites the mind to follow a line of thought that returns it to the starting point, so there is (dizzying) movement, within a self-contained whole. The circle-chiasmus is often melancholy in character:

> I am tired of thinking how thinking of you never tires me. (Petrarch)

(4) Chiasmus is experienced as a 'spiral' when the formal symmetry sets up a more dynamic process of movement, again, as in the circle-chiasmus, returning to the starting point, with the piquant difference that this starting point is no longer exactly what it was at the start – or *where* it was. The effect of the chiasmus is then not that of a self-contained whole but that of a form that has the capacity to open up thought and to transcend its balanced or antithetical terms. The effect is mind-opening, because the element of time-continuation is implicitly added, as in the following example:

> The inner world is formed by the outer and the outer by the inner.

It will already be clear that these four types of chiasmus are not hermetically sealed off from one another. Whether a given example is experienced as a cross, a mirroring, a circle or a spiral will in many cases depend on such factors as personal opinion, individual response and cultural orientation, and so will be a matter of emphasis and interpretation rather than unambiguous fact. That is in the nature of the material we are dealing with; the word 'scheme' might suggest something fixed and diagrammatic, but the workings of this rhetorical scheme constantly interact with consciousness, experience and human circumstance.

As suggested above, Keats's 'Beauty is truth, truth beauty' might be received as a cross-chiasmus or as a more complex type. For a clearer case of this sort of uncertainty let us take a sentence from T.S. Eliot's verse drama *The Family Reunion*:

> Accident is design / And design is accident / In a cloud of unknowing.

While formally similar to 'Fair is foul and foul is fair', and also presenting the mind with a challenge, Eliot's lines are problematic in a different way. 'Accident is design and design is accident' is philosophically puzzling, not rebuffing the mind with an insoluble double contradiction but inviting us to re-examine the normally opposed concepts that are here equated and thus put in question. We may be encouraged to take the words in this spirit by the context of the whole verse-drama in which they occur, and even by the immediate context quoted here, leading one in a philosophical direction, particularly if one recognizes in 'cloud of unknowing' the title of a fourteenth-century mystical prose work. If however one fails to respond to, or rejects, the author's philosophical intention, or finds it merely a baffling and insoluble contradiction, one will experience Eliot's line as a frustrating mirror-chiasmus. It might be argued that a stronger and more appropriate reading would see it as a circling rather than a mirroring, since it assumes an order of things above or beyond our understanding, in which the mind may move to and fro without necessarily arriving anywhere new. But if the text is found to offer not merely perplexity but some sort of illumination, its double reversal of expectation could be experienced as a spiral movement rather than a closed circling. If the idea that accident and design may be reversible or identical is experienced as fruitful and helpful, the line could be a means of arriving at new categories on a higher level of consciousness.

In what follows, my main and final concern is to consider chiasmus as it relates to life-experience; my use of literary texts as examples does not reflect a wish to return rhetoric to the literary fold, but rather a view of literature as providing conveniently compact models of experiential and existential material, and of verbal art as a highly focused response to the drama of life.

I shall now consider the four types of chiasmus in more detail.

Chiasmus as Cross-Shaped

Let us say that we tend to feel chiasmus as an X, a crossing, when it is an unambiguous assertion, a statement of community and mutuality for instance, involving no real contradiction and certainly no paradox, but indicating a desirable or satisfying relation between things.

Cicero, on returning from exile, addresses the *patres conscripti*, and celebrates them as the men 'qui mihi fratrem optatissimum, me fratri amantissimo, liberis nostris parentes, nobis liberos ... reddidistis' (You have restored my most longed for brother to me, me to my beloved brother, parents to our ˙children, our children to us) (Post Reditum in Senatu 1).

This assertion of a double restoration of the natural order may be felt as standing firmly on the feet of the X. On the face of it, Cicero's resounding words have little in common with the advertisement:

I am stuck on Band-Aid brand, 'cause the Band-Aid's stuck on me.

Yet this playful slogan works by drawing on the same power of the X-chiasmus to suggest, and embody, a solid rightness of relations. A similar coupling of chiastic reversal with verbal play is found in H.L. Mencken's definition of the task of journalism as to comfort the afflicted and afflict the comfortable. This is witty to a more intellectually serious purpose than the Band-Aid advertisement, giving striking and effective expression to a thought which involves a genuine and pointed antithesis. But here too, though the mind is invited to perform a complex reversal, and to reflect on what has been said, it is not entangled in conceptual difficulty or contradiction; the two halves of the statement add up to a whole which though complex is coherent and consistent.

Cross-chiasmus may also embody a strong and unambiguous statement when the chiastic crossing does involve a contradiction, but does so only to state a truth, reversing one formulation in order to arrive at another that is clearly to be preferred. For instance the standard ancient example already cited:

> Non ut edam vivo, sed ut vivam edo – I do not live to eat but eat to live.

The formula 'not A subordinate to B but B to A', clarifying and asserting a proper order of priorities, useful for moral and other injunctions,[4] recurs in the celebrated words from President Kennedy's 1960 inaugural address, very much in the Roman oratorical mode: 'Ask not what your country can do for you, but what you can do for your country.'

To resume: cross-chiasmus, if it uses effects of dissonance or ambiguity, does so only to resolve them; apparent contradiction is subordinate to agreement; doubleness to an overarching unity of statement. Cross-chiasmus may respond to our desire to see a proper and healthy order of things affirmed or restored, or it may help us to comprehend available alternatives. For instance, we must adapt means to ends or ends to means; the Stoic philosophers tell us that our dissatisfactions arise from unrealistic ambitions and desires; to remedy this we can 'either expand our means to attain our desires or reduce our desires to suit our means' (McMahon 2006: 57).[5] This chiastically stated rule of life is not merely a case of neat and thus effective rhetorical packaging; it is effective because it corresponds to a particularly crucial life-chiasmus. Desires and means stand in a chiastic relation to each other, and this clear iconic statement of the relation may help us to get a better grip on the whole large problem of means and desires, or at any rate give us the idea that we have a better grip on it, since we are presented with it in such a neatly packaged formulation.

Cross-chiasmus is a characteristic feature of English poetry of the early eighteenth century, the 'Augustan' period, when a high value was placed on order through the social virtues of 'politeness', reasonableness and common sense, and literature strove for classical dignity and authority. In Augustan chiasmus the balanced symmetry of chiasmus is what is salient, rather than other potentialities of the figure, such as to tease, baffle or perplex.

> The suff'ring eye inverted Nature sees,
> Trees cut to statues, statues thick as trees

writes Alexander Pope, describing 'The False Taste of Magnificence' in his Epistle to Burlington (Moral Essays, Epistle IV. To Richard Boyle, Earl of Burlington (1731), ll. 119–20). The poet makes a neat satirical point about the artificiality, the reversal of natural order, of a grand formal garden. As well as providing a precise mimesis of 'inverted Nature', the symmetrical balance of the line is satisfying and reassuring; a guarantee of the poet's (and the reader's) own good taste and sure judgement.

The same values pervade Pope's translations of Homer, which are a poetic equivalent of eighteenth-century grand opera. In Pope's Homer decorous and generalizing language tends to neutralize and dignify the content, as in the account of Cassandra's death:

> We groan, we faint; with blood the dome is dyed,
> And o'er the pavement floats the dreadful tide –
> Her breast all gore, with lamentable cries,
> The bleeding innocent Cassandra dies.
> (Alexander Pope, The Odyssey of Homer (1725), Book XI, ll. 521–24)

The chiasmus that runs from 'with blood' to 'tide' has no particular mimetic force: it looks like a piece of poetic automatism. It lacks the neat iconicity of 'Trees cut to statues, statues thick as trees', or the grave weightiness of Samuel Johnson's line from London (1738) (printed thus):

SLOW RISES WORTH, BY POVERTY DEPREST.

But whatever the degree of their mimetic effectiveness, none of these Augustan chiasmi presents a semantic or interpretive challenge. These poets aimed at clarity; the last thing they wanted to do was to involve the reader in any sort of perplexity.

Pope and Johnson were poets steeped in the classics, and who aspired to give the English language the permanence and authority of Latin, using Latinate diction and even syntax. As Norrman usefully points out, there is a radical difference between the force of chiasmus in an analytical language like English and in a synthetic language like Latin, sequential order being far more important in the former, so that in Latin chiasmus may be a matter of form only, while in English it tends to be one of both form and content. 'In the synthetic languages … chiasmus is likely to be something primarily ornamental or decorative; in the analytical languages something philosophical or psychological' (Norrman 1986: 2). But the eighteenth-century poets made their English more like Latin by the frequent use of inversion; their word order is more flexible than that of standard English, and the lines quoted are in a distinct 'poetic' dialect: no English speaker or prose writer of the eighteenth century would have said or written 'with blood the dome is dyed';

but it represents the standard poetic practice of its time, a practice in which rhetorical form is likely to be primarily ornamental rather than providing the sort of tensions – philosophical, psychological or existential – to be found in the chiasms and chiastic patterning of Shakespeare's *Macbeth*, James Joyce's *Ulysses* or T.S. Eliot's *Four Quartets*.

It should perhaps be noted here that it is not intended to equate the ornamental or decorative with the trivial. That is a false notion that took hold during the reign of realism in the arts; but as anthropologists know, and as much verbal and visual art demonstrates, ornament, patterning, decoration, are universal human impulses which often respond and correspond to the deepest needs and concerns of a culture. Artistic and rhetorical form is seldom if ever 'mere form', existing for its own sake.

Chiasmus as Mirroring

The mirror-chiasmus presents irreconcilable oppositions, bringing about stasis and a sense of life as fate or an insoluble riddle.

The mirroring aspect of chiasmus is present when the content of the second half contradicts that of the first, without (as in the Quintilian formula) making clear that the second is to be preferred, thus giving rise to a tension that is unresolved, and hence to doubt, stasis, perhaps even a sort of mental paralysis; the mind moves from thesis to antithesis, from statement to reversal, and back again, finding no easy way out and no way to a synthesis. The most famous, familiar and memorable literary example of a mirroring chiasmus involving mind-baffling contradiction is that from the first scene of Shakespeare's *Macbeth*:

> Fair is foul and foul is fair

The power of this line, its insoluble riddling effect, has to do with the absolute flatness of its contradictions. The statement that two things are each other's opposite brings about conceptual chaos. The line is semantically destabilising: it boggles the mind by at once inverting and equating two fundamentally opposed moral and ethical categories so that the very possibility of meaning and sense is denied. In six small words a radically unsafe world is suggested. A similar effect is achieved by George Orwell in *Nineteen Eighty-Four*, in which the three slogans of the Party – printed thus – are:

WAR IS PEACE

FREEDOM IS SLAVERY

IGNORANCE IS STRENGTH. (1954: 86)

The assertion that opposites are identical provides the clearest cases of mirror-chiasmus, but the pattern, widely present in life-experience, is often all the more insidious for being less easily identifiable. For instance it is surely a common experience to desire something only to find that once one has it, it is no longer desirable; desire might even be defined as the longing for that which is out of reach, and by definition not to be stilled, which is indeed Schopenhauer's view, and the view inherited by many of his successors. Possession does not bring satisfaction, or the assuaging of desire. Hence the discontents of consumerism, which are at heart mirror-chiastic: what I desire and pursue is beyond my reach; what is within my reach I no longer value or desire. This formula for dissatisfaction was already recognized as a feature of American democracy by Alexis de Tocqueville during his travels in the United States in 1831–32. The dilemma is beautifully encapsulated in the words attributed to Groucho Marx: 'I don't want to belong to any club that will have me as a member'. The latent or underlying chiasmus here is: 'I only want to belong to a good club, but no good club will let me belong to it'. Many of life's dissatisfactions and disappointments are of this type. A poor view of oneself cannot be remedied by success; rather than conferring satisfaction the success is immediately contaminated and devalued by belonging to the despised self.

A similar no-win strategy is personified by Bizet's Carmen when she sings 'Si tu m'aimes je t'aime pas, et si je t'aime prends garde à toi' (If you love me I don't love you, and if I love you you'd better watch out). This represents a sexual pathology at the opposite extreme of a balanced erotic reciprocity, just as Groucho's line represents the opposite of a balanced sociability. In these cases the nourishing, life-giving flow of love – love of self and love of the other – is blocked and thwarted. The subject hovers, unable to move in any direction, in the dead region between the two mirrors.

Desire at its most anguished and self-defeating is the theme of Shakespeare's great Sonnet 129, in which chiasmus serves to express mental torment and an inescapable circle of causes and effects (the chiasmi are here italicized for convenience of reference):

Th'expense of spirit in a waste of shame
Is lust in action, and, till action, lust
Is perjured, murd'rous, bloody, full of blame,
Savage, extreme, rude, cruel, not to trust,
Enjoyed no sooner but despisèd straight,
Past reason hunted, and no sooner had,
Past reason hated as a swallowed bait
On purpose laid to make the taker mad;

> Mad in pursuit, and in possession so,
> Had, having, and in quest to have, extreme,
> A bliss in proof, and proved, a very woe,
> Before, a joy proposed, behind, a dream.
> All this the world well knows, yet none knows well
> To shun the heaven that leads men to this hell.

In this short poem, one of Shakespeare's most powerfully concentrated achievements, chiasmus is woven into a tight web of language and allied to other forms of contrastive parallelism (spirit/shame; Enjoyed/despisèd; Past reason hunted/Past reason hated; Before, a joy proposed, behind, a dream; shun the heaven that leads men to this hell). Nagging repetitions of words (especially the crucial words 'had', 'have', 'having' and 'mad'), insistent alliteration, assonance and internal rhyme ('hunted... had... hated... bait... laid... make... taker mad') reinforce one another in the mimesis of sexual torment, the paralysing contradictions of lust which the mind is powerless to reason with.

This is the most austerely impersonal of Shakespeare's sonnets, in the most literal and demonstrable sense: a quick check reveals the startling fact that it is the only one of the collection (there are 154 of them) that contains no personal pronouns. In 129 there is no 'I', 'me' or 'thee', no 'he' or 'she' or even 'they'; this poem states general laws and delivers moral judgement. It presents a condition which afflicts all the world, which is 'extreme', beyond the grasp of reason, inescapable and self-perpetuating. 'Lust' is an autonomous and impersonal force the thinking individual is powerless to resist.

As well as being impersonal, 129 lacks the acute awareness of time, of day, night, hours, seasons, past, present and future, that pervades the sonnets. Yet a particular consciousness of time is built into the poem and its mirror-chiastic structure. A typical aspect of the mirror-chiastic situation is suspension in a state of timelessness, which this poem evokes by denying the reader the comfort of orderly temporal progression. The chiasmus of line 2 reverses chronological sequence (first 'in action', then 'till action'), as does line 10: 'Had, having, and in quest to have'. The effect is of a dreamlike anachronicity; dreamlike too, or nightmarish, is the sense of an urgent mad rush that gets nowhere, that is a form of stasis. The experience described is all feverish anticipation and disgusted retrospection with nothing between but an insignificant instant of 'action' which 'no sooner' occurs than it is 'despised' and 'hated'. Having hammered home its condemnation the poem then inverts the order of response one might expect by moving in its last four lines from the judgemental to the affective, naming the illusory allurements that make lust irresistible: 'bliss', 'joy', 'heaven'. This is hysteron proteron, or putting the cart before the horse; it conspires here with chiasmus to deny the possibility of action and forward movement.

The last words of the sonnet return it to where it started from, describing an inescapable closed circle. Nevertheless, the poem is not circle- but mirror-chiastic: there is no circling of the mind, which is held captive and disabled, buzzing like a wasp in a jam jar.

In his essay on Baudelaire, T.S. Eliot comments that 'in much romantic poetry the sadness is due to the exploitation of the fact that no human relations are adequate to human desires, but also to the disbelief in any further object for human desires than that which, being human, fails to satisfy them' ('Baudelaire', first published 1930, in Eliot 1953: 192). The search for the Grail, the voyage to Cithera, represent longings that cannot convince themselves, brief dream evasions of the sad hovering that is the romantic predicament. In the late nineteenth and early twentieth centuries, across which fall the long shadows of the nineteenth-century loss of faith and of the deeply pessimistic philosophy of Schopenhauer, that nineteenth-century romantic sadness condenses into a harder stoical pessimism, a sense of life as cage or treadmill, a condition that admits of no escape.

Shakespeare's twentieth-century heir as explorer of the torment of desire and the impossibility of its satisfaction is Marcel Proust. Proust shares the pervasive modernist association of chiasmus with despair and paralysis, providing a poignant example in *Albertine Disparue*, when the narrator tells us, 'ma séparation d'elle n'ouvrait nullement pour moi le champ des plaisirs possibles que j'avais cru m'être fermé par sa présence' (my separation from her did not in the least throw open to me the field of possible pleasures which I had imagined to be closed to me by her presence) (Proust 1989: 65).[6]

> A: ma séparation d'elle / B: n'ouvrait nullement / C : pour moi / X: le champ des plaisirs possibles / C: que j'avais cru / B : m'être fermé / A: par sa présence.

This sentence, moving backwards in time, tells us that the narrator is first prevented from going to Venice, for him the scene of imagined erotic delights, by Albertine's presence and that then her absence makes him prefer not to; so he is always prevented not merely from doing what he claims he longs to do, but even from wanting to. He contrives not to want to do what he wants to do. Proust's chiasmus embodies this paralysis of desire, endless return, and constant deferral of the unattainable real. In reading the sentence, if one reads it with careful attention, one finds oneself almost physically pulled back on reaching the full stop. Grasping the full sense of it requires a return; the sentence does not draw us on to what is to follow, nor does it reach out to an external reality; what is imaged here is the narrator's experience of reality rather than reality itself; the text describes and enacts the movements of his trapped mind, from a closing-off of desire in the present to a closing-off of possibility in the past, by opposite conditions, both identified with Albertine, the focus of his neurotic and self-defeating possessiveness and never-to-be satisfied desire.

The frequent association of chiasmus with a sense of paralysis and pessimism bordering on despair in early-twentieth-century writing means that when chiasmus has been the object of critical attention it has been presented above all as a figure of somewhat ill omen. 'The world of the chiasticist tends to be one of death, sterility, negation, unhappiness and destruction' states Norrman (1986: 20). In an essay on chiasmus in Joyce's *Ulysses*, W. Bronzwaer refers in passing to 'the despair and hopelessness that are characteristic of chiasmus' (Bronzwaer 1991). Not chiasmus in *Ulysses*, but chiasmus *tout court*. It is a view of chiasmus that would have surprised rhetoricians and critics of any time before the twentieth century; but it is unremarkable in the context of modernist writing, and, even more, of postmodern reading of modernist writing.[7]

Bronzwaer took his cue to investigate chiasmus as a defining presence in *Ulysses* from Paul de Man's chapter on Rilke (op. cit.). De Man identifies chiasmus as not merely a means of shaping the textual surface of Rilke's poems but as a 'determining figure'. He finds in Rilke's work a chiastic reversal of theme and figure; chiasmus is not the form Rilke finds for his themes, but both his starting point and his final subject: chiastic reversal is the 'source of Rilke's affinity with the myth of Orpheus'; he 'thematizes chiasmus'. There being a void at the heart of chiasmus, for the poet impelled to write chiastically 'it follows that only negative experiences can be poetically useful. Hence the proliferation of a thematics of negative experiences that will proliferate in Rilke's poetry: the insatiability of desire, the powerlessness of love, death of the unfulfilled or the innocent, the fragility of the earth, the alienation of consciousness – all these themes fit Rilke's rhetoric so well, not because they are the expression of his own lived experience ... but because their structure allows for the unfolding of his patterns of figuration.'

Even if one accepts this deconstructive interpretation, that Rilke goes to Orpheus because he is hungry for chiasmus rather than vice versa, the question still remains as to why the poet is so possessed by his master-figure in the first place. If Rilke is insistently chiastic, like Joyce, is it not because chiasmus answers to his expectation of the world, if not his experience of it, and strikes in him a deep chord? If the poet's mind is chiastic it is, in the first place, because he finds life chiastic. The poem is not, indeed, an incidental container for material which could just as well have been stated in another form, but neither is it a beautiful casket whose content is secondary. The life of the poem inheres in the interaction and even identity of form and theme. Joyce's masterly story 'The Dead' is no less chiastic in its total structure as in its details than any of Rilke's poems, or Shakespeare's *Macbeth*; but there is no reason to suppose that the chiasticist Joyce necessarily began with a pattern of figuration and found themes to fit it, rather than finding a correspondence between his view of existence and his figure. One's experience of reading the story, with its balance of meticulous realism and poetic form, suggests that the relations between its linguistic structure and its referential and thematic material constitute a more complex web of cause and effect, stimulus and response, form and philosophy, than de Man's theory of language will allow.

That a writer's work may be to some extent shaped by his style and language was pointed out by Aldous Huxley:

> *Le style c'est l'homme.* No doubt. But the converse is also partly true. *L'homme c'est le style.* Because we have a gift for writing in a certain way, we find ourselves, in some sort, becoming our way of writing. We mould ourselves in the likeness of our particular brand of eloquence. Eckhart was one of the inventors of German prose, and he was tempted by his new-found mastery of forceful expression to commit himself to extreme positions – to be doctrinally the image of his powerful and over-emphatic sentences. (Huxley [1946] 1958)

This sensible account of the interactions between a writer's personality, his style, and the matter of the text provides a useful counterweight, or antidote, to deconstructionist overstatements.

Chiasmus as Circling

The circle-chiasmus brings one back to the starting point; there is mental movement within a closed system. The characteristic effect is one of melancholy, the sense of life as a labyrinth. The labyrinthine (and melancholy) masterpieces of modernist literature are circular. I have mentioned Joyce's 'The Dead', which is a single huge circle-chiasmus, and refer below to the circular aspect of Molly Bloom's monologue that concludes *Ulysses; Finnegans Wake* is unending, beginning midway through a sentence and ending with the beginning of that sentence. Proust's *Search for Lost Time* also ends where it begins, and is enclosed within the dimension of time, its first word being 'Longtemps' and its last, 'temps'.

Long before Proust, and long before Shakespeare, chiasmus was wedded to (or thematized by?) the frustrations of love in the sonnets of Petrarch, who invented the form, and established it as a genre dedicated above all to the delineation of desire. Number 74 of his *Canzoniere* begins with a riddling chiasmus that is iconic of the labyrinth into which it leads. The whole poem is a single long sentence that loses itself and dwindles away into a maze of weariness and doubt, with the poet finding himself in the end back where he began:

> Io son già stanco di pensar si come
> I miei pensier' in voi stanchi non sono ...
> (I am already weary of thinking how / my thoughts of you do not weary me.)

The emotional world of Petrarch's Laura poems is dominated by doubt, a melancholy quest for the unattainable, a weary stumbling through a maze in the company of Amor, 'ragionando con meco, ed io con lui' (talking to me, and I to him) (poem 63).

The 'circling' of Petrarch's poem is unlike the turning and twisting of Shakespeare's Sonnet 129. Petrarch's chiasms are certainly not reassuring Xs, but neither do they figure the state of a painful hovering between thesis and antithesis and of the mind driven violently back on itself as Shakespeare does in his sonnet. They figure the movement of a mind, not getting anywhere perhaps, but at any rate moving around in the labyrinth. The main theme of Petrarch's love sonnets is not so much 'love' itself as the turning of his mind around the theme of love (in this Petrarch resembles Proust!); that of Shakespeare's Sonnet 129 the paralysis of the will brought on by the contradictions of 'lust'. Thinking and reflection – and the exercise of poetic art – are themes that offer indirect consolation: the thoughts may themselves be uncomfortable, but they display consciousness in action, and put the reader in contact with the living, feeling human subject reflecting on and attempting to deal with his predicament.

This is the consolation of Petrarch, and it is also that of much Romantic poetry, however dark or uncertain its thoughts may be. Leopardi's 'L'infinito' for instance is a meditative poem in which the poet's mind moves between pairs of oppositions: closeness and immense distance, nearby sounds and infinite silence, thought and emotion, death and life – all resolved and dissolving together in the last two chiastic and breathtaking lines (which are also the only moment when the poet breaks into metaphor). The emphasis is mine.

L'INFINITO
Sempre caro mi fu quest'ermo colle,
E questa siepe, che da tanta parte
Dell'ultimo orizzonte il guardo esclude.
Ma sedendo e mirando, **interminati**
Spazi di là da quella, e **sovrumani**   5
Silenzi, e profondissima quiete
Io nel pensier mi fingo ; ove per poco

Il cor non si spaura. E come il vento
Odo stormir tra queste piante, io quello
Infinito silenzio a questa voce   10
Vo comparando: e mi sovvien **l'eterno,**
E le morte stagioni, e la presente
E viva, e il suon di lei. **Così tra questa**
Immensità s'annega il pensier mio:
E il naufragar <u>m'è dolce</u> in questo mare.   15

THE INFINITE
<u>Always dear to me was</u> *this lonely hill,*
And this hedge which conceals from view
A large part of the uttermost horizon.
But sitting here and gazing, **boundless**
Spaces beyond that, and ***more than human***   5
Silences and deepest calm
I figure in my thought, whereby the heart
Is almost filled with fear. And as
I hear the wind that rustles through these shrubs, that
Infinite silence *to this voice*   10
I now compare: and I recall the **eternal,**
And the dead seasons, and the present
And living one, and the sound of it. **So amid this**
Immensity my thought is drowned:
And shipwreck <u>to me is lovely</u> in this sea.   15

'L'Infinito' is structured around its pairs of oppositions. Besides its closing chiasmus, the poem contains a number of chiastically arranged parallels and pairs, with the words 'm'è dolce' in the last line making a pair with 'caro mi fu' in the first line. The whole poem is chiastic, its centre, the axis on which the chiasmus turns, being line 7: 'Io nel pensier mi fingo' – the poet's thought process – just as 'il pensier mio' forms the axis of the closing sub-chiasmus. The poet's thinking is the central fact of his poem, which like Petrarch's sonnet reflects on reflection; the poet is present as a figure in the landscape, as in one of Caspar David Friedrich's paintings, sitting and gazing, between on the one hand these nearby, plainly named, ordinary things, 'this lonely hill', 'this hedge', the wind in 'these shrubs', and on the other, endless spaces, infinite silence, eternity and immensity.

We have here moved on some way from chiasmus conceived as iconic of entrapment, paralysis, a recursive inescapable fatality, the unending reflection of reflections (Leopardi's active reflection *on* reflection is something quite different), the despairing stasis at the dead centre. 'L'infinito' presents us with the human mind brought up against the mysteries of existence, almost giving way to existential terror but at last surrendering to the insoluble, and letting thought drown in the immensity of the mystery of the universe. Whether we experience the poem as a circle-chiasmus, a movement of the mind within a maze that has no exit, or as something else, depends on how we understand the last two lines. Are 'the drowning and sweet shipwreck of thought' a version of the Romantic swooning into oblivion as the only escape from life's pains and perplexities, a form of death seen as a release?[8] Or do they represent something philosophically more positive and hopeful, a moment of transcendent union with the universe, an orgasmic submission – a 'little death' of the mind – to the oceanic oneness of the infinite? In the first case, 'L'Infinito' is a closed system, in the second, it is open. If the poem culminates in a moment of transcendent bliss, then the speaker has broken out of life's labyrinth into a state of enlarged consciousness and meditational ecstasy. Ecstasy comes from the Greek ékstasis, etymologically, the state of being put out of one's habitual mode – 'oneself' – changed, altered; in this case, the speaker of the poem finds himself outside the confines of the mind within which thinking is condemned to move in circles, and his consciousness is altered.

Chiasmus as Spiral

The spiral-chiasmus involves an open-ended movement, returning the mind to a starting point that is now changed, whereby a further movement is initiated, a process which may continue indefinitely, generating new possibilities. As we have just seen, Leopardi's 'L'Infinito' could be read as a spiral-chiasmus. For another example:

> The world had a beginning
> And this beginning could be the mother of the world.
> When you know the mother
> Go on to know the child.
> After you have known the child
> Go back to holding fast to the mother,
> And to the end of your days you will not meet with danger.
> (Lao Tzu, Tao te Ching, LII, translated by D.C. Lau)

In cultures dominated by Aristotelian logic, by theological or scientific dogma and by the aspiration to live in the clear light of reason, chiasmus is most appreciated for its outer qualities of formal balance and symmetry, as we see it used by the Romans and by eighteenth-century English poets. In a time of political and cultural pessimism, philosophical despair and emotional anxiety, the mirror aspect of the figure comes to the fore, being an ideal vehicle for the expression of the predominant experience of the period, so that it becomes natural for Ralf Norrman to state that chiasmus provides thesis and antithesis but never synthesis, and thus gives rise to instability and to the discomfort of a symmetry that denies the possibility of choice and further progress. This, while often the case, particularly in modern writing, is not always so.

The commentators mentioned earlier – de Man, Norrman and Bronzwaer – take the chiastic condition to be one of sterility and paralysis. But thinkers who welcome and embrace paradox (rather than being themselves held in its grip) employ chiastic reversal either to free themselves from the received wisdom, as Montaigne often does, or to transcend reason, as do the paradoxes of the Tao te Ching, Heraclitus[9] and Nicholas of Cusa.[10] As well as a mirror mirroring another mirror, or a closed circle, chiasmus can be a dynamic figure, neither continually returning to where it started, the end point being the same as the starting point, nor turning around a dead centre where no movement or life can exist. But there is also the chiasmus that might be more appropriately seen as a wheeling around an axle. When we think of chiasmus as a spiral, its centre is not a still, dead centre, but the life-giving force that starts movement, the axis on which the spiral chiasmus turns, and is given the impulse to turn again.

As suggested above, interpretation of modernist writing that assumes a direct relation between chiastic patterning and negative experiences may on occasion prejudge the issue on the basis of an incomplete view of chiasmus, and find itself imprisoned within a circular argument. To interpret Joyce's writings in terms of their internal relationships is certainly a highly appropriate response to an author so fanatically dedicated to the arranging and structuring of the text. Circularity is indeed everywhere in his work, at every structural level, and is of thematic relevance. But this stylistic propensity does not justify a reading of Joyce as the purveyor of an exclusively negative vision of existence. Even if one were to take the deconstructionist position that Joyce thematizes the figure, that chiasmus is essentially what his novel is about, as de Man claims for Rilke's *Neue Gedichten*, this would certainly not be equivalent to saying that *Ulysses* presents life as a form of death. For one thing, any such interpretation of *Ulysses* depends on ignoring the book's last forty or so pages, Molly Bloom's oceanic monologue, which is nothing if not life-affirming. It is also conspicuously lacking in chiasmus, though it too comes in a characteristically Joycean full circle, beginning and ending – ecstatically! – with the word 'yes'.

Life and death are polarities with which Joyce is much concerned; but death is not the point on which everything in the novel converges. This could be discussed at length but I shall confine myself to one tiny example. In *Ulysses* occurs the sentence, 'In the midst of death we are in life'. Here Joyce characteristically reverses the order of words from the service of burial in the Anglican Book of Common Prayer, 'In the midst of life we are in death'. The Christian perspective on the facts of mortality sees life within the context of death; we are exhorted to live in the consciousness of our approaching end, for the beginning of life is also the beginning of death:

> Our life is ever on the wing,
> And death is ever nigh!
> The moment that our lives begin,
> We all begin to die.

Thus the eighteenth-century poet and hymn writer Isaac Watts; his contemporary Edward Young puts the matter more succinctly: 'Our birth is nothing but our death begun'. Although not a formal chiasmus, this is certainly a chiastic thought.

The chiasmus set up by Joyce's inversion of the words of the funeral service is in a different spirit from the conventional Christian memento mori; it constitutes a larger reflection, potentially unending, on the ways death and life coexist inseparably and interdependently, each in the midst of the other, which is also the theme of the very elaborately chiastic story 'The Dead', the concluding story of *Dubliners*, the work that preceded *Ulysses*.[11] Taken as a pair, the two statements, 'In the midst of life we are in death; in the midst of death we are in life', add up to a compact yet full and suggestive poetic embodying of our mortal condition.

By reversing, without necessarily denying, the truth of a statement, chiasmus can generate further truths. Thomas Paine, reflecting on the sublime and the ridiculous in *The Age of Reason*, finds that they 'are often so nearly related that it is difficult to class them separately. One step above the sublime makes the ridiculous; and one step above the ridiculous makes the sublime again.' The close-relatedness of the apparent opposites, their way of morphing into each other, invites chiasmus; or else it is that chiasmus opens our eyes to the relatedness – and shows how sublime and ridiculous could go on indefinitely generating each other at ever-higher levels: Paine envisages a climbing spiral.

So the perception of a chiastic relationship or process, the placing of terms within a chiasmus, alerts us to the exchanges and interchanging of categories we might have supposed to be far from related. Chiasmus may help us to grasp how oppositions may be identical or interchangeable, to construct models of reality in which familiar categories are superseded. For instance, the reality in which your young self (yourself at twenty, say) is old and your old self (at whatever age you have now reached) young. What is it after all to be old or young, what is age and what is youth? You could see yourself as an accumulation of layered selves, from youngest (i.e. oldest) to oldest (i.e. youngest). Each of us is a walking chiasmus and paradox.

To realize this fully might be to liberate oneself from the tyranny of a mental one-way system, to achieve an ideal openness to the possibility of an all-round view of things, the whole truth of which may be more clearly perceived when out of focus, the way an artist gets a full view of a landscape by squinting at it through half-closed eyes.

"'No reason but has its contrary,'" says the wisest of the schools of Philosophy',[12] Montaigne tells us (1993: 694; 1965: 362), referring to the Pyrrhonian Sceptics. Merleau-Ponty says of Montaigne's scepticism that it

> has two faces. It means that nothing is true, but also that nothing is false … Destroying dogmatic, partial or abstract truth, it introduces the idea of a total truth, with all the necessary facets and mediations. If it multiplies contrasts and contradictions, that is because the truth demands it. Montaigne begins by teaching that every truth contradicts itself, and perhaps ends by recognizing that contradiction is truth. (Maurice Merleau-Ponty, Preface to Montaigne, *III*, 1965: 7)

> (Le scepticisme a deux faces. Il signifie que rien n'est vrai, mais aussi que rien n'est faux … Détruisant la vérité dogmatique, partielle ou abstraite, il insinue l'idée d'une vérité totale, avec toutes les facettes et toutes les médiations nécessaires. S'il multiplie les contrastes et les contradictions, c'est que la vérité l'exige. Montaigne commence par enseigner que toute vérité se contredit, peut-être finit-il par reconnaître que la contradiction est vérité.)

Montaigne's radical independence of mind and his capacity to turn thoughts around and see them from the other side, his sceptical chiasticism, allowed him for instance not only to realize that 'the Cannibals' of the Americas were not necessarily any more barbaric than their European conquerors but even to achieve a detached view of mankind's anthropocentric arrogance, to question why man should be the ruler of creation and to perceive the possibility of a sort of equality between man and other species: 'When I play with my cat, how do I know that she is not passing the time with me rather than I with her?' he asks, and 'Why should it be a defect in the beasts not in us which stops all communication between us?'[13]

In the 'Apology for Raymond Sebond', Montaigne cites a dialogue (which like many other *exempla* he took from Erasmus' *Apophthegmata*) between the Cynic philosopher Diogenes and the more worldly Aristippus who did not, like Diogenes, eschew the company of the powerful. 'Diogenes was washing some cabbage leaves when he saw Aristippus go by: "If you knew how to live on cabbage," Diogenes said, "you would not be courting a tyrant." Artistippus retorted: "You would not be here washing cabbages if you knew how to live among men."' Montaigne comments: 'That is how Reason can make different actions seem right. Reason is a two-handled pot: you can grab it from the right or the left.' And chiasmus is a two-handled pot that can be picked up by both handles.

Aristippus employs the style of riposte that reverses the argument to provide a counter-truth. A strong instance of such a refutation, claiming not merely that a statement is untrue, but that the opposite is true, is Marx's answer to Hegel, 'nicht das Bewußtsein bestimmt das Sein, nein, das Sein bestimmt das Bewußtsein' ('it is not the consciousness of men that determines their being, but on the contrary their social being that determines their consciousness'; from the Preface to A Contribution to the Critique of Political Economy).[14] But if one dwells for a moment on this, seeing it not so much as thesis and antithesis but as a single, two-handled chiastic statement, one may find that neither half, neither Hegel nor Marx, offers a satisfying final truth: is not the whole truth rather that 'Das Bewußtsein bestimmt das Sein, das Sein bestimmt das Bewußtsein'; or, even better, 'Das Bewußtsein bestimmt das Sein, das das Bewußtsein bestimmt' – and so on? This chiastic sentence provides a double surprise by not merely reversing what one thought to be true, showing that the opposite may (also) be true, but waking us up to a third possibility, the single more complex new truth arrived at when we perceive, in the spirit of Montaigne, and of his admired Pyrrhonian Sceptics, that the two halves of the sentence are at once both untrue and true. Of course if one is committed to either the Hegelian or the Marxian view of consciousness one will not be attracted to the total, spiralling statement, one will have no need for it. They are opposed views: while taking over Hegel's theory of dialectic, Marx sets out, as Engels said, to 'stand Hegel on his head'.[15] 'Marx does not construe consciousness as Hegel does. For him it is already socialized and material in nature, and to speak of consciousness is to speak of how men treat objects and each other' (Hamlyn 1990: 69). So Marx's reversal of Hegel's priorities is the assertion that matter, not spirit, is the driving force: material conditions determine ideas. But if one finds the choice between Hegel's idealism and Marx's (anthropocentric, utopian) materialist idealism unappetizing, and would prefer another line of thinking, the spiralling chiasmus that results when their opposed views are put back to back has the power to suggest such another possibility. What the spiral chiasmus leads to is not a synthesis but, rather, an embrace, not of the separate components but of their open-ended and progressive dynamic interactivity. This suggests a recycling – or rather, a further spiralling – of Heraclitus' notion, taken up by Hegel, of the dynamic and cyclic interplay of opposites, and the unity arising from the combination of opposites.

In the wider view of the spiralling *nascimento*, new ideas of both being and consciousness, embracing contradictions, oppositions and paradoxes, can emerge and continue to expand and mutate, the idea of a total or final truth constantly drawing us on and extending our grasp. Seen in this light, what Keats called 'Negative Capability' is the most appropriate and enlightened way of confronting life: 'Negative Capability, that is when man is capable of being in uncertainties, mysteries, doubts, without any irritable reaching after fact and reason.'[16]

So the spiral chiasmus has the power to release us from having to choose between Diogenes and Aristippus, or Marx and Hegel. As a habit or principle of thinking it can open up fuller views of life and death, the sublime and the ridiculous, cabbages and kings, being and consciousness. Some sort of fuller view, transcending both materialism and idealism, while recognizing the degree to which we at once 'live in a world we ourselves create' (Herder) and are ourselves created by the world we find, might take us beyond certain sterile contemporary debates or dialogues of the deaf, might even succeed in raising us above our chronic myopic anthropocentrism and failure to take on board Montaigne's penetrating understanding of the status of man as but one species among many. It might be applied to embrace oppositions and transcend contradictions we have not yet recognized, to bring us some way to achieving a wholeness still difficult to imagine.

Chiasmus and Experience

It seems natural for us to understand ourselves and the world as made up of contrastive polarities which define each other – past and present, male and female, joy and pain, birth and death, hunger and satisfaction, and so on. This human doubleness or self-contradiction often involves us in the double contradictions of chiasmus: we know what it is to feel painful pleasure and pleasant pain; we can all sing along with the words, 'Sometimes I love you, sometimes I hate you, but when I hate you, it's 'cause I love you …'. The universality of chiasmus (perhaps it is just because it is so universal that it remained so long unseen and unrecognized) reflects the divided and contradictory condition of human beings, our fascination with our own dividedness, and our deeper longing to recover the wholeness that we conceive ourselves to have once had and whose memory haunts us.

Both individual experience and the collective experience of communities and cultures are suffused with and shaped by recursions and reciprocities, that is to say by chiastic patterns: the inner world is formed by the outer and the outer by the inner; the worker has to earn his wage while the wage has to be an adequate payment for the work; no gift can be given unless it is received, nor received unless it is given; it is only when we give up the idea that we are in control of our lives that we may hope to gain control over them, and so on.

Once it is seen to be a deep structure of life-experience, chiasmus becomes a key to explicating and structuring life's paradoxes and problems. Once we recognize forms of entrapment, personal and collective, in psychic, relational, systemic and social mirror-structures or circular labyrinths, we can start looking for the way out; understanding of spiral-chiastic phenomena and processes may encourage awareness of the balances, logic, connection and inescapable laws that underlie life's conflicts and apparent randomness, disorder and fragmentation. Many of the seeming contradictions of experience which arise from the paradoxical interrelatedness and interpenetration of oppositions such as loving and hating, waking and sleeping, being born and dying, may be better understood and transcended once the chiastic nature of the interrelatedness has been identified. The moment when one recognizes the chiasticity, in which life as we experience it is caught up, might mark the turn or twist by which one ceases to be mastered by rhetoric and by life, and even ceases to struggle to master them, but becomes instead their partner and ally. To help ourselves to live in harmony with patterns and structures of existence that represent the total truth, to which partial and abstract truths and all reasons with their contraries are subordinate, is perhaps the purpose of our present collective project.

Notes

1. For an account of Vico's posthumous reception and influence, and Michelet's discovery and advocacy of Vico, see Berlin 1976: 90–98.
2. De Man's study of Rilke is founded on the insight that 'The determining figure of Rilke's poetry is chiasmus' (38).
3. 'There are some authors whose fondness for chiasmus is so extreme that it deserves to be called an obsession. I shall call these authors *chiasticists*, and their state of mind *chiasticism*' (3).
4. A pedagogic example of this sub-type of chiasmus: 'Liberality ... submitteth her wealth, to herself, not herself to it, as the covetous man, doth' / 'Liberalitas ... subjicit opes sibi, non se illis, ut avarus' Johann A. Comenius, *Orbis Sensualium Pictus* (Visible World), translated into English by Charles Hoole, London 1658, twelfth edition 1777, facsimile edition Tokyo 1981: 150.
5. McMahon provides other witty and pointed chiastic reversals, in something like the spirit of Marx rebutting Hegel (see below 47 and n. 24), e.g., 'Whereas for most men and women at the dawn of the modern age, God was happiness, happiness has since become our god' (267), and '"Who would willingly possess genius?" Byron asks, with typical self-indulgence. "None, I am persuaded, who knew the misery it entails". Something like the opposite would seem to be the case. In smoke-filled

cafés, how many dark-clad youth have willingly taken up misery ever since – in the hope of knowing the genius that it might entail?' (282).

6. English translation by C.K. Scott Moncrieff and others, Harmondsworth, Penguin, 1983.

7. A conveniently compact diagnosis of the absence so often at the centre of modernist writing is given by Terry Eagleton: 'The typical modernist work of art is still haunted by the memory of an orderly universe, and so is nostalgic enough to feel the eclipse of meaning as an anguish, a scandal, an intolerable deprivation. That is why such works so often turn around a central absence, some cryptic gap or silence which marks the spot through which sense-making has leaked away. One thinks of Chekhov's Moscow in *Three Sisters*, Conrad's African heart of darkness, Virginia Woolf's blankly enigmatic lighthouse, E.M. Forster's empty Marabar caves, T.S. Eliot's still point of the turning world, the non-encounter at the heart of Joyce's *Ulysses*, Beckett's Godot, or the nameless crime of Kafka's Joseph K.' (Eagleton 2007: 100). Eagleton could also have mentioned the ever-undiscovered meaning of a writer's oeuvre in Henry James's story 'The Figure in the Carpet'; it might also be interesting to trace the 'central absence' in the visual arts and in music during the modernist period.

8. Cf. Keats's lines in the 'Ode to a Nightingale':
   Now more than ever seems it sweet to die,
   To cease upon the midnight with no pain.
   A nicely ambivalent instance of the poet simultaneously resisting and strongly stating the desire for oblivion is provided by the first line of his 'Ode to Melancholy': 'No, no, go not to Lethe, neither twist ...' where, as William Empson ([1930] 1977: 239) pointed out, 'it tells you that somebody, or some force in the poet's mind, must have wanted to go to Lethe very much, if it took four negatives in the first line to stop them'.

9. For instance, 'Mortals are immortals, and immortals are mortals, the one living the other's death and dying the other's life' (Russell [1946] 1969: 59).

10. The philosophical writings of Nicholas of Cusa, who is now best known for his notion of 'docta ignorantia' (learned ignorance), are full of reversal, paradox and oxymoron. He defines God as that in which oppositions become identical: the infinitely small is also infinitely large, and (blending mathematics with mysticism) infinity is a circle, any section of whose circumference is a straight line.

11. For an account of the chiastic structuring of 'The Dead', see Paul 1992: 174–80.

12. From the essay 'Que notre désir s'accroît par la malaisance' (That Difficulty Increases Desire): 'Il n'y a raison qui n'en ait une contraire, dit le plus sage parti des philosophes'. Montaigne comments more extensively on the Pyrrhonians in the 'Apology for Raymond Sebond'.

13. Lévi-Strauss hails Montaigne as the progenitor of the human sciences and the pioneer of cultural relativism in *Histoire de lynx*, ch.18, 'en relisant Montaigne'.

14. Cf. Montaigne (1993: 607) 'Whenever a case is fought from preliminary assumptions, to oppose it take the very axiom which is in dispute, reverse it and make that into your preliminary assumption. For any human assumption, any rhetorical proposition, has just as much authority as any other, unless a difference can be established by reason.'

15. Marx often used chiastic reversal as a technique of argument. For example his critique of Pierre-Joseph Proudhon's *The Philosophy of Poverty* is entitled *The Poverty of Philosophy*.
16. John Keats, letter to George and Thomas Keats, 21 December 1817.

References

Berlin, Isaiah. 1976. *Vico and Herder, Two Studies in the History of Ideas*. London: The Hogarth Press.

Bronzwaer, W. 1991. 'Het chiasme in James Joyce' *Ulysses*', *De Revisor* 18(5): 68–76.

Eagleton, Terry. 2007. *The Meaning of Life*. Oxford: Oxford University Press.

Eliot, T.S. 1953. *Selected Prose*. Harmondsworth: Penguin.

Empson, William. (1930) 1977. *Seven Types of Ambiguity*. Harmondsworth: Penguin.

Frankfort, Henri, Mrs Henri Frankfort, John A.Wilson and Thorkild Jacobsen. (1949) 1951. *Before Philosophy*. Harmondsworth: Pelican Books.

Hamlyn, D.W. (1987) 1990. *The Penguin History of Western Philosophy*. Harmondsworth: Penguin.

Huxley, Aldous. (1946) 1958. *The Perennial Philosophy*. London and Glasgow: Collins.

McMahon, Darrin. 2006. *The Pursuit of Happiness: A History from the Greeks to the Present*. London: Allan Lane.

Man, Paul de. 1979. *Allegories of Reading: Figural Language in Rousseau, Nietzsche, Rilke, and Proust*. New Haven, CT: Yale University Press.

Montaigne, Michel de. 1993. *The Complete Essays*, translated by M.A. Screech. Harmondsworth: Penguin.

Montaigne, Michel de. 1965. *Essais*. Paris: Gallimard.

Norrman, Ralf. 1986. *Samuel Butler and the Meaning of Chiasmus*. Basingstoke: Macmillan.

Orwell, George. (1949) 1954. *Nineteen Eighty-Four*. Harmondsworth: Penguin.

Paul, Anthony. 1992. *The Torture of the Mind, Macbeth, Tragedy and Chiasmus*. Amsterdam: Thesis Publishers.

Proust, Marcel. (1925-1927) 1989. *À La Recherche du temps perdu* IV. Paris: Gallimard.

Russell, Bertrand. (1946) 1969. *History of Western Philosophy*. London: Allen and Unwin.

Vico, Giambattista. (1744) 1977. *La Scienza Nuova*. Milan: Rizzoli.

CHAPTER 2

WHAT IS A CHIASMUS? OR, WHY THE ABYSS STARES BACK

Robert Hariman

■ ■ ■ ■ ■ ■ ■

> When you stare into an abyss, the abyss also stares into you.[1]
> – Friedrich Nietzsche, *Beyond Good and Evil*

Chiasmus usually is not seen as an important trope or as a trope at all. Even Paul de Man's use of it involved a sleight of hand – chiasmus was featured initially in *Allegories of Reading* to dismantle the idea of transcendental signification, but the real action in deconstruction proved to be elsewhere.[2] Twentieth-century rhetorical theory was focused on metaphor, metonymy, irony, and (less so) synecdoche, and, with that, the notion of 'master tropes' that are far more important than the many minor figures sprinkled throughout speech (Burke 1969a; White 1973).

Chiasmus seems caught at this crossroads between profundity and mere rhetoric. It evokes the deep patterning of the human mind at the limits of representation, yet when piled up in quotation books the device quickly appears vapid (cf. Grothe 1999). This ambivalence is indicative of the paradoxical status of figuration more generally, something that is put on display by chiasmus because it is the most visual of verbal devices. A chiasmus can epitomize how language can be used to order reality for rational reflection, and yet it obviously is a device, an artificial form that is crafted according to some intention that comes from outside the situation being described.

So it is that chiasmus is both a trope and a figure, a small device and a generative form, and its combination of rhetorical power and evident artificiality leads to restricted use. Chiasmus is found in Biblical narrative, Renaissance drama, modern poetry, urbane conversation, and great oratory, but rarely on the street. People admire it, scholars study it, writers practise it and play with it, but you can be immersed in newspapers, television, email, and the many other venues of ordinary speech for months and never see it or notice it. Nor is this because the figure is hard to use. Unlike jokes, for example, which are far harder to write (and deliver) than to enjoy, anyone could bundle words into the ABBA form if given a few examples and some small incentive: we should make our words fit our ideas, and our ideas fit our words; I don't like snow in the winter, but I don't like winter without snow; put a song in your heart, and your heart into a song. Do this occasionally, and you can acquire a reputation for having a way with words; keep it up and you will drive people nuts.

The point of these observations is not to locate the proper place for this or any other verbal technique in a pantheon of tropes, figures, schemes, or other discursive forms. Instead, the chiasmus invites consideration of the nature of rhetoric itself, and there of how compositional devices can be both small and large, full and empty, static and generative, encompassing and self-limiting, social and narcissistic, alien and all too human.

The rest of this essay develops an answer to the question, 'What is a chiasmus?' The answer will not be a definition but rather a discourse on why the chiasmus is particularly well suited for representing the gap between language and reality, and thus for representing language itself – and language divided against itself, as de Man argued. None of this is news, but I hope to make two small contributions to the literature on chiasmus: first, that it involves the generation of a third term, often although not necessarily unstated, that grounds an ontological claim; second, that it involves a guarded relationship between self and other that nonetheless reflects the profoundly social character of human communication. Chiasmus makes a claim about the world that cannot avoid falling into the abyss; strangely, however, the intention to communicate is redeemed when the abyss stares back.

CHIASMUS IS NOT FOUND IN NATURE

This claim would seem to be either obvious or nonsense: it is obvious because no figure, pronoun, dash, schwa, or other linguistic element occurs independent of human artifice; it is nonsense because nothing humans do exists outside of the natural forces shaping every molecule of their bodies and all neural activity. And yet the claim needs to be made, because the chiasmus can suggest deep affinity between art and nature, and because the figure has been enlisted as a means for thinking about the relationship between language and reality. The first of these associations stems directly from the visual salience of the term. One can see crossings scattered throughout the natural world: a floral array, the four-limbed body, or the dark X in 'photo 51', the X-ray diffraction image of DNA taken by Rosalind Franklin at King's College London in 1952.[3] Surely the symmetrical logic of the verbal figure is mapping some cosmic order.

Except that Franklin's image of the X is an artefact of optical technology, and all of the other examples one might provide testify, not to the presence of a specific form in nature, but rather to the marvellous ability of the human mind to see patterns and to pattern what it sees. This aesthetic aptitude, which is one subject for tropology, is what underwrites use of the chiasmus to think about the relationship between language and reality. De Man is illustrative, as his discussion of Rilke constructs a paradox between, on the one hand, the poetic freedom that comes from not being 'hampered by the referential constraints of meaning' and, on the other hand, the constraint that 'a language entirely freed of referential constraints is properly inconceivable' (de Man 1979: 47, 49). Chiasmus – 'the crossing that reverses the attributes of words and of things' – is presented as 'the determining figure of Rilke's poetry', and the point of the story, not surprisingly, lies in reversal of a prior model: instead of fixing meaning in a totalizing structure, even a mirror image, poetic truth is immersed in 'the dissolving perspective of the lie' that makes any connection between word and thing subject to a vanishing temporality and all the anxieties that come with that (de Man 1979: 38, 56).

The use of chiasmus becomes even more entangled with the problem of representation in the most philosophical of American poets, Wallace Stevens, to whom we will turn later. In these and other cases, chiasmus seems to be a figure of choice for thinking about how the mind apprehends nature, and the result is not merely a celebration of form. Instead, the chiasmus is enlisted because of a prior rupture, and even the possibility of crossing over from one realm to another (things in words, words in things) becomes marked by an obvious device. In place of a natural order, the chiasmus reveals that at the centre of the human encounter with reality there is only emptiness. 'Chiasmus ... can only come into being as the result of a void, of a lack that allows for the rotating motion of the polarities' (de Man 1979: 49).[4] What will come from that, however, remains an open question. Empty space can be crossed, and decorated, and might even become capable of more, if one stares long enough.

Chiasmus is an Ornament

Now this really is stating the obvious, but let us embroider the idea anyway. Just let them pile up and the artifice becomes all too evident:

> The greatest orator among lawyers, the greatest lawyer among orators.
> There are amusing people who do not interest, and interesting people who do not amuse.
> A wit with dunces, and a dunce with wits.
> Stars don't make movies, movies make stars.
> We're not better because we're bigger; we're bigger because we're better.

All such examples lie athwart Aristotle's maxim that speech is more persuasive as the artistry is hidden.[5] Any verbal technique can be too evident, of course, but even a striking metaphor may transfer its distinctiveness to its object, irony seems to lie in the situation or the speaker rather than in the technique, narrative structures consciousness automatically, and so it is with much ordinary usage. The chiasmus announces its craftwork, however, which may be why it is used so infrequently and quoted so often. Use of the figure is a sign that more than the usual intentionality has preceded the statement. Moreover, the device is obviously intended to please: witness the neat arrangement, the formal precision, the deft turn, the decisive binding together of contraries, the satisfying resolution of an argument or other complex relationships.

The figure becomes a rhetoric in miniature: intentional artistic use of a discursive form to instruct, please and move an audience. It is notable that rhetorical advice has been packaged in chiasmi:

> One must destroy one's adversaries' seriousness with laughter, and their laughter with seriousness.

> People don't care how much you know until they know how much you care.

Like technical rhetoric more generally, the chiasmus seems designed for portability. It becomes one of the small forms of public speech along with the maxim, the aphorism, the joke, the proverb, the parable and the quotation; or perhaps it is more accurate to say that it is a technique often used in small form composition. This classification allows us to see that the small form is suited to more than carrying the small thought, although that certainly remains the function of some use of the chiasmus.[6]

> To finish first, you must first finish.

Oh, so true, so true! Of course, even small thoughts can do heavy lifting from time to time as they prove to be apt tools for managing a situation, but the suspicion remains that the speaker is at the limit of his powers of invention.

Whatever the weight of the idea expressed, a chiasmus cannot wholly escape its decorative status. The neat phrasing or symmetrical organization appears unnecessary, features verbal craft, or adds aesthetic panache to more routine discourse. This decorative capability has tactical value in a culture of conversation, and there the figure may be most at home: its use draws attention to the speaker, but that is the point. Elsewhere, however, the obviously artistic composition and, with that, the tension between simplicity and excess is more destabilizing.

CHIASMUS IS A FIGURE OF THOUGHT

It is not news to say that the chiasmus can be both a verbal ornament and a means for more serious thinking, but the basis for the distinction remains murky. Ralf Norrman states that 'In the synthetic languages, then, chiasmus is likely to be something primarily ornamental or decorative; in the analytic languages something philosophical or psychological' (1986: 2). The linguistic tendencies are certainly in place, as word order counts far more in the one system than in the other, but the historical record requires significant caveats.[7] The obvious appreciation of the trope in English has led to a lot of merely decorative use, while few would argue that use of the form by the Psalmists, Plato, or the Gospel writers is primarily ornamental (think of the crossing pattern in *Protagoras*, or of the statement that 'The sabbath was made for humanity, not humanity for the sabbath'). And on the cusp, as usual, there is Cicero, who used ornamentation unabashedly while also revealing a mind that was at once both annoyingly prevaricating and capable of moving powerfully back and forth across two sides of a complex argument. Thus, both linguistic and idiosyncratic factors (not least with Norrman's example of Samuel Butler) will be at work in the range of usage, but there is need for an intermediate account of how the figure works.

Let me suggest that whatever philosophical work chiasmus can do, it does because it is a small device and visible. There are many small devices, of course, and much of the labour of composition can go into discursive visualization (*enargaia*), but the chiasmus proves to be a remarkably compact and powerful engine for organizing, inflecting and generating ideas. The chiasmus is small because of its symmetry requirement: unlike narrative or any of the 'master tropes', any increase at one point has to be doubled, which might be thought of as doubling the cognitive load. The advantages of doubling are significant, and include both an iron-clad organizational device and a clear guide for subsequent invention, but every addition also multiplies the complexity, mnemonic requirements and artificiality of the representational form. If the chiasmus is to be a figure of thought, it has to adhere to the same requirement for its being an ornament: it has to remain small enough to not become unwieldy.

This requirement also keeps the figure visible. Not many rhetorical devices are named after a shape, and the X is particularly distinctive as a shape. Again, this feature lends itself to decorative display, but it can also perform an important representational function, which is to shift composition from 'saying' to 'showing'.[8] Thus, the chiasmus is able to coordinate two fundamental modalities of representation. Metaphor and other figures can do the same, but not automatically – the effect depends on the artistry. In chiasmus, however, one is automatically directed to dual apprehension. We can both follow the logic and see it, which in turn can prompt both delight and a reflective attitude in the audience (the fact that the logic may be largely fabricated is beside the point). This showing can then be put to additional uses as well. For example, Elie Assis argues that Biblical chiasmus is used to reveal character and thereby to persuade by suggesting that the character's actions have been planned deliberatively. This indirect composition of ethos works because 'Chiasmus often directs the reader to the fact that the text is constructed, and not necessarily to the center of the structure' (Assis 2002: 273–304, 287). In short, the discourse works by showing a discursive pattern that requires premeditation, deliberation and self-control, rather than by saying outright that the character has those qualities.

One might well ask why this indirection is necessary, that is, why the verbal form should do the work typically ascribed to the content of a statement. The answer in the particular case will have to include the historical context (language, cultural conventions, and the like), but there is a tropological consideration as well. The unique function of the chiasmus as a figure of thought will be that it is suited to those things where both saying and showing are needed or useful. There will be a number of variants. The basic motivational value is obvious: where visualization has special value (whether in aesthetic or emotional matters, or due to literacy deficits in the audience, for example), then multimodal discourses will be preferred. But showing also is needed because saying is somewhat interdicted or inadequate for other reasons, and where the speaker wants to communicate that either something is being overlooked or that what needs to be said eludes representation.

The compact visualization that defines chiasmus is particularly useful in respect to the figure's performative coordination of binaries. Indeed, the chiasmus seems to turn everything it touches into binary oppositions, but in fact it is marking and arranging items in terms of available pairings. 'Jack loves Jill, and Jill Jack', and so two individuals become arranged in terms of subject/object, active/passive, male/female, desire/fulfilment, and perhaps other distinctions as well.[9] Given the importance of binary opposition within human cognition, social structuration, and rhetorical training, the work to be done can be specified directly. Norrman features several basic functions for chiastic thinking, including dualism, antithesis and inversion, and goes on to identify an 'ambilateralist' mentality that is obsessively committed to symmetry and uniquely vulnerable to the 'existential chiasmus' that profoundly destabilizes the principles of similarity and difference (Norrman 1986: 14). Other writers identify other basic mental operations that are activated or employed via chiastic composition, and some also posit a mentality grounded in the figure, often one that is relativistic or intersubjective.

It seems safe to say that as chiasmus operates as a figure of thought, it activates contrasting attitudes toward thinking itself. On the one hand, the figure is used to organize very specific ideas, to create a stable array that will carefully articulate similarity and difference in a demarcated mental space of comparison:

Failure is the foundation of success, and success is the lurking place of failure.

On the other hand, the chiasmus turns ideas on one another, and does not allow one to settle on either side of the equation:

Fair is foul, and foul is fair.

Worse yet, it sets up and shows a pattern that can only be taken as a whole, which proves to be a process of continual movement secured only in the illusory permanence of the gaze. The chiasmus moves one towards a centre that proves to be empty, a space only for crossing. As one thinks with chiasmus, the doubled modality of the term offers stability only to oscillate and then to spin off something beyond the binary, something asymmetrical.

Chiasmus is Generative

When celebrating the generative character of language, attention is usually paid to metaphor, and understandably so. Furthermore, the chiasmus seems to appeal to a contrary motive, the desire for visible order. The chiasmus joins terms together into a neat, symmetrical, balanced, self-contained arrangement, each item in its place in a small box with a bow on top:

Love makes sex better, sex makes love better.
Judge not, that ye not be judged.

What more do you need to know? Surely a rhetorical advantage of using the device comes from its implication that the pertinent area of concern is under control, indeed, that the mind of the speaker is capable of encompassing and mastering anything inchoate, complex, confusing, in flux, or otherwise troubling:

Fear cannot be without some hope, nor hope without some fear.

We might respond subconsciously, 'Whew, I'm glad that's settled, glad that these looming, volatile emotions in fact have an ordered relationship.'

This ordering function is powerful, but it does not account entirely for the operation of the trope. Let me suggest that the chiasmus works not simply through a logic of crossing or exchange between two terms, but also through the generation of a third term that becomes the bridge between the original pairing. Thus, in the ABBA format, A and B are not changed into one another, but generate a third term, C, to mediate their relationship. Of course, other and often very subtle adjustments and reverberations between the two primary terms can be triggered by their arrangement in the mirror image format, but the generative power of the reversal comes from consciously having to supply *something* to cross the chasm between the original set and its inverted double. The crossing pattern proves to be most powerful not because it compares by inverting binary terms, but because in doing so it supplies a new term as the common ground on which the contrasting propositions can stand together.

Any of the classic examples of the chiasmus should provide an example. The generative power is most evident in an example having perfect symmetry: 'Fair is foul and foul is fair'. Anthony Paul (1992) and others have carefully examined the role of this statement in the context of *Macbeth*, and particularly how it captures the reversal of values and the disorientation, desperation and brutality of that tragedy.[10] One unintended result is that the statement acquires a hermeneutical miasma. When looking for the third term, however, the answer becomes startlingly clear: when fair is foul and foul is fair, the third term is power. That is, this chiasmus makes an ontological claim: power exists and alters all that it touches, which in Macbeth's world is everything. Whatever ethics may be, power is now dominant in the world and capable of bending anything to that end. Likewise, power emerges as the ontological ground of the statement and acquires presence within one's consciousness, capable of pushing the audience where it may not want to go.

For another example, consider the adage from Cicero/Quintilian, 'I eat to live rather than live to eat'. The figure obviously contrasts eating and living, and one way of living (and eating) with another. None of this will have been news within the original context, however. Thus, the importance of a third term: the self that is formed through personal discipline and, most importantly, by a practice of self-control that was the centre of individual identity in the speaker's class. By the clever pairing of eating and living, common to all life, the speaker is able to generate a primary claim to his own existence as an individual human being – and one who is defined neither by eating nor living, but rather by self-control defining intentional action. The third term, then, is that 'I' at the start of the maxim – but as it is transformed into a richer sense of the 'I' at the other end. And note also how the third term is both present and absent in this text: there at the start of the crossing but not there at the end. This small, easily overlooked break in the lexical symmetry of the statement (in English) is indicative of how the term being generated can be present, absent, or both present and absent in the text of the chiasmus. More to the point, a broken symmetry can be one clue to identifying the third term being generated by the figure.

This play of presence and absence will prove to be a crucial element of the chiasmus, not least because of how it allows the generation of the unexpected and then of the limits of representation. Not to put too fine a point on it, but the cross pattern ultimately lends itself to mystification, where what once seemed clear and final – death, for example – can be transformed into something enduring though ineffable – say, eternal life. This is also the time to note the correspondence of chiasmus with metonymy (which underwrites the shift from chiasmus to the metaphor–metonymy relationship in de Man's tropology). The visual X, evident in the Greek letter *chi* that forms the root of the word, can stand easily for the metonymic relationship of all signs to their meanings. In particular, the axis of implication is from letter to spirit (or body to mind), and from the explicit terms in the figure to a third term signifying an excess – something implied by and yet exceeding the patterned relationship. No wonder, then, that the chiasmus is taken up by those who are fascinated with the problem of representation.

Wallace Stevens is judged by many to be one of the great poets of the twentieth century, and, among the Americans, both the most philosophical and the most attentive to rhetoric. Stevens was fascinated by the problem of how language mediated the relationship between mind and world. His poetry could imagine 'an abstraction blooded, as a man by thought', and so use the chiasmus and other tropes to suggest deep, paradoxical connections between meaning and reality that can be revealed but not quite grasped (Stevens 1972: 212). His poem 'The Motive for Metaphor' is a signature achievement in this regard. It would also seem to be a tailor-made exercise in tropology, as it creates a powerful oscillation between metaphor and metonymy that is in turn mediated by a series of chiastic transformations.

You like it under the trees in autumn,
Because everything is half dead.
The wind moves like a cripple among the leaves
And repeats words without meaning.

In the same way, you were happy in spring,
With the half-colors of quarter-things,
The slightly brighter sky, the melting clouds,
The single bird, the obscure moon—

The obscure moon lighting an obscure world
Of things that would never be quite expressed
Where you yourself were never quite yourself
And did not want nor have to be,

Desiring the exhilarations of changes:
The motive for metaphor, shrinking from
The weight of primary noon,
The A B C of being,

The ruddy temper, the hammer
Of red and blue, the hard sound—
Steel against intimation—the sharp flash,
The vital, arrogant, fatal, dominant X.

Wallace Stevens, 'The Motive for Metaphor' (1972: 240)

This poem is about metaphor and is rich in metaphoric display, yet the final X is a metonym emblematic of multiple crossings and their terminus in cancellation and what comes after. The strong form of address – to 'you' – and explicit figuration make the poem self-consciously, even arrogantly rhetorical, while its subject is language itself. Every word serves the powerful progression from your (our) tepid experience in ordinary language, dulled by routine habituation, to the hard, vital reality that can be revealed in poetry. He does not say 'poetry', but that is the third term of the most fundamental crossing in the poem. In brief, the chiastic relationship of language and reality reveals the ontological primacy of poetry. To get there, the poem supplies not a logical nor even a stylistic progression, but rather movement through a series of chiastic patterns.

One cannot readily see the successive iterations of an ABBA syntax so much as feel them, as the crossings are predominately semantic. Thus, 'everything is half dead' is mirrored by the wind moving like a cripple, half-able, and 'you' liking something in autumn, when trees are without leaves, is mirrored by a wind that now can speak to utter words without meaning. In the same way, the 'half colors of quarter things' are mirrored by the half-toned sky and melting clouds, and you stand alone like a single bird or the moon. The pattern is more obvious in the middle stanza's middle lines, as an obscure world not quite expressed is mirrored by you not quite yourself not wanting the world that is to come. The tensions are more pronounced in the fourth stanza as 'motive' and 'weight' are coupled via both opposition and identity with 'the exhilarations of changes' and the 'A B C of being'. The fifth stanza offers more of an intensification across the 'hard sound'/'steel against inti-mation' couplet, but the oppositional pattern is at the same time developed across the fourth and fifth stanzas, creating the tension between changes and the X, which then reveals that the entire poem follows the same pattern across all five stanzas.

Anthony Paul's four-fold typology of chiasmus (this volume) provides the tools needed to explicate the poem's chiastic structure. Each of the first two stanzas are examples of his first type, the simple *cross-shaped figure*: 'a single coherent statement with no inner contradiction'. The same applies to the two stanzas together, further reinforcing the sense of 'reciprocation, bal-ance, and the orderly relation of things'. Dulled mind, dulled nature; muted world, muted experience; in autumn, as in spring. One might expect to come to a stop, except that the second stanza does not end with a period but instead crosses to the third stanza, which is itself (and following from the second) what Paul labels a *mirroring*. This is the second type of chiasmus, which is 'associated with blockage, stasis or paralysis'. The obscure moon, which mirrors the sun's light, illuminates the obscure world, and so two forms of obscurity mirror one another – one might even imagine a reflection of the moon in dark water. In like manner, the obscure world is mirrored in obscure language that cannot quite express things, and you are likewise mirrored in that language, as half expressions can only illuminate half selves. Stasis seems to prevail, and the user of language appears trapped in half articulateness.

At exactly that point, the sentence cascades over into the next stanza, and now a strong *circling* pattern begins, a third type of chiasmus that provides 'movement' within 'a self-contained whole'. One has circled from stasis to the exhilaration of changes, from inexpressiveness to metaphor, from moonlight to the sun's 'weight at primary noon'. The celebrated change would seem to be complete: indeed, the cycle of the seasons has led to a perfect circle of language and reality, the 'A B C of being'. The poem has travelled from 'words without meaning' to pure language expressing pure being in perfectly symmetrical reciprocity. But this order is not what it appears. Indeed, to get here one had to accept a logical error, and the perfect symmetry proves to be something else, something excessive. And instead of stopping, the poem spills forward, turning into a *spiral* form that is not a self-contained whole but rather something that continues in time (as de Man would expect) to trouble its balanced terms. Paul calls the effect of this fourth type 'mind-opening', and adds, in words that could be a gloss on Stevens, that 'the inner world is formed by the outer and the outer by the inner'.

Thus, Paul's anatomy of the trope of chiasmus allows one to explicate Stevens' use of the trope to articulate both his poetics and his distinctive poetic effect. To see fully what is involved in the poem, we need to return for a moment to the fourth stanza and the logical sleight of hand that occurs there. The distinctive crossing can be identified by asking, 'who is shrinking?' One would expect from the structure of the poem that the answer would be 'you', the addressee who settled for half-measures and did not desire the exhilarations induced by metaphoric invention. You did not want change, so you would shrink from change and thus lack the motive for metaphor. That interpretation has to be reconstructed, however, as the direct reading of the line points to another answer: it is the motive for metaphor that shrinks from what follows. The grammatical relationship is that of apposition, which can both link ideas while also enacting the minor figure of hyperbaton, which intentionally creates disorder in the sentence structure for other effect. Thus, 'shrinking' would also refer back to the authorial subject of the poem, whose motive for metaphor rightly pulls back from the stasis of reality without shadow, interpretation or change.[11]

Whatever is being said, the poem is showing something more, and resolution does not come from a simple choice between you and the more enlightened author. The weight of primary noon is itself metaphoric, and the subsequent appositions are demonstrably, emphatically so.[12] Thus, the desire for changes logically leads away from the 'half colors of quarter things' to 'the weight of primary noon', and metaphor is aligned with the A B C of being. But isn't 'half colors of quarter things' a description of leaves as they turn? Aren't autumn and spring the time of evident change? And (again, as we are crossing and re-crossing) isn't primary noon a fixed thing? Shouldn't the motive for metaphor move away from a fixed, final alignment of word and things, away from the A B C of being?

And so it does. The poem teeters at this logical conundrum, and then a torrent of figuration is released.[13] The hammer of red and blue, the hard sound, and so on (even 'the sharp flash' as it can be a flash of insight): these are all things that exist primarily in language and yet seem to be revelations of pure being. This poem, and particularly its final metaphor of the living letter X, is Stevens' poetics in metonymic form and enacts his most distinctive effect. As Frank Doggett has summarized, Stevens placed poetic meaning 'a little beyond determination' because he believed that that although poetry could communicate a sense of objective reality, that reality could never be known in itself (Doggett 1980: xii). No wonder that the final X is tauntingly empty – dare one say 'obscure'?[14] It is the epitome of literal truth, to announce that truth cannot be literal. Truth cannot be literal in this case because the subject of the poem, the motive for metaphor, is self-contradictory: metaphor both turns towards and shrinks from primary meaning, just as the mind does with matter. More to the point, these polarities are linked in chiastic oscillation, with the moment of perfect equipoise itself a supreme fiction. (The pertinent philosophical claims are that pure being is pure transformation, and that neither can be known, but that the relationships between language and reality can be revealed by poetry if it is known to be fictive.[15]) No wonder that much of the time people settle for half colours and repeating words without meaning, and that poets labour to release the transformative potential of those same words.

As the chiasmus becomes the representative trope, whether in Stevens or Rilke, it becomes a figure of transformation and thus involves risk. For example, destabilizing the horizon of 'primary noon' on behalf of generative flow can lead to mystification.[16] In place of fixed relationships, the third term always carries excess energy that can be a sign of additional yet undefined meaning. One can trade clarity for possibility and possibility for obscurity. That is not the only outcome possible, however. More simply (though not in Stevens), the third term is often expressed as laughter that in turn is a welcome mystification of social relations. The frequency of the chiasmus in comedy, both in witty repartee and in the mirrored inversions of many comedic plays, is testimony to this effect. But that is the bright side. Ultimately, it takes Stevens to the edge of his modernist faith in unified mediation via the symbol.[17] And it takes him farther still. Note how the poem begins with 'you', and then takes you to one point of equipoise where things are not quite expressed and you are not quite yourself, and then takes you through a vortex to the centre of being and back out again on the other side of where you began, but then ends not with 'you', but with your mirror image: 'X'.[18] You stare into the abyss, and it stares back into you.

CHIASMUS IS A PHILOSOPHICAL FIGURE

This is not to say that it is a favourite of philosophers or even of philosophical poets. The prevalence of the form in the wisdom literature should be noted, but that may merely reflect conventions of instruction developed within oral cultures. Closer to home, chiasmus is featured in recent work on phenomenology that emphasizes the utility of the figure for explicating the split subject and other paradoxical conditions of consciousness (Evans and Lawlor 2000;

Doyle 2001; Erdinast-Vulcan 2007: 395–409). Chiasmus also has some service as an organizational device in discussions of pragmatism: pairing Dewey and Stevens or law and poetry to better articulate the aesthetic elements of pragmatist thought (Grey 1991; Levin 1999; Kestenbaum 2002). Any of these alignments can seem incidental, however, and thus the philosophical tenor of chiasmus must lie in the design itself.

The chiasmus can be philosophical in several senses. First, there is the merely rhetorical motive, in that its deft ordering of a semantic field supplies a patina of cognitive mastery in that realm. Philosophers, both amateur and professional, need to appear philosophical, and their performance of their mentality is inseparable from its most distinctive accomplishments (Hariman 1986: 38–54). Second, the chiasmus is an organizational device particularly well suited to arranging ideas. In its small form, it manages the binary distinctions that are central to all analytical thinking; in more extended form (such as ABCCBA), it can array binaries while recording additional nuances in the situation; in its long form (such as with extended ring construction in the Bible or Thucydides), it provides an extensive cognitive architecture for structuring understanding.[19] In addition, the crossing pattern is particularly well suited to reflexive interpretation: as noted above, it not only says but shows; the pattern obviously makes ideas capable of being compared with their contraries; the fixed array implies both a bounded semantic space and a sense of its limit or beyond; the distinctive positions and double movement require the reader to choose where one might stand in that space.

That might be enough to qualify a figure for serious thinking, but the invitation to enter into the figure leads to trouble and so to a richer sense of its intellectual potential. Is one a butterfly dreaming of being a human being, or a human being dreaming of being a butterfly? Is it the time to preserve order amidst change or change amidst order? (This paraphrase of a chiasmus by Alfred North Whitehead could serve as the basic question about chiasmus itself, which can be used to advance either attitude.) If you should respond to seriousness with laughter and to laughter with seriousness, is nothing or everything serious? The answer in every case cannot come from either of the polar positions, nor does the pairing offer dialectical resolution or a programme for fine-grained comparative analysis or a middle ground for negotiated compromise. As noted earlier, the chiasmus works in part by generating a third term (and the social energy animating that term), and in its more philosophical moment that third term is a mentality. Thus, the Chinese aphorism identifies the consciousness that is the subject of philosophical idealism; Whitehead is articulating a conception of progress (the third term is explicit in his literal statement); Gorgias is identifying neither laughter nor seriousness but rather strategic thinking. Thus, the chiasmus operates as a way of staking an ontological claim (rather than merely stating one); curiously, it does so by inviting the reader into a space that is itself uninhabitable. The chiasmus does not settle things so much as it generates a process of thinking that will necessarily lead one past resolution of the two (or more) terms presented.

The chiasmus is a philosophical figure not simply because it generates a third term; that 'term' often registers entirely as laughter, delight, awe or other emotional responses that are appropriate to the speech situation. The philosophical potential of the figure stems from its capacity to imply an additional dimension of thought, experience or social organization in which incommensurables can be joined harmoniously or productively. This is not a dialectical resolution, moreover, in that the basis for resolution is always signified only by the crossing, which itself supplies no principle of resolution but rather perpetual oscillation. (The principle of resolution is located in an absent signifier.) Thus, the chiasmus is a philosophical figure precisely because it is disposed to mystification. The value is not the mystification itself, but its usefulness for communicating an unavoidable excess within the semantic space that cannot be accommodated by the terms of analysis. In the most quotidian sense, the figure thus is available anytime one needs to suggest that there remains more work to do. There will be a bias beyond that, however, in favour of process philosophies or philosophies that are relatively marginal within a larger intellectual dispensation. All this is too serious, however, as perhaps the better philosophical value of the device is its potential for scandal, and that, too, comes from the crossing pattern.

Chiasmus is the Play of Language

The more rhetorically astute discussions of chiasmus all converge on the fact that the figure is defined by a symmetrical crossing pattern that contains, at its centre, nothing. This is the tropological equivalent of Christianity's scandal of the empty cross. Worse, that centre is the place for a continual pingponging back and forth, like a primitive video game running automatically whether anyone is in the room or not. Gorgias' adage is reverberating yet, and what could stop it?

Playfulness can evoke a mood of celebration, and celebrations evoke a mood of playfulness. (*What? Yet another chiasmus – how did that happen?*) An essay should culminate in a good conclusion, and a good conclusion will be the culmination of an essay. (*Oh, no, it happened again.*) How can I finish this argument, without this argument finishing me? (*Help, someone, get me out of here!*) And so another paradox emerges, which is that the playfulness of the chiasmus is closely related to its being a small prison house of language.

Thus de Man's sense of Rilke's urgency: his chiastic intelligence needed to escape from the eternal recurrence of the crossing pattern. When trapped in a linguistic form, play becomes a means of transformation and escape. One plays with language to escape its dull routines and unwitting conventions, its autopoetic power to reproduce discursive forms endlessly. De Man features the escape into temporality, and the anxieties of temporality, and with that breaks out of modernist conceptions of representation as well. Any third term can be a breakout, however, particularly when accompanying laughter or other pleasures.

The chiasmus shows not only its terms and a model of symbolic order, but also the artificiality of representation. That formal awareness can be quite serious, as with the Biblical writer – although there will have been pleasures of composition and interpretation that were an important part of that craft. More often, it lends itself to the comic attitude of good conversation. The writer or speaker appears not only skilful but playful, willing to elevate an ordinary turn of conversation into wit. When Isadora Duncan suggested to George Bernard Shaw that they should reproduce in order to grace the world with someone having her body and his brains, Shaw responded, 'Yes, but what if it had your brains and my body?' Shaw did not need to supply a direct, explicit critique of eugenics or extricate himself from the social predicament or otherwise redefine the situation. The attitude of playfulness is rhetorically powerful precisely because it obtains a reversal within such constraints. And when the retelling occurs, it is likely to pass that attitude along rather than serve any didactic purpose. The chiasmus, particularly in its most common articulations in quotation books, Shakespearean plays, and other repositories of wit, enacts linguistic playfulness.

The chiasmus also disciplines that playfulness, keeping to a relatively conservative sense of play, one with clearly demarcated rules, dedicated space, and almost ritual enactment (Huizinga 1966). Again, the play of language is, in the chiasmus, caught in reciprocal interaction with language's impersonal control of consciousness. Play acquires room to move because the centre of the chiastic relationship is empty, and it becomes necessary because the walls of figuration cannot be breached. In this, Stevens and Rilke are agreed that 'the mind's power is indistinguishable from its abiding powerlessness' (Levin 1999: 198).[20] Once the fixed form is exposed as having no fixed referent, once the reciprocity between terms, or between the first position and the last, supposedly identical, position is known to have shifted, the only remaining alternative is the 'incessant creation' of language itself, its playfulness within the prison house of available forms.

A classic piece of graffiti states, 'God is dead – Nietzsche. Nietzsche is dead – God'. Here the joke is on Nietzsche, but it is also on God, who has to kill people to put them in their place and will do so to get the last laugh. Better to simply recognize that Neitzsche could be too serious for his own good, that arguments ended can remain unanswered, and that graffiti are written more for fun than for philosophy. As Stevens, also too serious for his own good, nonetheless understood: 'being includes death and the imagination' (Stevens 1972: 323–24).[21] The chiasmus exemplifies the play of language, both the incessant refiguring of meaning inside forms that remain fixed, and the use of those forms to playfully reframe situations so that they do not become tyrannical, however inevitable they may be. If the cross is empty, all that can remain is the laughter.

CHIASMUS IS FOUND IN SOCIAL CONSCIOUSNESS

Rather than the unity of word and thing, the chiasmus presents a visible ordering of terms that signify a set of binary relations bounded by the limits of representation. I eat to live rather than live to eat, and so I am ratified as an individual capable of intentional action and self-control, but at the same time a world of excess is implied, lurking beyond my person and within my person. The chiasmus is not part of that larger world – none of the world's inchoate powers need flow through a crossing pattern – but it is a figure of social interaction. Indeed, as Norrman observes about the extreme case of chiastic thinking, 'only relations are real', and that could be the motto of an acutely social intelligence.

Of course, it could be a cosmological principle as well, and as acknowledged earlier, society is not exempt from the forces of nature. It is important to emphasize the social character of the chiasmus, however, to fully understand its significance and limitations. This social articulation is itself paradoxical, as there is something asocial about the figure. Gerald Bruns, in a critical essay about Stevens, faults the poet for being fundamentally turned away from other people; the important point is that what is widely acknowledged as a feature of Stevens' personality is claimed to be inseparable from his poetics (Gelpi 1985: 24–40).[22] To the extent that those artistic principles culminate in the 'vital, arrogant, fatal, dominant X', we may have a problem. The case of Samuel Butler is more telling: Norrman's exposition of the incredible inventional resources of chiastic thinking also identifies a corresponding pathology: narcissism. Butler's excessive love of symmetry is also an inability to choose between opposites and so to make any commitment. Again, this trait is not merely idiosyncratic: chiasmus both activates and thwarts desire for meeting in the middle, for melding with another. Indeed, as Norrman also notes, it seems suited to frustrating expectations and expressing cruelty (Norrman 1986: 98–100). Laughter can be savage, and though in a binding pattern inversions can be used to cut.

Even so, there are less vicious though still restricted forms of chiastic sociality. The figure's implied relationship with the audience, for example, generally is one of admiration of rather than identification with the speaker. The chiasmus refers the audience to its own cultural capital but not to shared experience, and the figure acts as a bar between speaker and audience: something that stands between them precisely because it is obviously crafted. The chiasmus is a linguistic screen, and its mood is that of spectatorship; the audience is entertained and edified but kept at a distance from the speaker. Attention is focused on the subject – the sabbath, for example, and the audience's relationship to that ritual form – but the speaker remains on the other side of the speech. Bruns notes that 'language in the world is structured like a conversation rather than like a grammar', and the peculiar sociality of the chiasmus makes conversation seem to be an exercise in grammar (Gelpi 1985: 30).[23]

This relatively impersonal or asocial tendency is paradoxical, and not merely because all speech is inherently social. The deeper conundrum can be identified by asking how the chiasmus, like any trope, is a mental form of bodily experience; that is, how it reflects a discursive mapping of the body in order to anchor thought (Fernandez and Huber 2001: 10; Lakoff and Johnson 1980; Lakoff 1990). That is, if the chiasmus is a trope (and not only an ornament), there must be a bodily correlate to the verbal form, whether in the specific case (the metonym 'all hands on deck', the metaphor 'burning with passion', the catachresis 'leg of a table') or in the basic design. Obviously, many chiastic statements are highly ideational, and the phenomenological grounding seems rather abstract. Perhaps the form originates in the symmetry of the human body, and especially in the four limbs, two by two. That makes sense, and the body's thick, inchoate interior may be coded as the empty space of chiastic inversion – but such analogies seem awkward. Instead, the experiential correlative becomes clear when thinking of one person looking at another, or, better yet, looking into a mirror.

The inverted symmetry and reciprocal exchange defining a chiasmus is precisely analogous to the visual experience of looking at another person or at one's mirror image. One sees the same, but different; and difference, but the same. When looking at another, the correlative symmetries (eyes, ears, arms, legs) suggest a common identity independent of other variations in visage, size, colour, and so forth; and when looking at the self, the same correlates confirm the difference between oneself and one's image since each side is the inversion of the other (my right is its left). The most important part of these doublings, however, is the space between: the observation depends on both proximity and distance, and on there being empty space between one and one's double. Most important, this relationship models the paradigmatic condition of human communication as it was identified by Protagoras. The radical subjectivism of 'the human being is the measure of all things' should preclude communication, as one can never perfectly replicate the experience of another (even one's double). Instead, it is a condition of possibility, for communication emerges as the means for bridging the gaps created by radical subjectivity. More specifically, one can understand by observing similarities and making transpositions across an empty space, and by coding that experience into discursive form.

This process has been condensed into the small form of the chiasmus, which imitates the transposed subjects of the speaking situation and generates a third term that can serve as a temporary basis for commensurability. The aesthetic formalization of the exchange may alleviate ignorance and alienation – if the exchange is always partial, at least it can be elegant. But the form can work only as there is no principle for the permanent determination of the meaning of the terms and no basis for communion outside of an obviously artificial pairing in time. So it is that Nietzsche's chiasmus may be the most representative: by reversing seeing and being seen, subject and object, meaning and meaninglessness, he reveals the figural potential of language, not least its ability to turn opposites into complements. That potential issues from the chiastic structure of speech itself, the pattern seen when speaking to another or looking into the social mirror where one can see both self and other, but always separate and ineffable.[24]

Thus, the chiasmus is profoundly social but perhaps disturbingly so. It activates the cognitive reciprocity of interpersonal exchange prior to all other social patterning, and yet always keeps the other at a distance allowing continued observation. The other – and, in the mirror, the self – becomes identifiable on one's own terms and yet remains fundamentally beyond determinate meaning. Thus, a small device for pairing and inverting terms becomes an emblem of the pathos of human communication. We do communicate, which we can do because we both are and are not the same as others, and because we can recognize ourselves in the other and the other in oneself, but never to eliminate the empty space between us. More to the point, the chiasmus as figure generates its own themes, which are that duplication is never the same, that inversion is never resolution, and that the inchoate without mirrors the inchoate within.

Notes

1. Friedrich Nietzsche, *Beyond Good and Evil*, part IV, section 146 (1886). My translation is one variant among many like it that are in circulation (e.g., as evident from a Google search for the phrase.) The original text reads: 'Wer mit Ungeheuern kämpft, mag zusehn, dass er nicht dabei zum Ungeheuer wird. Und wenn du lange

in einen Abgrund blickst, blickt der Abgrund auch in dich hinein.' (*Jenseits von Gut und Böse:Vorspiel einer Philosophie der Zukunft, from Digital critical edition of the complete works and letters*, based on the critical text by G. Colli and M. Montinari, Berlin/New York, de Gruyter 1967, edited by Paolo D'Iorio, Nietzsche Source, http://www.nietzschesource.org/texts/eKGWB/JGB). In the widely available English translation by Walter Kaufman, this becomes 'Whoever fights monsters should see to it that in the process he does not become a monster. And when you look long into an abyss, the abyss also looks into you' (Nietzsche, trans. Kaufman 1989: 89). The circulation of the second sentence by itself probably reflects both the linguistic erosion that occurs during circulation and the durability of the chiasmus within process. The elision of the first sentence in the epigram has significant implications for how one reads the aphorism, however, as does the loss of the surrounding text from *Beyond Good and Evil*.

There are two issues here. The first involves the relationship between the two sentences in the full epigram. As the first sentence would seem to be good advice, one is tempted to see the second statement as mere elaboration for didactic effect. Indeed, Nietzsche's tone then seems rather light, albeit reflecting the ease of one who has been there and back more than once. Nietzsche is writing philosophy, however, and not an advice book. In my use of the quotation, we should keep both the light tone and the more philosophical rather than didactic implication. The point of the aphorism is not merely 'do not brood too much' or 'avoid projecting meaninglessness into your own life'. That is there, but there is more as well which can be suggested by drawing on analytical claims developed later in this essay. The aphorism goes on to depict something in the predicament of self-consciousness that is carried by the third term of its chiasmus: time. The condition described is that of looking long or staring rather than merely looking. Time is essential to gaining knowledge, but it becomes a curse when one learns that consciousness has no transcendental ground. Both the existential and pragmatic interpretations of the maxim coexist in the anxiety of temporality that emerges when one lives in language known to be in flux. That could lead to not looking into the abyss at all, which would be a mistaken application of Nietzsche. Instead, one might suggest that the better alternative is to take the advice but not assume it will save you.

This pathos acquires a deeper bite when epigram 146 is read back into its textual context, where it is the middle of five passages devoted to denigrating women. Nietzsche's misogyny is being given its rein, and the middle passage appears to be the abstract formulation of that antagonism. Women are monstrous, and despite the powerful desire for that Other in the battle of the sexes, one must beware of becoming one's enemy. And now the second line is particularly telling: the real danger is to have a woman staring into you, a reverse penetration capable of producing an alien knowledge of oneself. That is what it would mean to become a monster, apparently: to know what women would see, which is that one is an empty shell who can only bluster or dominate rather than be oneself. And thus the aphorism is symptomatic of another feature of its chiastic form that is mentioned later in this essay: the troubled attempt to manage self-consciousness that is inherently dependent on communicative exchange with and imperfect knowledge of other persons who are and are not like oneself.

2. De Man (1979) uses chiasmus to thematize 'trope', yet it is the generic term and not the specific device that is given titular status, unlike what happens with metaphor. The lack of nomination is all the more interesting when one considers how the chiastic logic is central to the metaphor-metonymy alteration that is the core example of de Man's deconstructive method.

3. The image is available at http://www.pbs.org/wgbh/nova/photo51/pict-01.html#fea_top. See also http://www.nocaptionneeded.com/?p=561.

4. De Man adds: 'As long as it is confined to objects, this structural necessity may seem harmless enough … But Rilke's figuration [and Stevens'] must also involve subject/object polarities, precisely because it has to put in question the irrevocability of this particularly compelling polarity' (de Man 1979: 49). Sanford Budick emphasizes the point: 'chiasmus creates a species of absence between its binary terms. … Chiasmus is the figure of a mind that cannot be made up, by itself, in any present moment' (Budick 1993: 964–65).

5. Aristotle, *Rhetoric*, 1404b.15.

6. For examples of the small form doing important work, see Kenneth Burke's (1973: 293–304) analysis of the proverb and Gary Saul Morson's studies of the quotation (2011) and the aphorism (2012).

7. The extensive use in ancient literature is beyond doubt and qualifies the analytic–synthetic distinction. See Welch 1981; Welch and McKinlay 1999. Welch provides a concise summary of the utility of the form in oral cultures and liturgical practices (Welch 1981: 12), and discusses methodological issues (Welch and McKinlay 1999: 157–74). A critical counterpoint is provided by David A. deSilva (2008: 242–71).

8. This now commonplace distinction stems from Ludwig Wittgenstein, where it was fundamental to his critique of language from the *Tractatus* through *On Certainty*. In Wittgenstein, the distinction involves corresponding shifts from truth to sense and from propositional content to the form of representation. 'There are, beyond the senses that can be formulated in sayable (sensical) propositions, things that can only be shown. These – the logical form of the world, the pictorial form, etc. – show themselves in the form of (contingent) propositions, in the symbolism and logical propositions, and even in the unsayable (metaphysical, ethical, aesthetic) propositions of philosophy. "What can be shown cannot be said." But it is there, in language, even though it cannot be said.' 'Ludwig Wittgenstein', *Stanford Encyclopedia of Philosophy*, http://plato.stanford.edu/entries/wittgenstein/ (entry first published 8 November 2002; substantive revision 23 December 2009).

9. This point follows from Norrman's discussion of linguistic binaries (Norrman 1986: 2).

10. On chiasmus in Shakespeare, see also Davis 2005: 237–58; Clark 2007; Engel 2009.

11. 'Recall the familiar critical distribution of sun and moon as figures respectively of reality and imagination in Stevens' symbology – a polarity imposed upon us by his poetry as well as his criticism, but a polarity which is as systematically undone as it is systematically inscribed' (Riddel 1988: 156).

12. Riddel notes that 'the "primary noon" of "The Motive for Metaphor" is an "X", that is, already a trope, a chiasmus, an originally doubled or extended figure' (Riddel 1988: 156).

13. This capacitance/cascade shift is insufficiently developed in the literature on chiasmus, although Norrman pegs it with his account of 'toppling-over': how

unidirectionalism causes a growing strain until it triggers a catastrophic reversal (Norrman 1986: 47).

14. The answer to this question is, not surprisingly, yes and no. The chiastic interweaving does allow for reuse of the term and so opens a door for criticism of Stevens' comfort with obscurity (a door many have walked through), but the larger argument of the poem is on behalf of movement from a weak imagination and empty words to a vivid imagination and words that strike sparks. And why could he not just say that? Because he is saying – and showing – much more as well, not least the poetic philosophy outlined here.

15. 'The final belief is to believe in fiction which you know to be a fiction, there being nothing else. The exquisite truth is to know that it is a fiction and that you believe it wittingly' (Stevens 1957: 163).

16. Despite his rigorous composition, mystification was a risk that Stevens was willing to take: 'Overall, the semantic form of a poem by Stevens seems to be a development of thought toward disclosure that remains a possibility' (Doggett 1980: 135). See also Kenneth Burke's analysis of mystification: *A Rhetoric of Motives* (Burke 1969: 101–27).

17. On the modernist valorization of symbol (and corresponding devaluing of allegory), see de Man 1969: 173–209. The literature on Stevens' modernism, including symbolist influence on his work, includes Benamou 1972; Gelpi 1985; and Surette 2008.

18. Walsh argues that 'the extremes may be as important as, if not more significant, than the center of a chiasm' (Walsh and McKinlay 1999: 174 n.9).

19. Scholarship on extended chiastic construction in Biblical texts is indexed by text and chiastic pattern in Welch and McKinlay 1999. On ring construction in Thucydides, see Rawlings 1981.

20. De Man has a similar insight: 'In conformity with a paradox that is inherent in all literature, the poetry gains a maximum of convincing power at the very moment that it abdicates any claim to truth' (de Man 1979: 50). Riddel captures the problem in Stevens' modernism in a manner that parallels de Man on key points: 'the poem ["Credences"] states by metaphorical indirection that the ideal of pure or unmediated perception is a philosophical construction and would be realized in a poem only if the poem purified its own means or burned away its own representational language' (Riddel 1988: 155).

21. Wallace Stevens, 'Metaphor as Degeneration'. The omission of 'both', as in 'both death and the imagination', may be significant: the two are presented as continuous rather than as separate realms.

22. To get a sense of the range of criticism on Stevens, see Axelrod and Deese 1988: 1–25.

23. Bruns is taking his lead from Mikhail Bakhtin's (1981: 275 ff., 286) critique of the monological attitude and its alignment with poetry.

24. Once again, de Man is instructive if one considers the implication of placing chiasmus, as he does, under the sign of allegory. Whereas the crossing pattern could be taken as a sign of pure identification between sign and reality, I am emphasizing how it involves 'the *repetition* (in the Kierkegaardian sense of the term) of a previous sign with which it can never coincide'. Thus, 'whereas the symbol postulates the possibility of an identity or identification, allegory designates primarily a distance in relation to its own origin, and renouncing the nostalgia and the desire to coincide, it establishes its language in the void of this temporal difference. In so doing it prevents

the self from an illusory identification with the non-self, which is now fully, though painfully, recognized as a non-self' (Singleton 1969: 190–91).

References

Assis, Elie. 2002. 'Chiasmus in Biblical Narrative: Rhetoric of Characterization', *Prooftexts* 22.

Axelrod, Steven Gould, and Helen Deese (eds). 1988. *Critical Essays on Wallace Stevens*. Boston: G.K. Hall.

Bakhtin, Mikhail. 1981. *The Dialogic Imagination*, ed. Michael Holquist, trans. Caryl Emerson and Michael Holmquist. Austin: University of Texas Press.

Benamou, Michael. 1972. *Wallace Stevens and the Symbolist Imagination*. Princeton: Princeton University Press.

Budick, Sanford. 1993. "Chiasmus and the Making of Literary Tradition: The Case of Wordsworth and 'The Days of Dryden and Pope,'" *ELH* 60: 964-965.

Burke, Kenneth. 1969a. 'Four Master Tropes', in *A Grammar of Motives*. Berkeley: University of California Press.

Burke, Kenneth. 1969b. *A Rhetoric of Motives*. Berkeley: University of California Press.

Burke, Kenneth. 1973. 'Literature as Equipment for Living', in *The Philosophy of Literary Form: Studies in Symbolic Action*, 3rd ed., Berkeley: University of California Press.

Clark, Ira. 2007. *Rhetorical Readings, Dark Comedies, and Shakespeare's Problem Plays*. Gainesville: University Press of Florida.

Davis, William L. 2005. 'Structural Secrets: Shakespeare's Complex Chiasmus', *Style* 39: 237–58.

deSilva, David A. 2008. 'X Marks the Spot? A Critique of the Use of Chiasmus in Macro-Structural Analyses of Revelation', *Journal for the Study of the New Testament* 30: 242–71.

Doggett, Frank. 1980. *Wallace Stevens: The Making of the Poem*. Baltimore: Johns Hopkins University Press.

Doyle, Laura (ed.). 2001. *Bodies of Resistance: New Phenomenologies of Politics, Agency, and Culture*. Evanston, IL: Northwestern University Press.

Engel, William E. 2009. *Chiastic Designs in English Literature from Sidney to Shakespeare*. Surrey, UK: Ashgate.

Erdinast-Vulcan, Daphna. 2007. 'That which 'Has No Name in Philosophy': Merleau-Ponty and the Language of Literature', *Human Studies* 30: 395–409.

Evans, Fred, and Leonard Lawlor. 2000. *Chiasms: Merleau-Ponty's Notion of Flesh*. Albany: State University of New York Press.

Fernandez, James W. and Mary Taylor Huber (eds). 2001. *Irony in Action*. Chicago: University of Chicago Press.

Gelpi, Albert (ed.). 1985. *Wallace Stevens: The Poetics of Modernism*. Cambridge: Cambridge University Press.

Grey, Thomas C. 1991. *The Wallace Stevens Case: Law and the Practice of Poetry*. Cambridge: Harvard University Press.

Grothe, Mardy. 1999. *Never Let a Fool Kiss You or a Kiss Fool You: Chiasmus and a World of Quotations that Say what they Mean and Mean what they Say*. New York: Viking; http://www.drmardy.com/chiasmus/welcome.shtml.

Hariman, Robert. 1986. 'Status, Marginality, and Rhetorical Theory', *Quarterly Journal of Speech* 72: 38-54.

Huizinga, J. 1966. *Homo Ludens: A Study of the Play-element in Culture*, Boston: Beacon.

Kestenbaum, Victor. 2002. *The Grace and Severity of the Ideal: John Dewey and the Transcendent*. Chicago: University of Chicago Press.

Lakoff, George. 1990. *Women, Fire, and Dangerous Things*. Chicago: University of Chicago Press.

Lakoff, George, and Mark Johnson. 1980. *Metaphors We Live By*. Chicago: University of Chicago Press.

Levin, Jonathan. 1999. *The Poetics of Transition: Emerson, Pragmatism, and American Literary Modernism*. Durham, NC: Duke University Press.

Man, Paul de. 1979. *Allegories of Reading: Figural Language in Rousseau, Nietzsche, Rilke, and Proust*. New Haven, CT: Yale University Press.

Man, Paul de. 1969. 'The Rhetoric of Temporality', in *Interpretation: Theory and Practice*, ed. Charles S. Singleton. Baltimore: Johns Hopkins University Press.

Morson, Gary Saul. 2011. *The Words of Others: From Quotations to Culture*. New Haven: Yale University Press.

Morson, Gary Saul. 2012. *The Long and the Short of It: From Aphorism to Novel*. Stanford: Stanford University Press.

Nietzsche, Friedrich, trans. Walter Kaufman. (1966) 1989. *Beyond Good and Evil: Prelude to a Philosophy of the Future*. New York, Vintage.

Norrman, Ralf. 1986. *Samuel Butler and the Meaning of Chiasmus*. New York: St. Martin's.

Paul, Anthony. 1992. *The Torture of the Mind: Macbeth, Tragedy, and Chiasmus*. Amsterdam: Thesis Publishers.

Rawlings, Hunter R. 1981. *The Structure of Thucydides' History*. Princeton: Princeton University Press.

Riddel, Joseph N. 1988 'The Climate of Our Poems', in *Critical Essays on Wallace Stevens*, ed. Steven Gould Axelrod and Helen Deese. Boston: G.K. Hall.

Singleton, Charles S. 1969. *Interpretation: Theory and Practice*. Baltimore, MD: Johns Hopkins University Press.

Stevens, Wallace. 1957. *Opus Postumus*. New York: Knopf.

Stevens, Wallace. 1972. 'Notes Toward a Supreme Fiction', in *The Palm at the End of the Mind*, ed. Holly Stevens. New York: Vintage.

Surette, Leon. 2008. *The Modern Dilemma: Wallace Stevens, T.S. Eliot, and Humanism*. Montreal: McGill-Queen's University Press.

Welch, John H. (ed.). 1981. *Chiasmus in Antiquity: Structures, Analyses, Exegesis*. Hildesheim: Gerstenberg Verlag.

Welch, John H., and Daniel B. McKinlay (eds). 1999. *Chiasmus Bibliography*. Provo, UT: Research Press.

White, Hayden. 1973. *Metahistory: The Historical Imagination in Nineteenth-Century Europe*. Baltimore, MD: Johns Hopkins University Press.

CHAPTER 3

Chiasmus and Metaphor

Ivo Strecker

■ ■ ■ ■ ■ ■ ■

The Timeliness and Promises of Chiasmus

Chiasmus is an excellent rhetorical tool to move and 'turn' people's minds and emotions. Since Antiquity, this figure has been widely used in verbal and written communication, yet discourse about its stylistic features and role in human life has remained confined to select circles of poets, literary critics, rhetoricians, anthropologists and scholars of the mind. Publications explicitly devoted to it are accordingly few, and when you ask the proverbial man in the street what a chiasmus is, the most likely answer will be 'I have never heard of it'.

It is different when it comes to other figures. Irony, for example, is a term deeply entrenched in Western everyday discourse, both practical and theoretical. People employ irony, and they reflect and comment on its use. Although most will be hard-pressed if asked to clearly define irony and explain how it works, they will nevertheless be ready to answer and will have interesting things to say. Academically, irony has attracted much attention past and present, and especially during the last decades has generated a rich and fast-growing literature (Gibbs and Colston 2007; Bender and Wellbery 1990).

Metaphor has similarly been in the limelight, and in the wake of the various linguistic, performative, rhetorical and other 'turns' that preceded the change of the millennia, it has begun to play an even more prominent role in Western intellectual life. It is now popular in spiffy conversation, social and cultural commentary, literary criticism, political debate and the like. In fact, today metaphor is something of a buzzword. People comment on its appropriate or inappropriate use, speak of 'profound' or 'shallow' or 'misfiring' metaphors and generally consider discourse on metaphor the hallmark of learnedness. With this growing popularity goes a prolific production of publications, which, like those on irony, come from a variety of disciplines such as linguistics, literature, philosophy, psychology, history and anthropology (see the online bibliographies of metaphor and other tropes).

As stated earlier, chiasmus has lingered in the background but is now coming to the fore. Like metaphor, its appearance suits the present Western mood, which has lost much of its belief in plain style and univocal logic. Or, expressed differently, the newly developing interest in chiasmus corresponds to the awareness that we live in 'an age not of rhetoric, but of rhetoricality, the age, that is, of a generalized rhetoric that penetrates to the deepest levels of human experience' (Nienkamp 2001: 3, referring to Bitzer and Black 1971: 208; see also Bender and Wellbery, in Bender and Wellbery 1990).

■ ■ ■

In order to show something of the spirit in which I embark on this chapter I should like to quote from some of the correspondence I have had with Anthony Paul, contributor to and co-editor of this volume:

(1) *Ivo to Anthony*
Can one call the following sayings/thoughts/events/experiences interesting chiasmi?
'I like you, you like me'; or 'I hate you, you hate me';
'They cross swords: Eric strikes at Shawn, Shawn strikes at Eric';
'Friend becomes foe, foe becomes friend'.

(2) *Anthony to Ivo*
A loves/hates/strikes B and B loves/hates/strikes A embodies an important truth about human relations and interactions. Because of course it isn't a simple matter of symmetrical reciprocity but of a response that reinforces the first emotion or action and leads to more of the same and so on, escalating or bifurcating exponentially. So the simple chiastic formula is like a basic building block of personal/social/political/historical relations.

(3) *Ivo to Anthony*
Chiasmus, I think, is a powerful rhetorical device because it mirrors some of our strongest experiences, the experiences of reversal, of utter surprise

that things can be opposite to what we expected. Or rather doubly so: not only does fair turn out to be foul, also foul turns out to be fair. My interest is to explore how we experience this double surprise in real life, while your interest has been to explore the way in which the double surprise has been used on the stage. But world and stage are in turn chiastically related as we can read in William Shakespeare and Victor Turner. One topic that interests me is the relationship between chiasmus and metaphor theory, as well as the theory of emphasis (see what Stephen Tyler has to say about this in *The Said and the Unsaid!*).

(4) *Anthony to Ivo*
In response to your latest thoughts about chiasmus: it seems we are going down two interesting roads. We want to know what it is we want from a chiasmus, and we are interested in the relations between chiasmus and existence. Relevant is the point that while every chiasmus is a mirroring, not every mirroring is a chiasmus. More has to be going on; some kind of reciprocity, a giving back, a turn of meaning often involving paradox. These conditions are present in good chiasmi. They satisfy because they make a little dazzle, don't they? For a moment they make you blink: what is cause here, what is effect? But then you see how they dance together and augment each other. When it comes to chiasmus and existence, the drama of life, I think we may be on the edge of great discoveries.

■ ■ ■

There are various kinds of chiasmus, many of them trite. As Robert Hariman observes:

> Anyone could bundle words into the ABBA form if given a few examples and some small incentive: we should make our words fit our ideas, and our ideas fit our words; I don't like snow in the winter, but I don't like winter without snow; put a song in your heart, and your heart into a song. Do this occasionally, and you can acquire a reputation for having a way with words; keep it up and you will drive people nuts. (Hariman, this volume)

Yet how is one to decide whether the meaning of a chiasmus is shallow or deep? Does not, for example, 'words fit ideas, ideas fit words' hide deep epistemological puzzles; and does not 'song in your heart, heart in your song' invite reflections about the way in which cause and effect mutually imply one another? In other words, it is hard to decide whether a particular chiasmus is just an empty ornament or a true trope, which 'turns' sentences in such a way that they enrich both mind and emotion. The following examples of productive chiasmi may serve as orientation as we embark on a study of the more meaningful role of 'chiasmus in the drama of life':

> To shut what is open, to open what is shut. (Apocrypha)
> Life leads to death, death leads to life. (Apocrypha)
> I do not live to eat, but eat to live. (Quintilian; Wiseman and Hariman, this volume)
> Fair is foul, foul is fair. (Shakespeare; Paul and Hariman, this volume)
> We may lack land for living, but land for dying will never lack. (Montaigne; Usher, this volume)
> All art must become science, all science, art. (Schelling; Wiseman, this volume)
> Not consciousness determines being, but being determines consciousness. (Marx; Paul this volume)
> Friends make gifts, gifts make friends. (Sahlins; Wiseman, this volume)

In 'From Stasis to Ékstasis: Four Types of Chiasmus' (this volume), Anthony Paul has analysed a variety of such meaningful chiasmi, which led him to distinguish (1) Cross-shaped chiasmi that spring from and induce a sense of balance as in 'Man is made for woman and woman for man'; (2) Mirror-shaped chiasmi that express and generate feelings of paralysis as in 'Fair is foul and foul is fair'; (3) Circling chiasmi that are both cause and effect of melancholy, as in 'I am tired of thinking how thinking of you never tires me'; and (4) Spiraling chiasmi that are mind-opening and themselves the product of open minds as in 'The inner world is formed by the outer and the outer by the inner'.

Spiralling chiasmi such as the one mentioned above are especially attractive, says Paul, in that they wake us up

> to a third possibility, the single more complex new truth arrived at when we perceive ... that the two halves of the sentence are at once both untrue and true ... What the spiral chiasmus leads to is not a synthesis but, rather, an embrace, not of the separate components but of their open-ended and progressive dynamic interactivity. This suggests a recycling – or rather, a further spiralling – of Heraclitus' notion, taken up by Hegel, of the dynamic and cyclic interplay of opposites, and the unity arising from the combination of opposites'. (Paul, this volume)

In similar fashion Boris Wiseman has argued that spiralling chiasmus plays a constitutive role in anthropology. Taking the work of Claude Lévi-Strauss as an example, he has shown how 'the anthropological journey, real or in the mind, is construed in terms of a switching of positions of self and other' (Wiseman 2009: 93). It entails:

a chiasmic inversion of the poles of the far and the near: the far becomes near and the near, far ... It is this chiasmic switching of positions – other becomes self, self other – which explains the paradox inherent in anthropology: if the other remains other, I have no way of understanding him/her; but if I understand him/her, he/she is no longer other. (Ibid.: 99; see also Tyler this volume)

[However,] anthropology only appears to be an impossible task when theorized in terms of the two polar situations hypothesised by the paradox: *absolute* otherness or *absolute* sameness. Ordinarily, though, the ethnographer does speak the other's language, and mediation is possible. Here ... there is a third position between the two polar extremes, a mid-point in the anthropologist's journey where self and other ... are at the right distance from one another to be able to engage in a meaningful exchange. ... The ethnographic conversion of 'other' into 'self' and 'self' into 'other' is a *process*, one that implies a gradual transformation which, even if it is ultimately circular (assimilation, in reality, is never total), is nevertheless a source of understanding and knowledge. The return to the point of departure – self-other; other-self – is not a return to the same. The point of departure has been modified. (Ibid.: 100–101)

In my own life I have also been subject to these enabling and constraining conditions of the 'ethnographic chiasmus'. In fact, I recently published a collection of essays under this title, saying on the back of the cover that chiasmus is part of ethnographic practice, which involves constant surprise and reversal of position during fieldwork, and which is the reason why trans-cultural understanding can come about only as a meeting, touching, or crossing (Strecker 2010). But although I find spiralling chiasmus the most fruitful and important in my own life and hope to further explore its potentials within the context of the 'rhetoric culture project' (Strecker and Tyler 2009), which is itself also based on a chiasmus (culture shapes rhetoric, rhetoric shapes culture), the present contribution is devoted to 'mirror-shaped' chiasmus, an important figure for inward and outward persuasion that also plays a role in magic and other manifestations of what Lévi-Strauss has called the 'savage mind'. I also intend to show how the newly developing study of chiasmus can gain from the more advanced theory of metaphor.

THE INTERNAL DRAMA OF METAPHOR AND CHIASMUS

To begin with, chiasmus resembles metaphor in that it is based on the art of 'collocation', 'displacement' or 'juxtaposition'. In metaphor, I.A. Richards tells us, 'two things belonging to very different orders of experience' are put together, and as the two things put together 'are more remote, the tension created is, of course, greater. That tension is the spring of the bow, the source of the energy of the shot' (Richards 1936: 124–25).

David Sapir similarly stresses that in metaphor two separate domains are brought into juxtaposition. His description of the process runs as follows:

> By replacing a term continuous to a topic with one that is discontinuous, or by putting the two in juxtaposition, we are compelled ... to consider each term in relation to the other, and it is at this point that we are aware of the metaphor. In establishing a relationship two processes operate: first, the reduction of the terms to their shared features – to what makes them alike; secondly, the transference from one to the other, but mainly from the discontinuous to the continuous, of what they do not share – of what makes them unlike. The first process, which is basic, gives the metaphor its specificity. On hearing George the Lion we are compelled to consider what we know about lions and to select those features that would apply to George, thus learning something very specific about George. In contrast, the second process gives a metaphor, for want of a better word, its *colour*. It allows us to consider the continuous term for what it is not, to assume for a moment that, although George is 'really' like a lion only in certain specific ways, he might be a lot more like a lion in just those ways. We are given the means to imagine George as a real lion, straight and simple, even down to his tail. (Sapir 1977: 9)

As long as one focuses on the bundle of features which both terms share with each other (mammal, strength, courage), 'George the Lion' is an 'internal metaphor', but if one relates first each term to its own domain and then goes on to compare the two pairs with each other, creating the analogy 'George : men :: lion : animals', one arrives at an 'external metaphor' (Sapir 1977: 22). This 'interactional theory' (implicit already in Richards 1936, and explicit in Black 1962) points out that metaphor creates a 'new entity', or a mental and emotional space that induces the mind to oscillate between the poles of likeness and non-likeness. Note how close this is to what Robert Hariman says:

> Chiasmus works not simply through a logic of crossing or exchange between two terms, but also through the generation of a third term that becomes the bridge between the original pairing. Thus, in the ABBA format, A and B are not changed into one another, but generate a third term, C, to mediate their relationship. Of course, other and often very subtle adjustments and reverberations between the two primary terms can be triggered by their arrangement in the mirror image format, but the generative power of the reversal comes from consciousness having to supply *something* to cross the chasm between the original set and its inverted double. The crossing pattern proves

to be most powerful not because it compares by inverting binary terms, but because in doing so it supplies a new term as the common ground on which the contrasting propositions can stand together'. (Hariman, this volume)

One of the examples Hariman provides is the chiasmus at the beginning of *Macbeth* (minutely analysed by Anthony Paul [1992]) where the witches chant, 'Fair is foul and foul is fair'. To Hariman it is 'startling clear' that here the 'third term' is *power*: 'That is, this chiasmus makes an ontological claim: power exists and alters all that it touches, which in Macbeth's world is everything. Whatever ethics may be, power now is dominant in the world and capable of bending anything to that end' (Hariman, this volume).

Yet Hariman states elsewhere that (a) the 'void' or 'abyss' between the two primary terms of a chiasmus produce 'reverberations', and (b) that chiasmus generates a 'continual movement secured only in the illusory permanence of the gaze ... And so as one thinks with chiasmus, the doubled modality of the term offers stability only to oscillate and then to spin off something beyond the binary, something asymmetrical' (ibid.). If (a) and (b) are true, then there cannot really be a single, clear and stable third term, and chiasmus must be considered to be a thoroughly multi-vocal trope. Its rhetorical strength would derive from its power to cause oscillations and reverberations in ways that are similar to metaphor. As Richards pointed out when he considered

> what happens in the mind when we put together – in a sudden and strik-
> ing fashion – two things belonging to very different orders of experience.
> The most important happenings – in addition to a general confused rever-
> beration and strain – are the mind's efforts to connect them. The mind is a
> connecting organ, it works only by connecting and it can connect any two
> things in an indefinitely large number of different ways. (Richards 1936:
> 124–25)

Thus, 'reverberation' and a concomitant state of mental and emotional 'confusion' are characteristic of both metaphor and chiasmus. This is perhaps the reason why Paul has based his chapter (this volume) not on univocal definitions but on images that are in themselves suggestive of multi-vocal meanings: balance, mirror, circle and spiral allow for a kind of abundance or even excess of meaning to which Hariman himself calls attention when he writes of chiasmus: 'In place of fixed relationships, the third term always carries excess energy that can be a sign of additional yet undefined meaning' (Hariman, this volume).

To better understand what we are grappling with here, let us recall what Richards said about the relationship between the two parts of a metaphor. First he noted that there were:

no agreed terms for the two halves of a metaphor, in spite of the immense inconvenience, almost the necessity, of such terms if we are to make any analyses without confusion. For the whole task is to compare the different relations which, in different cases, these two members of a metaphor hold to one another, and we are confused at the start if we don't know which of the two we are talking about. (Richards 1936: 96)

Then he introduced the term 'tenor' for the first and 'vehicle' for the second part of a metaphor, adding:

The co-presence of the vehicle and tenor results in a meaning (to be clearly distinguished from the tenor) which is not attainable without their interaction ... Vehicle and tenor in co-operation give a meaning of more varied powers than can be ascribed to either ... With different metaphors the relative importance of the contributions of vehicle and tenor to this resultant meaning varies immensely. (Ibid.: 100)

In *Anatomy of Metaphor*, Sapir followed Richards' train of thought and referred to his terminology but replaced it with his own. 'To have a metaphor at all,' he wrote, 'the discontinuous term (vehicle) must be stated along with the topic and/or the continuous term (tenor)' (1977: 7). The first part is 'continuous' with the topic (as George in 'George the Lion'), and the second is 'discontinuous' in that it involves a different semantic domain (as Lion in 'George the Lion'). When we perceive a metaphorical expression, we 'depart' from the continuous term, 'arrive' at the discontinuous term, and then, realizing that the 'two terms are one in that they are alike, two that they are not alike' (ibid.: 9), our mind switches back and forth between the two terms to examine 'the bundle of shared features' (ibid.: 6).

Richards' and Sapir's analyses lead to some terminological clarity, yet the terms 'vehicle', 'continuous' and 'discontinuous' seem strange because they do not do justice to how we experience metaphor. 'Tenor' is different, for it connotes music and accords well with the way in which we 'tune in' with the meaning of a metaphor. However, it would be better not to use 'tenor' for the first term but rather for the 'thrust' of a metaphor as a whole; for its multivocal meaning that cannot and must not be arrested; for its 'colour' as Sapir would say, or, better still, for its 'sound' and 'aura'.

So how should the two different parts of metaphor be called if we want to do justice to the underlying social and psychological realities? I suggest we speak of a 'pathetic' (first) and a 'sympathetic' (second) part. 'Pathetic' refers to states of affairs that are in one way or other 'distressingly inadequate' (*Collins Dictionary*), and it is precisely a feeling of distressingly inadequate communicative competence that acts as the source and motive for metaphorical production. Social life abounds with situations where people are at a loss for what to say, where plain, univocal speech will just not do, and where they strain their imagination to find the right rhetorical figures that help to overcome the impasse.

To give an example: George (a favourite in the discussion of metaphor) may have had success in a wrestling contest. But before we utter any words of praise we may well pause for a brief moment while searching in our mind for the appropriate expression. Sensing that 'George you are strong!' would be 'distressingly inadequate' to convince George of our admiration, we may eventually come up with, 'George you are a lion!' When he hears this, George will probably be pleased, for the metaphor with its multi-vocal aura of prowess and invincibility provides a more than adequate recognition of his personal achievement.

Thus, the first term (George) remains 'pathetic' until the semantically appropriate expression (lion) is found, which 'sympathetically' answers the needs of the topic of discourse (praise of George).

∎ ∎ ∎

The point I am trying to establish is that the internal organization of tropes is dramatic, and that in order to understand both metaphor and chiasmus we need to have a closer look at the relationships pertaining between their different parts. So far we have seen that the first part of metaphor is 'pathetic' and the second 'sympathetic'. As they act upon each other, both parts generate an ephemeral whole, the quality of which cannot be precisely described but may be evoked by metaphors such as 'colour', 'aura', 'sound' or 'tenor'. Generally, the two parts of metaphor uphold a positive relationship characterized by resonance, response and cooperation, and what may be called 'semantic sympathy'.

This 'semantic sympathy' comes out clearly in Stephen Tyler's theory of metaphor, which says that 'by means of metaphor speakers bring together concepts ordinarily separated and consciously violate semantic categories to convey and approximate in imagination what was previously unfamiliar. Without such intention one cannot really speak of metaphor' (Tyler 1978: 320). Furthermore, 'Metaphors have dual representation; they work not only by drawing our attention to a comparison, but also by pointing to a particular emphasis either by explicitly naming the appropriate attribute, ... or by implying it' (ibid.: 325).

The internal dynamics of chiasmus on the other hand are very different, for the two parts of this trope are characterized not by consonance but by dissonance, not by stabilizing resemblance but destabilizing antinomy. Again this can be best understood with the help of Tyler, especially his outline of meaning schemata: meaning schemata of existence, attribution, function and comparison 'are the pillars of our naive realism'. They 'deal with what exists, what it is made of, what it does and is for, and how it relates to other existents'. And, very importantly, meaning schemata 'have a certain psychological and linguistic reality' because 'they reflect our natural metaphysical disposition to think of the world as consisting of things more or less real, known by their attributes, and characteristic patterns of aggregation' (Tyler 1978: 240).

Attribution and function are the most immediate schemata, which come into play as we perceive the world and talk about it. Then follow sequence schemata of temporal and spatial comparison, as well as schemata of resemblance where attributions and functions are compared and matched.

Also, these schemata play a fundamental role in figuration: metaphor includes categorical relations of part to whole, cause to effect, and quality to substance, which 'mutually imply one another, for we may know causes by their effects, substances by their qualities, and wholes by their parts because wholes have parts, substances have qualities, and causes have effects. Naming one aspect of the relationship implies the other, and the metaphoric relation of substituting one for the other seems clearly logical' (Tyler 1978: 317).

Grafted onto these schemata are the schemata of antinomy, which oppose, negate or convert what has previously been established, especially by means of the schemata of attribution, function and resemblance. In other words, interlocutors employ metaphor (as well as simile, synecdoche, metonymy and the like) on one side to establish and affirm the conventions they live by, and on the other side, they use chiasmus to throw each other's received wisdom into question. This often amounts to what Brown and Levinson have called a 'face-threatening act' (Brown and Levinson 1978: 56–324), for nothing is more overbearing, more self-assertive, more arrogant than to tell someone not only that what he has considered until now to be true is not true, but that in fact the very opposite of what he held to be true is the case.

Hariman has similarly noted this provocative, even 'asocial tendency' of chiasmus, a figure which 'refers the audience to its own cultural capital but not to shared experience', prohibits an 'identification with the speaker', and 'acts as a bar between speaker and audience'. Wallace Stevens, says Hariman, has perfectly expressed this superiority of chiasmus in his poem 'The Motive for Metaphor', which in its very last line refers to 'The vital, arrogant, fatal, dominant X' (Hariman, this volume).

However, not only chiasmus but even the use of other tropes may involve some kind of affront, although more soft and subtle. Grice called this 'flouting' (showing open disregard, mocking, scoffing) and explained it as follows: in conversation, participants are expected to follow a basic principle of cooperation, which demands, 'Make your conversational contribution such as is required, at the stage at which it occurs, by the accepted purpose or direction of the talk exchange in which you are engaged' (Grice 1975: 45). This requires adherence to four different conversational maxims: be as informative as required (maxim of quantity); be true (maxim of quality); be

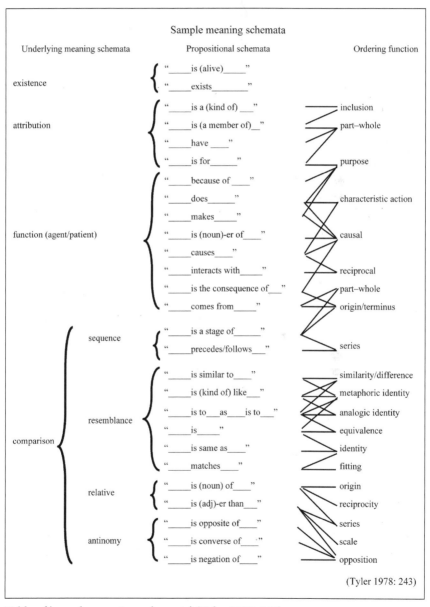

Table of 'sample meaning schemata' (Tyler 1978: 243).

relevant (maxim of relation) and be perspicuous (maxim of manner). As they converse, people often deliberately violate these maxims, and by doing so they offend each other. But the offence does not last long because its sympathetic intention is quickly understood: a conversational maxim has been flouted to get some additional meaning across:

> On the assumption that the speaker is able to fulfil the maxim and to do so without violating another maxim ... is not opting out, and is not, in view of the blatancy of his performance, trying to mislead, the hearer is faced with a minor problem: How can his saying what he did say be reconciled with the supposition that he is observing the overall *cooperative principle*? This situation is one that characteristically gives rise to a conversational implicature; and when a conversational implicature is generated in this way, I shall say that a maxim is being *exploited*. (Grice 1975: 49 – his emphasis)

Here we can see that implicatures involve some kind of offence and demand mental submission of the hearer to the speaker, if only for brief moments. For this reason they cannot be used in all social situations: persons of lower social status are expected to use no implicatures but only plain style as they speak upwards, while their superiors may make use of them as they communicate downwards (Strecker 1988: 162–70).

Generally one can say that all implicatures are to some extent mind teasers (as well as mind pleasers), but the teasing involved in chiasmus is the strongest, and the feelings that accompany it involve the highest intensities of pleasure and pain.

CHIASMUS COMBINED WITH METAPHOR

In the light of the internal dynamics of metaphor and chiasmus outlined in the second part of this chapter, we can understand why chiasmus combined with metaphor must be doubly multivocal: the first multiplication of meaning is enshrined in the structure of the chiastic expression itself, the second multiplication derives from the reverberations between the pathetic and the sympathetic parts of the metaphors used in the chiasmus.

Shakespeare's line, 'Fair is foul and foul is fair', which Paul has chosen as a paragon of mirror chiasmus, carries such doubly multi-vocal meanings. This is why I think that the line does not produce stasis (as Paul has it), nor is it 'startlingly clear' that it 'makes an ontological claim: power exists and alters all that it touches' (as Hariman argues). Rather, its chiastic use of metaphors fires the imagination, lets both mind and emotion spin, and generally has a 'bewitching' effect.

One might object, saying that 'fair' and 'foul' do not carry any multi-vocal meanings and should not be understood as metaphors. True, 'fair' and 'foul' have a long history and are so well established in Anglo-Saxon discourse that they may be called 'dead' metaphors and therefore do not carry any real metaphorical meaning anymore. 'Much of our use of metaphors is not really metaphoric,' writes Tyler, 'for either we are unaware that we are using a metaphor or the metaphor has become so stale that no one takes it metaphorically' (Tyler 1987: 320). But 'dead' metaphors are often not quite as dead as they seem, and the transfer of meaning from one semantic domain to another may not be as complete as it seems. Great poets like Shakespeare (and many other writers and orators) know how to exploit this. They use the latent metaphorical meanings of certain terms to create hidden undercurrents in their texts, or they breathe new life into what was thought to be 'dead' metaphors.

This applies also to 'Fair is foul and foul is fair'. 'Fair' and 'foul' originally derive from different kinds of sensation. 'Fair' pertained to vision and referred especially to the beauty of women. This visual feature was then transferred to other domains, which were partly concrete and real like 'fair weather' or imaginary and abstract like 'rules of fair conduct'. 'Foul' on the other hand pertained to smell and referred to the stink, the odour of rotting substances. This feature was then transferred to other domains, again partly to concrete and real phenomena such as 'foul weather' or to more imaginary, moral realms where it signified wickedness, a break of rules, disgrace and dishonour.

All these meanings are contained in the 'resonance chamber' (Maranda 2010) of 'Fair is foul and foul is fair'. But there is more to it: the perception and appreciation of a drama such as *Macbeth* – and generally the drama of life – always involves retrospective and prospective thinking and feeling. Lines like 'Fair is foul and foul is fair' make us look forward and anticipate either with horror or with joy what is going to come. And later, as things unfold, we look back and see what happened earlier in a new light. Because the chant of the witches occurs right at the beginning of the play there is no apparent topic of discourse to which 'fair' and 'foul' could refer and act as 'sympathetic' terms. But later, as the tragedy develops, and as one begins to realize the awesome schemes of Macbeth and Lady Macbeth, the metaphorical power of the two terms begins to develop.

As I have already mentioned, in my view Shakespeare's witches neither want to arrest anyone's mind nor make any ontological claim. Rather they want to throw a magical spell over the country so that not fairness but foulness may 'hover through the fog and filthy air'. In their chants they mix mysterious rhetorical ingredients together like chiasmus, metaphor, contradiction, alliteration, ironic reference to tautology, and so on, and this is how they achieve their magical end.

The nexus between metaphor, chiasmus and magical spell becomes apparent when we recall what the anthropologist Julian Huxley and the rhetorician Kenneth Burke have said about the matter:

> Magic, in the strict anthropological sense, is based on the belief that both nature and man can be brought under compulsion and controlled by psychological means through spells, incantations, prayer, sacrifice, and special personal or professional powers. … Magical belief-rituals survive and play a part even in the highest and most scientific cultures of today … And when we say that we are 'under the spell' of beauty or great music, or call a view of a work of art 'magical', we are acknowledging the existence of magic, in the extended sense of non-rational, emotional and often unconscious formalizing or patterning forces, which are essential for all transcendent experience. (Huxley 1966: 264–65)

> Since the effective politician is a 'spellbinder', it seems to follow by elimination that the hortatory use of speech for political ends can be called 'magic', in the discredited sense of that term. As a result, much analysis of political exhortation comes to look simply like survival of primitive magic, whereas it should be handled in its own terms, as an aspect of what it really is: rhetoric … The realistic use of addressed language to *induce action in people* became the magical use of addressed language to *induce motion in things* (things by nature alien to purely linguistic orders of motivation). If we then begin by treating this *erroneous* and *derived* magical use as *primary*, we are invited to treat a *proper* use of language (for instance, political persuasion) simply as a vestige of benightedly prescientific magic. To be sure, the rhetorician has the tricks of his trade. But they are not mere 'bad science'; 'they are an art'. (Burke 1950: 54–55)

From what these authors explain it follows that all well-formed tropes are 'magical' in that they captivate, enchant, and mysteriously persuade us. As the example of 'Fair is foul and foul is fair' shows, mirror chiasmus – one of the most complex tools available to the art of rhetoric – intensifies this experience.

But before moving on to another example of the 'magical' and 'bewitching' power of mirror chiasmus combined with metaphor, one further rhetorical strategy of the witches should be noted: in 'Fair is foul and foul is fair' they echo and invert the tautology, 'Fair is fair and foul is foul'. Tautologies of this kind play an important role in social discourse. By uttering 'patent and necessary truths', speakers encourage listeners 'to look for an informative interpretation of the non-informative utterance' (Brown and Levinson 1978: 225). Penelope Brown and Stephen Levinson have provided examples where tautologies are used for excuses, criticisms, refusals, complaints, approvals and encouragements, but I should like to quote here what I have observed among the Hamar, an agro-pastoral people of southern Ethiopia:

> I was struck from the start by the role tautologies play in Hamar discourse, and after a while I began to understand that tautology is an assertion of authority and an affirmation of the status quo. It is not for the young and inexperienced to utter tautologies but only for the old and wise. Thus, when in 1973 Baldambe (our host, friend, teacher and mentor in Hamar) gave a lecture for the children of his friends in Berlin, he closed with the words, 'bad is bad and good is good'. These words were not only the message of the lengthy speech but also the resumé of a long life in which Baldambe had come to realize the limits of relativism. The young and inquisitive naturally question all 'patent' truth. They say, 'bad is good and good is bad' and try to discover how far they get with these contradictions. But having gone through this process there comes the time when certain things really are what they seem, and it is this that gets expressed by tautologies in Hamar. (Strecker 1988: 133)

To put myself once again in the position of the witches: they knew very well that in Medieval England a decent person, especially one of great social standing and authority, would have insisted that 'Good is good and bad is bad'. But they taunted the moral order and ironically inverted the tautology, stirring yet another rhetorical potion into their magical broth.

■ ■ ■

Paul has observed that mirror chiasmus provides a means to deal with 'life's paradoxes and problems'. It addresses 'forms of entrapment, personal and collective', and it serves 'to express mental torment and an inescapable circle of causes and effects' (Paul, this volume). In this final section, the thesis will be supported with an ethnographical case recorded during my fieldwork in Hamar. It reveals yet again the 'magical' effect of mirror chiasmus when it is combined with metaphor. But this time chiasmus is not meant to destroy as in the chants of the witches. Rather it serves as a vehicle for lamentation and in this way helps to alleviate social stress and personal sorrow. First the case, then follows my interpretation:

> As evening comes I sit outside in front of the house on my cowhide. Soon the goats will come and later the cattle. Already even before it really gets dark, the moon and the male and female stars become visible. They have been 'sitting in a semi-circle as in a public meeting' and that means trouble.

These heavenly bodies would not sit together like this if everything in the country was fine, for then there would be no reason to hold a meeting. In the silence of the night Baldambe, contemplating some deep-seated conflict with his brothers, suddenly exclaims, 'The hyena – its son is a lion; the lion – its son is a hyena!' (Lydall and Strecker 1979: 226)

Years later, but still long before I became fully aware of the role of chiasmus in the drama of life, I interpreted this case as follows:

What Baldambe uttered that night was not a unique statement unheard before. On the contrary, it is a proverb, which encodes an old knowledge about Hamar social organization and its weakness. It is used whenever people need to comment on certain latent or manifest conflicts within the family. The proverb, a neatly constructed chiasmus, indicates that lions are related to hyenas as fathers to sons and as sons are to fathers. Lions and hyenas compete over carcasses as fathers and sons compete over cattle. Lions and hyenas are similar in that both are meat-eaters but stand in contrast in their major roles as hunters and scavengers. Translated into the social relationships of Hamar the proverb seems to say: there is a mutual opposition between fathers and sons. It expresses the identity of members of the same and alternate generations and the opposition between members of adjacent generations.

But this is not all. When I asked Baldambe what he had meant when he made the statement, his explanation was as follows: he used the proverb because he wanted to get his anger about his brothers off his chest without saying precisely what he meant and without attacking anyone in particular. In Baldambe's eyes their father Berinas (Gino) had been a true 'lion'. During his lifetime he had been a strong, self-assured, competent and generous provider of food. He had been a distinguished hunter, raider and herdsman, and in his homestead there had been always food which guests and everyone of the family could share. Baldambe felt that he and his brothers were not like his father. That is why he said, 'The hyena, its son is a lion; the lion, its son is a hyena' when thinking of the way in which he and his brothers were quarrelling about the cattle they had inherited from their father.

They were quarrelling over matters concerning these cattle, he thought, as hyenas quarrel over the carcass slain by a lion. Thus, Baldambe was not so much thinking about the opposition between father and son, but rather about the competing interests of older and younger brothers. His father was already long dead and it had been an argument with his older brothers, which had prompted him to pronounce the proverb. Yet the proverb actually starts with hyena-father. When I pointed this out to Baldambe, he laughed, agreed and indicated that it is here where the mystery lies. Out of all the many 'hyenas' born in Hamar, miraculously some will beget sons who will turn out to be 'lions'. Then, not miraculously at all, the sons of these 'lions' will again be the usual Hamar 'hyenas' who are greedy and quarrelsome. Also, many fathers are seen by their sons as 'hyenas' because they do not pass on the cattle which they themselves have inherited from their fathers and older brothers. They devour them like 'hyenas' and do not share them with their sons. (Strecker 1988: 146–47)

CONCLUSION

As we have seen, mirror chiasmus – especially when combined with metaphor – is an amazing figure, and its use in social life can be magical (as in 'Fair is foul and foul is fair') or cathartic (as in 'The hyena, its son is a lion; the lion, its son is a hyena'). But returning to spiralling chiasmus and its dramatic role in our lives, we see it is a figure of surprise and emphasis, and already the fact that it is 'mind opening', as Paul says, indicates that it may have some dramatic effect in our brain. Tyler once pointed out something similar to me when we first began to talk about chiasmus:

> Chiasmi involve the idea of opposition – which is common everywhere – but they are more than opposite, they are linked in a kind of mobius strip. Perhaps there is a range of complexity here – the simpler ones are sexed-up oppositions, and the more interesting, complicated ones are like the mobius strip. I am always tempted, as you know, by spirals in which the movement of opposition is not just dialectical – onward and upward à la Hegel – but involves 'turns and returns' which do not close. Anyway, as Lévi-Strauss somewhere observes about something else, these are 'good to think'.

This cognitive potential of chiasmus was used by Tyler in his essays assembled in *The Unspeakable*, where he criticized anthropologists for their compliance with the ruling epistemologies of the natural sciences and spoke of 'the world that made science, and that science made' (1987: 200) and suggested that postmodern ethnography is a 'fantasy reality of a reality fantasy' (ibid.: 211). His provocative use of chiasmi made a considerable stir at the time, and drove – to paraphrase Hariman – quite a few readers nuts. That is, those who were not prepared to put their minds to these complicated spiralling chiasmi dismissed them as 'mere rhetoric'. But others, who understood that they were meant as mind teasers, used them to better understand the complexities involved in the study of culture and of social life.

More dramatic is, of course, the social use of spiralling chiasmus. Here I refer back to what Paul has said about the Marxian chiasmus, 'It is not the consciousness of men that determines their being, but on the contrary their social being that determines their consciousness'. And after pointing out that, 'This chiastic sentence provides a double surprise by not merely reversing what one thought to be true, showing that the opposite may (also) be true, but waking us up to a third possibility', he goes on to say:

> Marx's reversal of Hegel's priorities is the assertion that matter, not spirit, is the driving force: material conditions determine ideas. But if one finds the choice between Hegel's idealism and Marx's (anthropocentric, utopian) materialist idealism unappetizing, and would prefer another line of thinking, the spiralling chiasmus that results when their opposed views are put back to back has the power to suggest such another possibility. (Paul, this volume)

True, the two parts of the chiasmus can be 'put back to back', as Paul suggests, and in this way lead to rich cognitive results. But this is not what happened and caused the chiasmus to emerge. Rather, the two parts were put face to face to serve as weapons in an ideological confrontation. Hegel was 'made to stand on his head' so triumphantly because this allowed Marx and his followers to assert that a complete turnover of the social order was a historical necessity, and revolution inescapable. In other words, this particular chiasmus developed its rhetorical power at a particular moment in time.

We can generalize, and say that each historical period allows – even demands – its own chiasmus. Examples abound, but I shall mention only two, which I especially like: (1) 'People were not created for the state, but the state for the people', attributed to Albert Einstein and formulated at a time when totalitarian regimes ruled over most of Europe and parts of Asia. (2) 'Do I have all I need, do I need all I have?' This short and unimposing line, found on posters of the Green Movement, may at first be understood only as good advice for travellers, or for students who periodically have to move from place to place. But after a while it begins to sink in and one starts to realize its broader relevance: it is a warning to reflect on the need to consume less and develop a new kind of economy that may help to save our embattled planet.

This '*kairos* of chiasmus' can be observed on a grand historical scale as in the examples given above. But, of course, it also applies to social interaction on a minute scale, in fact to all 'rhetorical situations' (Bitzer 1968) in which the assertion of will and the exercise of social power play a role. Remember what Hariman has said about the 'asocial' nature of chiasmus, and how the line in Stevens' poem – "'The vital, arrogant, fatal, dominant X' – was explained as an outcome of the meaning schemata of antinomy used to oppose and invert the cherished positions held by others. Here, in its potential to shatter expectations and conventions (and establish new ones), lies the raison d'être as well as the pleasure and pain of chiasmus.

Without shattering, there is no opening of the mind, no search for appropriate 'third terms', no spiralling thoughts about mutual oppositions! Shattering provides the rhetorical energy of chiasmus. It energizes the mind first in a flash, which 'dazzles' and 'makes us blink', as Paul says. For example, 'I do not live to eat but eat to live' (attributed to Quintilian, and analysed by Hariman, this volume) must have first 'shattered' the aristocratic Roman youths to whom it was indirectly addressed and who it admonished not to forget their social and especially their public duties. But as they then began to ponder the statement, they may well have smiled and even mocked its prudish sentiment, saying that there can surely be no better reason for living than to enjoy life.

References

Bender, John, and David E. Wellbery. 1990. 'On the Modernist Return of Rhetoric' in John Bender and David E. Wellbery (eds), *The Ends of Rhetoric: History, Theory, Practice*. Stanford: Stanford University Press.

Bitzer, L.F. 1968. 'The Rhetorical Situation', *Philosophy and Rhetoric* 1: 1–14.

Bitzer, Lloyd, and Edwin Black (eds). 1971. The *Prospects of Rhetoric*. Englewood Cliffs, NJ: Prentice-Hall.

Black, Max. 1962. *Models and Metaphors*. New York: Cornell University Press.

Brown, Penelope, and Stephen Levinson. 1978. 'Universals in Language Usage: Politeness Phenomena', in *Questions and Politeness: Strategies in Social Interaction*, ed. E. Goody. Cambridge: Cambridge University Press.

Burke, Kenneth. 1950. *A Rhetoric of Motives*. New York: Prentice-Hall.

Gibbs, Raymond, and Herbert Colston (eds). 2007. *Irony in Language and Thought: A Cognitive Science Reader*. Hillsdale, NJ: Lawrence Erlbaum Associates.

Grice, Paul. 1975. 'Logic and Conversation', in *Syntax and Semantics*, vol. 3: Speech Acts, eds P. Cohen and J.L. Morgan. London: Academic Press, pp. 41–58.

Huxley, Julian (ed.). 1966. 'A Discussion on Ritualization of Behaviour in Animals and Man', Philosophical Transactions of the Royal Society of London. Series B, Biological Sciences, no. 772, vol. 251, S. 247–526. London: Royal Society, pp. 264–65.

Lydall, Jean, and Ivo Strecker. 1979. *The Hamar of Southern Ethiopia, Vol. I: Work Journal*. Hohenschäftlarn: Renner-Verlag, pp. 204–5.

Maranda, Pierre. 2010. 'Echo Chambers and Rhetoric', in Christian Meyer and Felix Girke (eds), *The Rhetorical Emergence of Culture*. New York and Oxford: Berghahn Books.

Nienkamp, Jean. 2001. *Internal Rhetorics: Towards a History and Theory of Self-Persuasion*. Carbondale: Southern Illinois University Press.

Paul, Anthony. 1992. *The Torture of the Mind*. Amsterdam: Thesis Publishers.

Richards, I.A. 1936. *The Philosophy of Rhetoric*. Oxford: Oxford University Press.

Sapir, David. 1977. 'An Anatomy of Metaphor', in Christopher Crocker and David Sapir (eds), *The Social Use of Metaphor*. Philadelphia: University of Pennsylvania Press.

Strecker, Ivo. 2010. *Ethnographic Chiasmus: Essays on Culture, Conflict and Rhetoric*. Berlin and Michigan: Lit & Michigan State University Press.

Strecker, Ivo, and Stephen Tyler (eds). 2009. *Culture and Rhetoric*. New York and Oxford: Berghahn Books.

Strecker, Ivo. 1988. *The Social Practice of Symbolization*, London: Athlone Press.

Tyler, Stephen. 1978. *The Said and the Unsaid: Mind, Meaning, and Culture*. New York and London: Academic Press.

Tyler, Stephen. 1987. *The Unspeakable: Discourse, Dialogue, and Rhetoric in the Postmodern World*. Madison: University of Wisconsin Press.

Wiseman, Boris. 2009. 'Chiastic Thought and Culture: A Reading of Claude Lévi-Strauss', in Ivo Strecker and Stephen Tyler (eds), *Culture and Rhetoric*. New York and Oxford: Berghahn Books.

PART II

EPISTEMOLOGICAL REFLECTIONS
ON CHIASMUS

CHAPTER 4

CHIASM IN MERLEAU-PONTY
METAPHOR OR CONCEPT?

Isabelle Thomas-Fogiel

■ ■ ■ ■ ■ ■ ■

Jacques Bouveresse, in *Prodiges et vertiges de l'analogie*, deplores the transference of concepts from one field of knowledge (e.g. mathematics or physics) to another (e.g. philosophy).[1] In his view, continental philosophy of the last half century has continually confused 'metaphor' and 'concept', 'analogy' and 'rigorous relations', thus leading the discipline towards 'connections which, from a cognitive point of view, hardly go beyond the level of the simple association of ideas' (Bouveresse 1999: 37).[2] But is the transference of notions from one field of knowledge to another really as arbitrary as Bouveresse supposes? Has the migration of concepts not given rise to fecund discoveries, not to say changes of paradigm in various fields of knowledge and in our very lives, such as, for instance, the invention of perspective which has spread from painting to architecture, from architecture to mathematics, from mathematics to philosophy, transformed and enriched by the multiple spaces it has passed through. Are metaphor (as transposition) and analogy (as association) so devoid of cognitive content and epistemic rigour? In this chapter I wish to study one of the numerous transferences which have been performed by philosophy in the course of its history and to test its meaning and its rigour.

I will look into the introduction of the notion of chiasm in philosophy, which accounts for its recent popularity in various human sciences such as history of art, psychology and sociology. This introduction has often been criticized in terms similar to those of Bouveresse: the notion is seen as metaphorical, born from an ill-controlled transposition from one field to another. Initially chiasmus is a figure of rhetoric which consists in placing two groups of words in reversed order, producing a reverse parallelism that can be represented as ABBA ('the power of representation, the representation of power', to borrow an example from Louis Marin, who made great use of this structure in his studies of painting).[3] Neglected by treatises of classical rhetoric, chiasmus was however over-abundantly used by the Romantics, particularly the French Romantics.[4] Victor Hugo, for instance, made it one of his main rhetorical tools. As well as in rhetoric, the term 'chiasm' is also used in physiology to denote the interlacing or intertwining of, for example, two nerves. In philosophy chiasm is raised to the status of a true 'philosophical concept' by Merleau-Ponty. One might even go as far as to say that the chiasm is the nodal concept of his philosophy, encapsulating both its appearance and its content. This is attested by its prominence in every account of Merleau-Ponty's terminology;[5] as it is by the title of a journal entirely devoted to his thinking, *Chiasmi*, in which the term becomes emblematic of the thinker; and it is shown by the many recent evocations of the chiasm in Merleau-Ponty's work.[6]

I wish to resume the discussion of this notion of chiasm in the light of a questioning of its status: is it a mere metaphor devoid of cognitive value produced by an analogical and arbitrary transference from one field to another, or is it a rigorous concept which may be experimented upon, reused or improved? If such is the case, what is the nature of this concept: descriptive, heuristic or even logical? The question is all the more pertinent since it is not only the most orthodox disciples of analytical philosophy, such as Bouveresse, who are likely to see in this transference of concept nothing but poetic licence. Indeed, the most respected commentators on Merleau-Ponty follow in the footsteps of the critics in seeing the chiasm as a literary metaphor. Whether they then reproach the philosopher for using it, as does even Saint Aubert, usually a scrupulous defender of Merleau-Ponty, who denounces 'the equivocity' (Saint Aubert 2004: 20)[7] of the notion of encroachment – the chiasm occupying pride of place among its modalities – or, on the contrary, glorify its literary allure, as does Isabel Matos Dias, who hails in this recourse to the chiasm, the fusion – legitimate, in her eyes – of art and philosophy (Matos Dias 2001: 87ff.),[8] the philosopher's central notion is seldom regarded as a concept based on a definite cognitive content, a univocal definition and a rigorous status. I shall therefore first examine the function of this concept in Merleau-Ponty's philosophy, then its extension, before finally attempting to determine its status: is the chiasm a metaphor or a concept? Is its function poetic or epistemic? It is only at the end of this study that I will be able to show how this notion may enlighten us as to Merleau-Ponty's leading concern: to produce a counter-model of Renaissance perspective and to promote a new category of relation, a concern which unifies all the apparently disjointed facets of his philosophy.

THE FUNCTION OF THE NOTION IN MERLEAU-PONTY'S PHILOSOPHY

The Nature of the Transference

With the notions of encroachment and intertwining, then of reversibility and finally of the chiasm, Merleau-Ponty undeniably imports notions from one field to another. It appears relevant, however, to note that if there is trans-ference with the notion of 'chiasm', it is less a transference from rhetoric or physiology to philosophy than, seemingly paradoxically, a transference from mathematics to philosophy. Indeed, if the notion of chiasm appears late in Merleau-Ponty's work and if it is de facto explicitly referred to the rhetorical figure (in particular as used by Valéry)[9] and to its biological use (optics), the fact that this notion is brought to the fore, the way it is used and its progressive extension follow from an initial transference of mathematical notions to the field of philosophy. It is the notion of encroachment, intertwining and revers-ibility which will gradually give Merleau-Ponty the idea of a category which threads various fields together, making them reversible, in the sense that when one has one, it is possible to find the other by inversion. True, the term 'chiasm' does not appear as such in *Phenomenology of Perception*, although 'encroachment' and 'reversibility' both do. It is nevertheless implicit in several of the analyses in the work, notably in that of sensation, where Merleau-Ponty uses the image of the loop to conceptualize the reversibility between the sens-ing and the sensed, hence their simultaneous identity and opposition. The chiasm, which appears late in his work, thus arises as a clarification and deep-enning of the notion of encroachment, of the Husserlian '*ineinander*' and of the intertwining formed by the relation between the sensing and the sensed. Merleau-Ponty goes further and turns the chiasm into a pure and simple synonym of intertwining, and of reversibility: 'The chiasm, reversibility, is the idea that every perception is doubled with a counter perception (Kant's real opposition), is an act with two faces, one does not know who speaks and who listens' (Merleau-Ponty 1968: 264–65).[10] Thus the chiasm is used as a spatial figure (as an exact synonym of intertwining and reversibility) rather than as a figure of rhetoric strictly following the ABBA pattern. It captures, par excellence, a figure of reversibility and is thus one of the modalities of the notion of 'proximity' ('voisinage'), understood as the spatial idea of being 'one next to the other' as well as 'one with the other', and even, partly, 'one in the other', as opposed to the notion of being 'one outside of the other or one facing the other', which designates the classical distribution between what is on the side of the subject (the sensed) and what is on the side of the object (the sensible). The chiasm as a figure of proximity which leads to intertwining is thus originally linked to an attempt at rethinking space. This rethinking started as early as in *Phenomenology of Perception*, in which Merleau-Ponty ([1945] 2002) considers space, more than time,[11] as a central problem. In this work he attempts to grasp space using topological concepts. Yet, as we know, topological concepts, which Merleau-Ponty will employ more and more as his work develops, are first and foremost mathematical concepts, aiming at thinking more concrete relations than those defined by space as conceived in Euclidian geometry.[12] In a strictly mathematical sense, the real development of topological questions was above all due to Poincaré, who deemed topology to be the most useful type of mathematics since it deals not with measurements but with concrete forms actually perceived by common consciousness, such as the intuitive notion of proximity, so central in topology, from Poincaré to the Bourbaki group. By using notions that are more intuitive than quantitative, mathematical topology attempted to give an account of the world in which we actually live, concretely and through our senses[13] in opposition to the world seen as a geometrically structured expanse. It is this which, as early as the *Phenomenology of Perception*, raised hopes in Merleau-Ponty who made explicit mention of the new mathematical discoveries, which he saw as opening the way to a possible redefinition of Cartesian space.

The first conclusion to be drawn from this initial analysis is that the idea of using, first, reversibility, then chiasm as philosophical concepts was born from a meditation on the limits of Euclidean space and from an interest in the mathematical notions of proximity, of encroachment understood as intertwining and reversibility. So we have here a double transference: the transference of an optical notion (intertwining of nerves), then, by association, that of a rhetorical figure to the philosophical field; but this transference is performed on the basis of a more fundamental one, that from mathematical notions to the philosophical field: Merleau-Ponty sincerely believed that the most recent research in mathematics as well as in physics could help him to fulfil his own philosophical project. In this respect, he welcomes, as early as *La Structure du comportement* 'the re-introduction of the most unexpected perceptual structures into modern science' (Merleau-Ponty 1942: 145), and then, in *Phenomenology of Perception*, goes on to take the recent inventions in non-Euclidean geometry as his guiding thread in his critique of Euclidean space (Merleau-Ponty [1945] 2002: 391). This attitude, far from being an expression of poetic licence, is, on the contrary, that of a rather 'positivistic' or even 'scientific' project, in a classical and neutral sense, that of drawing on mathematics as a paradigm which allows us to explain that which needs to be explained. Paradoxically, Merleau-Ponty seems to want to go beyond Euclidean space by borrowing tools from the extension of Leibniz's *analysis situs*, in order to extend the domain of intelligibility even further towards the concrete, the intuitive and the quotidian. So this initial conclusion on the transference from one field to another does not seem to agree with Bouveresse, nor with the general condemnation of metaphorical transference from one field to another. Merleau-Ponty's aim is simply (and very conventionally if we consider the history of philosophy) to produce more intelligibility within a previously neglected field: the concrete space of our day-to-day world as opposed to the abstract space of geometry. He achieves this thanks to the various concepts and instruments which science (the 'new' mathematics and physics of his day) rendered available to him. This is confirmed if we look further into the function of the chiasm as the means of a redefinition of Cartesian space.

The Conquest of the Sensible, Based on a Reading of The Dioptrics

Merleau-Ponty's philosophy is almost exclusively dedicated to rethinking the relation to the world which Descartes had established, a relation in which a sovereign and independent subject scrutinizes, masters and dominates an object offered to his eyes. Galileo's science and, before it, the invention of perspective, placed human beings in front of the world rather than in it. Man thus became a spectator of objects – in the same position as the Renaissance viewer placed in front of a figurative work of art, which he scrutinizes and enfolds in his gaze. This desire to find a way out of the Cartesian schema is derived from the concern to describe the sub-structures of consciousness in more depth, that is to say – if we rigorously analyse Merleau-Ponty's aims – by the desire to enlarge our field of intelligibility. What used to be relegated to the hazy field of sensation, of the living world, of the world pre-existent to language, will henceforth be decipherable through philosophy. Thus, Merleau-Ponty's desire to go beyond Cartesian dualism is to be understood in different terms than the same desire manifested by later deconstructionists, such as Derrida, who, following Heidegger, endeavoured to denounce philosophical modes of understanding judged to be metaphysical and 'violent'. That is the reason why Merleau-Ponty's criticism of Descartes doesn't aim to be 'destructive' but rather to 'amend', in the sense that he strives to complete or correct the Cartesian project, at least as far the relation to space is concerned. Let us look in more detail, by following his reading of *The Dioptrics*, at this critique by Merleau-Ponty which does not destroy but develops a dimension which is unthought but nevertheless implied by the Cartesian project.

The Dioptrics, as Merleau-Ponty explains, is indeed dedicated to phenomena of vision and more generally to light; nevertheless, Descartes's goal is not to describe these phenomena per se, neither to determine what they really are: 'Here there is no concern to cling to vision' (Merleau-Ponty 1964b: 7).[14] Descartes's aim is to produce 'artificial organs' that improve our vision. This technical and hands-on purpose determines the nature and the method of his inquiry and the way in which vision and light are apprehended. In this context, there is 'no questioning of light, of vision. We do not live in light. We give no thought to that phenomenon' (Merleau-Ponty 1996: 176). Descartes endeavours, rather, to determine the way in which light acts on our eye, the way in which it is in contact with it, in order to be able to act as a technician on this action by modifying it. Remaining faithful to the method that he laid out in the *Regulae*, Descartes constructed a model that aimed to master the phenomenon. The Cartesian reflection therefore distances itself from the field of the lived experience of vision and light so as to provide a translation of these phenomena in the shape of artificial 'figures' or 'models'. The models which Descartes constructed were quasi fictional, as he himself more or less admits at the beginning of *The World*: 'For a while, then, allow your thoughts to wander beyond this world to view another, wholly new, world, which I call forth in imaginary spaces before it' (Descartes 1998: 21). To build his model of vision, Descartes will postulate an analogy between vision and touch. In the same way as the blind manage to 'see with their hands' thanks to their canes, it is thanks to a contact with the eye that light can be thought and that the phenomenon of vision can be defined. Merleau-Ponty thus notes that Descartes 'eliminates action at a distance and relieves us of that ubiquity which is the whole problem of vision (as well as its peculiar virtue)' (Merleau-Ponty 1964b: 7).

For Merleau-Ponty this reductive conception of vision also explains the fact that Descartes multiplies the intermediate stages which little by little distance us from the sensible to the extent that the latter eventually disappears. This is evidenced by the famous figure of the man looking through the eye of a dead animal, at the process by which we pass from the figure (in nature) to the sensation (in the eye experiencing contact with the ray of light); in other words, the process by which we pass from the language of quantity associated with the figure to its transcription in qualitative and sensory signs. What we have here is indeed a spectacle which multiplies intermediaries and screens: our eye looks at the man who looks at the eye of the animal, which looks at the object. The multiplying of screens aims at distancing the sensible until it disappears as sensible and appears as a figure. It is, however, not this paradigmatic example which Merleau-Ponty brings to the fore to analyse this 'spectacularisation' of the world and this dismissal of the sensible, but the examples of line-engraving favoured by Descartes. The relation between the image of the object and the object itself is a relation of dissimilarity, so that we literally end up with what Merleau-Ponty calls a 'perception without an object' (Merleau-Ponty 1964b: 11).

In this connection, Merleau-Ponty notices how Descartes compares the process of transcription/translation of the figure into sensation to a language whose relation with what it signifies is intrinsically arbitrary. The image is as it is only because, just like the sign, it does not resemble what it designates. The image 'excites our thought to conceive', in the same way as signs and words 'which in no way resemble the things they signify' (Merleau-Ponty 1964b: 8). Thus line-engraving is an occasional cause and not an image resembling the object represented, it is an arbitrary sign and not a mimesis. Reality is no longer the sensible grasped through sensation but the length and the breadth of figures, geometric projections of algebraic relations, untouched by any irregularity, depth or obscurity. As the purpose of the explanation is to modify reality (to create artificial visual organs like lenses), it does not arrive at an understanding of the sensible, but rather strips it of its reality. Hence, the figure, the only thing that is real, renders unreal the entirety of the perceptible world.

Yet Merleau-Ponty does not reject this conception of space but merely grants it less importance. He believes in fact that it is necessary to be able to think, beyond any narrowly empirical considerations, an idealized space *partes extra partes* and exterior to the subject. This is why 'Descartes was right in liberating space: his mistake was to erect it into a positive being, beyond all points of view, all latency and depth, devoid of any real thickness' (Merleau-Ponty 1964b: 10). So he does not set out to undermine this conception of space, which after all he presents, in this text, as a systematization as well as a consequence of research on perspective that has been conducted since the Quattrocento, but to limit it, to confine it to a given field of validity, to raise again and differently the question of spatiality. Merleau-Ponty is so little concerned to criticize Descartes that he shows how Descartes, at the very moment he is suggesting the idea of space *partes extra partes*, implies an 'other' spatiality which cannot be reduced to the construction of figures ('that dimension … that Descartes opened up and so quickly closed again' [1964b: 12]).[15] He shows how the analyses of *The Dioptrics* presuppose a position of the spectator's body and hence a situation different from that of pure, disembodied vision. The spectator, however exterior he may be, is capable of determining 'where the parts of [his] body are, of transferring its attention from there to all the points of space that lie along the prolongation of [his] bodily members' (1964b: 11). This is why the body effectively appears as 'the place' from which objects will be defined as being 'there', at that point in space and not at another. The body is the fixed point, the 'here' which makes it possible to locate the different 'theres' of exterior bodies. Merleau-Ponty states that Descartes understood, in spite of his dualism, that the soul thinks with its body and from it, and that 'space, or exterior distance, is also stipulated within the natural pact that unites them' (ibid.). Thus Merleau-Ponty uses Cartesianism to demonstrate the necessity of, not transcending it, but of overflowing its limits. One has to retrogress to another level to think true vision 'of which we can have no idea except in the exercise of it, and which introduces, between space and thought, the autonomous order of the composite of soul and body' (1964b: 11). The inadequacy of his theory of vision is thus indicated by Descartes himself: vision is not only the act of a disembodied mind which decodes the signs of a world lying before it, but the act of a moving body, and it is in relation to its position that space unfolds; vision is 'knowledge by position or situation' (1964b: 12). What is now needed is to recover the sensible, to think its reality at its proper level, namely that of the body moving in the world that surrounds it.

> Space is not what it was in the *Dioptrics*, a network of relations between objects such as would be seen by a third party, witnessing my vision, or by a geometer surveying it and reconstructing it from outside. It is, rather, a space reckoned starting from me as the null point or degree zero of spatiality. I do not see it according to its exterior envelope; I live it from the inside; I am immersed in it. (Merleau-Ponty 1964b: 12)

What does this analysis tell us? It reveals the consistency and the purpose of Merleau-Ponty's thinking: the sensible, deprived of its status as reality by Cartesian thinking, has to reconquer some sort of intelligibility. We therefore have to extend the scope of our understanding to fields which have been ignored so far: the concrete world and how one's own body is related to other bodies, just as other bodies are interrelated. This purpose requires an extension of the limits of Euclidean geometry (not its destruction) and of the physics based on the figures which Descartes developed. This overflowing demands tools of a different sort but no less rational such as the topological concepts (proximity, intertwining, reversibility) which a mathematics of the concrete world provides us with, and of which Descartes had some intuition. It seems that Merleau-Ponty's most astute commentators do not take seriously his intention to find the seeds of his own theory in Descartes. Saint Aubert attributes this intention to a psychological, and thus contingent, particularity. It results, he explains, 'from the usual strategy of the art of the devious counter-example: let us recognize ourselves in him who seemed the most opposed to us so as to establish the validity of our theses all the better' (Saint Aubert 2005: 32). This amounts to giving little importance to the time-consuming task of unearthing, at the very heart of *The Dioptrics*, the necessity of overflowing, broadening and eventually completing this work. Similarly, in his important and decisive chapter devoted to Merleau-Ponty's 'topology of reflection', Matos Dias does not mention the analogy with mathematical concepts but rather insists on the power of the literary metaphors and the reference to Cézanne. In both cases, Merleau-Ponty's genuinely rationalistic trust in science (here, mathematical, elsewhere psychological) and in the explanatory potency of philosophy is belittled or ignored. It is not a question of 'destroying' or 'deconstructing' philosophy but quite the opposite, of extending its field of relevance by forging appropriate concepts. And these concepts (intertwining, reversibility, crossing) are themselves imported from mathematics, which confirms our initial conclusion: Merleau-Ponty shows himself to be a conventional rationalist (in the line of Descartes, Leibniz, even Helmholtz) since he expects mathematics to provide him with tools which may enable him to think the sensible space he has undertaken to conquer, drawing from what Descartes discarded, all the while saying: 'All the inquiries we believed closed have been reopened' (Merleau-Ponty 1964b: 12).

What conclusion can we draw from this inquiry into the function of the chiasm and encroachment other than that we are far from equivocation and metaphor, at any rate as much as Merleau-Ponty's intentions are concerned? It is true that there is transference of a notion from one field to another, but this transference is quite usual in philosophy just as it is in physics. Does Descartes not wish to study vision with 'two or three comparisons' as starting points? Moreover, such migration of concepts between the most apparently unrelated fields (mathematics, philosophy, rhetoric) can be found at the very beginnings of philosophy in Ancient Greece where, as A.G. Wersinger and Sylvie Perceau write, 'topological schemas were [equally] resorted to to represent logic: Aristotle used the figure of the knot and the chain when talking about aporia and reasoning as Plato had already done in the Timaeus' (Wersinger and Perceau 2010: 43).

Merleau-Ponty's concern is therefore to extend the field of intelligibility using concepts found in other sciences (here, mathematical topology, but elsewhere Piaget's cognitive psychology, or psycho-pathological studies). He imports and hybridizes notions in the interests of returning the perceptible world initially dismissed by Descartes to philosophical understanding and to ontic reality. It follows that the function of transference is on the one hand heuristic: to find the appropriate tools to think space via the most recent 'scientific' research (in the sense of specialized sciences), and on the other hand descriptive: to manage, by gradually refining these concepts (from proximity to intertwining, from intertwining to reversibility, and from the latter to the chiasm), to describe as accurately as possibly what is at stake in our relation to concrete space.

Now that we understand why Merleau-Ponty introduced the concept of chiasm in philosophy and how he used it, let us turn to the question of the extension of the concept for, as Saint Aubert complains, Merleau-Ponty ends up applying topological figures, such as encroachment, to everything and 'sometimes hovers near the margins of equivocation. This is all the more dangerous since the very meaning of encroachment tends to make previously separate fields overlap and blurs the boundaries between them. And when this figure, as is the case in Merleau-Ponty's work, becomes over-generalised, a new problem arises, namely that the concept becomes null and void through lack of anything to oppose to it, or through the absence of boundaries to contain it' (Saint Aubert 2004: 20).[16]

An Over-generalization?

The Process of Extension to all Fields

Let us try to grasp the logic of this extension. Encroachment, intertwining, reversibility or chiasm are, as all the commentators have pointed out, notions which are first used to think one's own body. This is again carried out in relation to the Cartesian construction of the world. Beyond the conception of man in *The Dioptrics*, which presents him as a disembodied spectator who transcribes a message by deciphering its code, Merleau-Ponty intends to 'go back to the working, actual body – not the body as a chunk of space or a bundle of functions but that body which is an intertwining of vision and movement' (Merleau-Ponty 1964b: 2). The body in the flesh, the lived body is an intertwining. In this regard, Merleau-Ponty will demonstrate how vision and motivity are linked to an original experience and cannot be dissociated as two distinct and independent operations. One calls for the other and intersects with it: vision implies movement and vice versa since eyes themselves move, just like the rest of the body, to connect with visible things visually. Thus, vision and motor function encroach on and intertwine with each other in the sensible experience. The concern to overflow the Cartesian position of the spectator exterior to the world is here obvious, since vision is no longer pure, theoretical vision, comparable to the attitude of a geographer contemplating his maps, but is inscribed in the world, contained and intertwined. This is why Merleau-Ponty no longer thinks of vision as an appropriation of the visible, as a mastering of the real, but as an opening to the world. Similarly, the world is no longer an independent in-itself, facing me, as in classical representationalism in which two independent entities (*res cogitans* and *res extensa*) face each other. Moreover, if there is an encroachment of vision on movement and of movement on vision, the two never truly coincide. In this sense, the gap which separates vision and movement is an integral part of their relation and their crossing. The term 'chiasm', which is synonymous with intertwining, as intertwining is with encroachment, is consequently used with a definite purpose: to express identity within difference, and even within opposition. Each of the terms, opposed or different to the other, is itself valid only in its relation to the other (reversibility and crossing). To show this intertwining of vision and movement consists in unveiling this fundamental experience by which the body 'which sees everything can also look at itself and recognize, in what it sees, the "other side" of its power of looking. It sees itself seeing; it touches itself touching; it is visible and sensitive for itself' (Merleau-Ponty 1964b: 3). This unveiling reveals a relation which is not a relation between two entities but one that confers identity on opposites.

It is this experience by which the body splits into two, becoming both body-subject and body-object, which will be presented as primordial, an original experience which not only expresses our relation to our body but also our relation to ourselves as subjects and to the exterior world in general. Let us consider this double extension. This experience of our body displays a circularity by which it reflects itself, becomes seeing and see-able, sensing and sensible (this is the loop of the *Phenomenology of Perception*). This encroachment of the body on itself exemplifies this relation of co-determination, in which the interconnection implies a fundamental gap between the two dimensions of the experience, which denies the possibility that the touching and the touched, for example, be one and the same within a relation of identity. When my right hand touches my left hand, an 'exchange' takes place between the two hands while excluding any possible perfect equivalence. We have here a reciprocal relation, in which one gives its reality to the other, excluding fusion and identity. Thus what this experience of reversibility essentially reveals to us is that one's own relation to oneself is blurred. The reflexive relation to the self cannot providean immediate access to the self (the transparency of the Cartesian system). The experience of reversibility implies an access to the self which is simultaneously a distance, a way of apprehending the self which, reciprocally, suggests a dispossession of the self. The result is a chiastic structure of possession/dispossession. Any relation of the subject with himself thus implies some integral opacity that dictates that he can only connect with himself through an internal distance separating self from self, which is the very origin of reflexivity. This is why Merleau-Ponty characterizes the subject in *Eye and Mind* as 'a self by confusion, narcissism, inherence of the see-er in the seen, the toucher in the touched, the feeler in the felt – a self, then, that is caught up in things' (1964b: 3).

Such a conclusion is obviously charged with implications as to the relation of the 'subject' with the exterior world. If the subject is already intrinsically visible and sensible to himself, the relation this subject entertains with the world can only be the prolongation, the extension of this reversibility. Because it is itself visible, the body is a thing amongst the things of the world; nevertheless it does not fuse with them. Here again, we should understand this relation in terms of both identity and opposition. Because the body 'moves itself and sees, it holds things in a circle around itself. Things are an annex or prolongation of itself; they are incrusted in its flesh, they are part of its full definition; the world is made of the very stuff of the body' (Merleau-Ponty 1964b: 3).

We therefore have an extension of topological notions from one's own body to the reflexive subject, then to the world in general, the world of objects and the world of others. The chiasm expresses my relation to the other: 'Chiasm, instead of For the Other: that means that there is not only a me–other rivalry, but a co-functioning. We function as one unique body' (Merleau-Ponty 1968: 215). Through these notions of encroachment, intertwining, chiasm and reversibility, Merleau-Ponty attempts to subvert all the classical oppositions of modern metaphysics. He rejects the whole system of opposition between an independent subject and an object (or another subject) placed facing him.

It follows that it is not only the Cartesian conception of space which is rejected but, beyond that, the position of the subject facing the world, introduced by perspective during the Quattrocento. Let us consider this fundamental point which will uncover the significance of extensions outlined in the preceding paragraph.

Intertwining as a 'Counter-model' to Perspective

Merleau-Ponty argues that perspective is a construction or invention of a world and not a mere transposition of real perception. To show this, he quite clearly relies on Panofsky's analyses which, in *Eye and Mind*, he contrasts with Descartes's analyses. As Hubert Damisch indicates, Merleau-Ponty was one of the first to introduce Panofsky's analyses in France; in addition to a text of 1950 criticizing Malraux's position, *Le langage indirect et les voix du silence*, Merleau-Ponty provided a reading and an analysis of *Perspective as Symbolic Form* in his lectures of 1954–55 on 'The Institution'. For Panofsky, perspective, mathematically conceived, is not the continuation or extension of the psycho-physiological experience of perception but an artificial, 'symbolic' construction (*perspectiva artificialis*) which aims at, as Merleau-Ponty comments, 'developing a practically usable construction of the flat pictorial image' (2003: 80). Perspective is therefore a 'symbolic form' as defined by Cassirer, who inspired Panofsky's art-historical studies. Panofsky has shown the 'abstract' and constructed character of perspective in relation to sensible, real space:

> In order to guarantee a fully rational – that is, infinite unchanging and homogeneous – space, this 'central perspective' makes two tacit but essential assumptions: first, that we see with a single and immobile eye, and second, that the planar cross-section of the visual pyramid can pass for an adequate reproduction of our optical image. In fact these two premises are rather bold abstractions from reality, if by 'reality' we mean the actual subjective optical impression. For the structure of an infinite, unchanging and homogeneous space – in short, a purely mathematical space – is quite unlike the structure of psychophysiological space. (Panofsky 1976: 30)

With perspective, objects become ordered in such a way as to fit onto one plane; they make space appear as pre-existent to them, a homogeneous space, an ordered space whose slow development, from Lorenzetti to Brunelleschi and Piero della Francesca, was later theorized by Alberti in terms of a recourse to the principle of intersection and to the plan of the visual pyramid. Merleau-Ponty, drawing upon Panofsky's analyses, takes up the idea of a historical construction and of a 'symbolic'[17] institution of space. Perspective has led to a general conception of the relation between the seeing subject and the object: we are in front of the world, we control it through our eyes and this relation is seen as a relation of exteriority (the two entities are independent and constituted before they are put in relation with each other) and of confrontation. In a nutshell, the invention of perspective has not only shaped our relation to space, but has also fashioned our thinking of the category of relation to any other (space, thing, the other). How am I in the world? Am I facing space, facing the object, facing the other? Merleau-Ponty substitutes a chiastic model in the place of the classic category of the relation associated with perspective. This allows us to understand the generalizing character of this relation. It is just as 'generalizing' as was perspective, which has progressively shaped all our thinking about relation: first our relation to space, then our relation to the world, then relation to the other. It is thus just as futile to reproach Merleau-Ponty for his extension or 'over-generalization' as to reproach perspective; for, after being first conceived as a relation to space (by the painters of Quattrocento), it went on to fashion the very category of relation as a face to face between two distinct and independent entities (me and the things, me and my body, me and the other). Merleau-Ponty's reading of Panofsky,[18] too little mentioned in the studies of the former, thus proves to be of utmost importance. It is the missing link which allows us to understand Merleau-Ponty's ambitions when he highlights intertwining and chiasm as encompassing categories. His purpose is no more and no less than to refashion our relation to the world just as perspective 'informed' the modern age and attuned us to it. One decisive fact confirms this interpretation: Merleau-Ponty's analyses of Cézanne. They have often been seen as the expression of an interest in painting and a foray into the field of aesthetics. This view is in itself obviously not untrue, but it lessens, to my mind, the fundamentally epistemic scope of his analyses of the painter. This involves no less than substituting another relationship to the world for the one inferred by Brunelleschi's invention and ratified by the philosophical conception of Descartes and then of Kant. Only by taking into consideration Merleau-Ponty's reading of Panofsky (who, once again, was first made known in France by Merleau-Ponty) can we understand the epistemological concern that underlies his studies of Cézanne. Let us examine this point to comprehend what Merleau-Ponty intends to do with his chiasm thinking, namely, to put forward a new category of relation, the ultimate and unifying aim of his analyses in many different fields (perception, painting, mathematics, psychology, etc.).

Cézanne and Epistemology

Noting, with no hint of ambiguity, the relation between the thinking of perspective and the Cartesian relation to the world, Merleau-Ponty writes: 'Four centuries after the "solutions" of the Renaissance and three centuries after Descartes, depth is still new, and it insists on being sought, not "once in a lifetime" but all through life' (1964b: 13). To the Renaissance and Cartesian view of things he opposes a painter's thinking since, as he points out, what is particular to Cézanne is to have kept looking for depth throughout his life. His work on Cézanne thus appears to be an epistemological inquiry in so far as it revolves purely and simply around verifying as well as extending his analyses of depth and its importance in our relation to the world, already developed at length in *Phenomenology of Perception*. If Cézanne is of interest to Merleau-Ponty it is as a counter-example to Descartes, in so far as his painting seeks to unveil a different spatiality from the Cartesian one, from space in itself, 'space as a homogeneous system' of which Panofsky spoke when talking about Renaissance painting. In place of this space, Cézanne substitutes depth, which will become the dimension through which things are in relation. Restoring depth means disrupting the relation that places a sovereign subject in a face to face relation to the world, looking down from the exterior with an 'all-encompassing' gaze. In this respect, Merleau-Ponty shows how the whole of Cézanne's work can be conceived as a meditation with variations on and against perspective. He tells us that Cézanne wants 'to put intelligence, ideas, sciences, perspective, and tradition back in touch with the world of nature which they must comprehend' (1964c: 14). For him, Cézanne is clearly concerned with our understanding ('to put ... sciences ... back in touch'). Cézanne is apprehended as the Husserlian painter par excellence, since he strives to restore the world in which we live upon which science is built. Cézanne's purpose is clearly conceived as a counter-proposition to the abstract construction of a world without depth, as an attempt to return to the lived experience of natural perception, that is, the very thing Descartes's *Dioptrics* had branded as both unintelligible and unreal through his thinking of the sign and the code: Cézanne as a critic of Descartes, we might say, whose paintings aim to restore the genesis of the world, the birth of the sensible negated by the code of Cartesian science. Going beyond the constructed world, Cézanne attempts to return to our native, primary perception, to our initial intertwining with the world and in the world. So Cézanne's work is indeed considered as an epistemological undertaking. This pictorial undertaking consists in recovering our 'primary' perception underlying the abstract construction fashioned by centuries of 'information' and, consequently, of cultural 'deformation'. Cézanne applied the chiasm, this 'system of exchanges' (Merleau-Ponty 1964b: 4), and Merleau-Ponty, like Descartes when faced with the invention of perspective, takes up the painter's endeavour to claim it as the truth of our relation to all things and, by extension, the truth of the very category of relation. Cézanne recovers the 'primordial expression' of 'the first cave painting', it being the prolongation of the child's perception – Piaget's studies having shown, in Merleau-Ponty's eyes, how the child's relation to the world was initially a topological one (Saint Aubert 2006: Ch. 6; Thomas-Fogiel 2008: Ch. 2). We can here appreciate how the meditation on Cézanne's painting cannot be dissociated from Merleau-Ponty's epistemological project as well as how consistent his thinking is. Initially derived from a meditation on topological concepts based on mathematical research, which were taken to be more in touch with the concrete world, the chiasm as a figure of reversibility becomes the relation which Merleau-Ponty opposes to the relation induced by the scientific and abstract construction of the modern world. Through this relation, raised to the status of a quasi logical category as it can be applied to numerous fields, Merleau-Ponty aims to gain access to this 'wild world', the world of our primary perception, the world the child experiences before he is informed by culture. The purpose of the chiasm is indeed to replace perspective and the category of relation which its implementation induced. 'Take topological space as a model of being. The Euclidean space is the model for perspectival being, it is a space without transcendence, positive, a network of straight lines' (Merleau-Ponty 1968: 210). The relation of intertwining of the subject and the world is the truth of the substructures on which science was built and to which Husserl wanted to return. This shows that Merleau-Ponty did choose to pitch Cézanne against Descartes and to turn the study of painting into an epistemological project, as was effectively the birth of perspective. The difference between Panofsky/Cassirer and Merleau-Ponty lies in the fact that the former consider our world as a construction and that any constructions other than perspective will also be elaborations or constructions of the world, that is to say 'symbolic forms'. To this Kantian vision Merleau-Ponty opposes the world of 'the primary', 'the primordial', 'the *infans*' or 'the primitive man'. I detect here a quasi 'naturalistic' concern in Merleau-Ponty's undertaking since what matters to him is to return to the original space and, beyond that, to promote a new category of relation.

These analyses demonstrate how, far from being an 'over-generalization', the extension of the concepts of intertwining and encroachment, of reversibility and chiasm is proof of an epistemological consistency maintained throughout the diversity of the fields explored: from *Phenomenology of Perception* which, in counter-position to Euclidean space, attempts to explore the succession of singular spaces, to mathematical topology, to Piaget's studies on the topological space of the *infans*, to Descartes's *Dioptrics*, to Panofsky's study of perspective, to the meditation on Cézanne's painting, we encounter the same concern again and again: to bring to the fore another category of relation that can more adequately describe our being in the primary world. This category of relation becomes a quasi logical category in the sense that we witness the development of a new logic, just as Hegelian logic undertook to rebuild the categories of relation in quite a different way. Merleau-Ponty's purpose is indeed to think a relation as identity of opposites and not as an interface between two distinct entities. The extension of this category is therefore not surprising in the least and is rather the mark of the consistency of Merleau-Ponty's project. As with Hegel, all the fields are from then on affected by this thinking of relation as identity within opposition, or opposition within identity, or crossing of opposites and reversibility. This thinking of the relation will even be used by Merleau-Ponty as a unifying tool for the relation between the various fields of knowledge (history, mathematics, neurology, psychology, philosophy, etc.). If philosophers, historians, scientists of all ilk enter a dialogue, such a dialogue will take place thanks to the figure of encroachment, which, *in fine*, will be the very definition of philosophy[19] and will express its 'relation' to all fields of knowledge.

CROSSING AS THE DEFINITION OF A RELATION

The Theses Involved

What do we learn from this second stage in our analysis of the extension of these notions (encroachment, intertwining, reversibility) which the notion of *chiasma* sums up? First and foremost we have a clear demonstration that the function of the notion is to replace 'the symbolic institution' of perspective. Thanks to this notion, another category of relation is promoted, one that is as encompassing and general as had become the relation as a secondary interface between two entities initially separated from and exterior one to the other (subject/space, subject/body, subject/world, subject/the other, but also relation of one discipline to any other).[20] To think identity within opposition, or opposition within identity is what the chiasm renders possible: 'Negativity/chiasm ... The negative exists only upon a ground of identity (identity of thing and of its reflection). Negative: the reverse side of identity ... me-world chiasm'; or similarly '[t]he idea of *chiasm*, that is: every relation with being is *simultaneously* a taking and a being taken, the hold is held; it is *inscribed* and inscribed in the same being that it takes hold of' (Merleau-Ponty 1964d: 266). It follows that this ambition is clearly gnoseological: to a truncated relation (the perspective of Euclidian geometry which Descartes defines as relation to all things), Merleau-Ponty opposes a 'veritable' relation, given as more 'primary' and authentic. The study of Cézanne works as the continuation of this epistemic concern: to restore our true relation to the world. Merleau-Ponty's consistency proves complete: far from 'overgeneralizing' he brings to the fore a new category of relation, capable, in his eyes, of replacing that put forward by modern philosophy, a relation of opposition or exteriority, a relation secondarily based on initial and constituted elements, a relation which the perspective of the Quattrocento had developed and which has been 'generalized' to all things by modern science and Descartes's philosophy. Merleau-Ponty's so-called over-generalization is contingent on a first 'generalization', that which derived from our entering the world of perspective from the Renaissance onwards, and which Merleau-Ponty does his best to let go of.

This is why at the end of this study on the functioning and the extension of the concept of chiasm, I come to a paradoxical argument, at least as regards mainstream commentaries of Merleau-Ponty or the continuers of his work who, following a French trend in phenomenology, have tended to place him among literary philosophers ('the phenomenology of writers') rather than scientific ones. In fact, Merleau-Ponty here seems to be almost 'positivist', with his trust in specialized sciences (mathematical and psychological, with regards to topological concepts) and 'naturalistic' in his concern to recover a primary nature, buried deep within our bodies of flesh under layers of culture.

Merleau-Ponty: A 'Positivist'?

We may consider him as a positivist for – as we have seen in the course of this analysis – Merleau-Ponty believes that recent discoveries in mathematics can help him to think space. He read, among others, Cassirer on the mathematics of his time (Poincaré and topology, non-Euclidian geometries, etc.). Through a thorough study of *The Dioptrics*, he attempted to overflow its theories by using the concepts of intertwining, encroachment and chiasm, so as to restore reality and intelligibility to the perceptible world – two qualities which Descartes had partially denied it. In this sense, his attitude seems quasi 'Leibnizian' as he extends our field of intelligibility thanks to tools better honed than those provided by Euclidian geometry.[21] Of course Merleau-Ponty is not a 'positivist' in the narrow sense of accepting only specialized sciences as paradigms of truth (as Carnap regards mathematics and physics, or Austin and Quine linguistics and psychology) and seeing philosophy as nothing but the pathological ramblings of failed artists. In this regard, Merleau-Ponty is rather a classical 'philosopher': all science can help us, as philosophers, to build tools to bring us closer to the reality which is there to be thought; thus, Piaget's psychology shows us how the child's space is initially a topological space and Poincaré's mathematics provides us with a handful of notions that help to grasp the changeability of the concrete world (proximity). Merleau-Ponty's aim is to foster communication between different fields of knowledge and to explore their mutual encroachments.

This concern, classically philosophical, rationalistic, even 'positivistic' in a wider sense of the term, that is to say in the philosophical sense used by Descartes or Leibniz, distances Merleau-Ponty from phenomenology, which, for Husserl, may not have recourse to specialized sciences in its analysis of phenomenality. Merleau-Ponty certainly means to recover a 'lived-in world', which is lost by science in the course of its constructions. In this sense, he is in line with the conclusions drawn by the *Krisis*, in which Husserl observes the hold of narrowly positivistic or scientistic rationality which consists in considering as true only what is determined in the shape of a quantifiable object, attributable to a cause, calculable according to laws, and which in the last instance can be manipulated (as in the mathematized world of Galilean science and Cartesian philosophy). Husserl believes that, by taking this view, Descartes, through the generalization of the object of physio-mathematical science, veiled or shrouded the meaning of the world. It is this considered choice of a single form of rationality which brings about the crisis of meaning and knowledge, because this Logos that measures and stakes out, dominates and manipulates, relegates to the category of non-sense whole sections of human experience, such as the lived-in world. For Husserl, however, the critique of this rationality requires that one enters a wholly different world, that of pure phenomenality, which, because it radically differs from the world of science, of the psycho-physiological subject, requires tools other than the limited tools of regional (specialised) science. Conversely, Merleau-Ponty does undertake to think the 'lived-in world', with the help of all the resources he can draw from regional sciences: mathematics, physics, psychology, psychoanalysis, history (of perspective and of painting), sociology, and so on. Merleau-Ponty is undoubtedly, in the exact sense of the term, less a phenomenologist than Levinas or, today, Marion. Indeed, if we sketch a short comparison of these authors, both Levinas and Marion undertake to promote a type of relation which is other than purely metaphysical (Cartesian exteriority as a face to face of the object and the subject). In both cases, as for Merleau-Ponty, a thinking of the relation as primary is developed, preceding and instituting the poles of identity: subject/world, subject/the other. Levinas does it through the elaboration of a primarily ethical relation which defines both subjects and precedes them. Marion does it through his definition of love as an ' intersecting phenomenon': 'Not only does the erotic phenomenon appear in common to him and me without a single egoic pole, but it only appears at this intersection. *Intersecting phenomenon*' (Marion 2003: 164).[22] Love as an 'intersection' (in which we again find the idea of intertwining and crossing) does indeed refer to the idea of a previous and constituting relation which, beyond the subject and the object, beyond the sum of two subjects, precedes and establishes one and the other. The projects, here, are the same: to bring to the fore a relation as 'crossing', unlike the face-to-face relation. But while the projects may be similar the approaches are radically different. Merleau-Ponty, constantly referring to other sciences, seems indeed not to want to assent to the strict division between phenomenology and regional sciences, when, paradoxically, Levinas and Marion prove to be more orthodox and undertake to describe the appearance as appearance with the sole resources of phenomenological description, without making use of the numerous tools of specialized sciences. This is also why Merleau-Ponty proves quasi logically to be more naturalistic in his approach.

Merleau-Ponty: A 'Naturalist'?

He is indeed a naturalist in as much as his nodal concern is to strive for something more 'primary', which he does through his recasting of the notion of relation. As I have shown elsewhere, the primary in Merleau-Ponty is clearly conceived as what comes first in time, as a past to discover – that of the *infans*, of the primitive – an initial lived experience shrouded by culture, the opposite of the concept which conceals, mutilates and betrays. The recurring image of the primitive man who instinctively finds his bearings in the desert,[23] like the evocation of the cave painter, like the study, via Piaget's analysis, of the *infans* and his behaviour, reveals to what extent Merleau-Ponty's concern is a concern with the primary, clearly understood as a time before the fall into objectivization, a time before manipulation, before the loss of the carnal body engendered by the Cartesian mathematization of the world. True, some will say that the search for that which is primary is an integral part of the project of phenomenology; some will claim that Husserl's followers have, as François David Sebbah writes: 'all, each in a completely different way, a quite obvious desire to unearth a primary more primary than the Ego ... an 'on this side' of the place where consciousness can be controlled' (Sebbah 2008: 28). Nevertheless the primary can be given different meanings and in Husserl nothing legitimizes referring it to the classic sense given to the notion of origin. But here again, if we briefly compare Merleau-Ponty's and Levinas's use of the term 'primary', we find a huge difference. For instance, in Levinas we find a 'primary', defined as the invisible which any visible summons and demands. If we must assume 'a hither side, a pre-original, an invisible' (259), this original does not have 'the status of origin' since it has no temporal meaning but is a condition. Likewise, when Marion (2007: 11) exemplifies the relation of the invisible and the unseen through the model of perspective which allows the visible to appear without, however, being the object of a seeing, he clearly interprets the unseen not in terms of time and history but in terms of a principle or condition. The invisible is everywhere, of all time, at every moment and in every place. Merleau-Ponty on the other hand clearly identifies that which is primary with a lost past (child, primitive) thus immediately interpreting the origin as a temporal modality, not as a principle or condition. Merleau-Ponty's categories are indeed those of 'before' mathematization and 'after' conceptualization which shrouds and mutilates our first relation. Merleau-Ponty is consequently led to think the movement of history and culture as a remembering of this buried primary:[24] 'Philosophy is a remembering of this being. Science is not concerned with it because it conceives of the relationship of being and understanding as those of the geometrical and its projections, and forgets the being which surrounds and invests us, and could be called the topology of being' (Merleau-Ponty 1964a: 22). Through philosophy, Merleau-Ponty tries to return to 'the first experience of the impalpable body of history', the 'primordial expression'. Art, and particularly painting, is the 'amplification' of this primary experience which the first 'cave painting' expressed,[25] itself a prolongation of the initial perception of the *infans*. This naturalistic tendency (in the sense that it seeks to recover the nature of man and his primary relation to the world) can be seen clearly in Merleau-Ponty's relation to Cassirer and Panofsky. As mentioned earlier, Merleau-Ponty carefully analyses Panofsky's arguments about the allegedly symbolic form of perspective. His point of departure from Panofsky and Cassirer is that the relation to space which he means to bring to the fore has in his eyes nothing to do with the construction of the subject, either in Cassirer's Kantian version (all is construction) or in Panofsky's version (which is a sort of conception of a historicized transcendence): all is historical construction. For Merleau-Ponty the relation he attempts to clarify through the concepts of intertwining and chiasm is indeed a truth of our 'primary' nature. As Hubert Damisch shows in *L'origine de la perspective*, if Merleau-Ponty dwells not on the influence which perception may have had on perspective but rather on the influence which perspective has had on perception itself, it is because of his corollary idea that there is a 'brute' or 'wild' perception.[26] We have thus three distinct lines of argument: perspective is either a symbolic and transcendental form (Cassirer), or a historically constructed, symbolic form (Panofsky), or a construction beyond which we have to go to attain brute perception, free of all cultural work (Merleau-Ponty). To return to buried nature is then very much Merleau-Ponty's concern here, as opposed to Cassirer's or Panofsky's. All these reasons show us how it is no exaggeration to speak of Merleau-Ponty's 'naturalism'.

CONCLUSION

Where has the above discussion taken us? We have studied the movement of concepts from one field to another and questioned the status of this transference. Through this analysis we have come to the opposite of Bouveresse's position on the arbitrariness of the use of analogy in philosophy. Indeed, Merleau-Ponty proves to be a very classical philosopher (Descartes, Leibniz) in so far as he borrows his concepts from various fields of knowledge, from various 'specialized sciences' (mathematical topology, psychology, history of perspective, etc.). This transfer of concepts, far from being arbitrary is, on the contrary, the rigorous consequence of the philosopher's main concern: to define another category of relation, the better to restore intelligibility to the sensible world, which Descartes had turned into an abstraction. The relation will no longer be a secondary interface between two previously constituted entities (the relation of classical representationalism) but an identity within opposition, a crossing that institutes the very elements it puts in relation. This thinking of the relation makes it possible to explore all the fields previously ignored by philosophy and so to extend its range of investigation. The extension of this new category of the relation as crossing is thus in no way an 'over-generalization', contrary to what Saint Aubert states, but rather, on the model of the Hegelian category of identity of difference and of identity, an implementation of a new logic: that of the sensible. This logic offers a counter-model of perspective. This enquiry has also led me to uncover a more unexpected aspect of Merleau-Ponty's philosophy: his philosophy expresses a genuine trust in the possibility for 'specialized sciences' to provide tools for philosophy, which for its part extends its field of intelligibility ever further. This recourse to specialized sciences distances Merleau-Ponty from a more 'orthodox' phenomenology but also confers on him his specific character: that of a phenomenology which paradoxically appears positivistic and naturalistic. More generally, all these results compel us to rethink the philosophical practice of the migration of concepts from one field to another under other auspices than those of indignation and condemnation.

Notes

1. See in particular the chapter entitled 'Les malheurs de Gödel ou l'art d'accommoder un théorème à la sauce préférée des philosophes'. Bouveresse, in this text, is not critical of Merleau-Ponty but of other less prestigious thinkers who in some cases do not even claim to be philosophers. Nevertheless the main purpose of the book is, on the one hand, to warn against transference from one field to another, while on the other hand Bouveresse often generalizes from these thinkers or essayists to 'French philosophy' (e.g. on p. 37, 'we know that logic is not given great importance in French philosophy' [my translation] just like 'empiricism') then goes on to generalize to a certain form of 'continental' philosophy, always tinged with 'literaristic' influences, which, for Bouveresse, are quite clearly derived from Heidegger's phenomenology.
2. All translations from the French are mine, unless otherwise indicated.
3. For this use of the notion of chiasm by Louis Marin, see Thomas-Fogiel 2011.
4. The alexandrine, with two hemistiches of equal length, obviously lends itself easily to effects of symmetry and parallelism.
5. See, to take a recent example, in France, the *Dictionnaire Merleau-Ponty* (Dupond 2008), which is part of a series of textbooks which aim briefly to present the key concepts of an author, and which devotes a very long entry to this term (among the 26 notions reviewed).
6. See for example: 'le chiasme *est sans doute la figure qui dirige le plus le discours de Merleau-Ponty*. Réversibilité, entrelacs, écart, déhiscence sont tous des accents chiasmatiques' (Bozga and Coperu 2003: 1), and in the same special issue the essay by R. Barbaras 'Le problème du chiasme'; or Olkowska 2006; Reynolds 2002; Hamrick 1999.
7. Saint Aubert speaks about a 'drift', about 'over-generalization', and underlines 'that the philosopher sometimes hovers near the margins of equivocity'; for the complete

quotation, see below. Saint Aubert will repeat this judgement in *Le scenario cartésien* (2004, p. 194, note 1).

8. David Sebbah (2008) opposes a 'phenomenology of writers' to a more scientific phenomenology derived from Husserl. Merleau-Ponty has often been associated with this phenomenology of writers and countless commentators have mentioned his 'poetic use' of language or his 'metaphors', whether or not in praise. It is this distinction between 'phenomenology of scientists' and phenomenology of writers which I intend to question here, at least so far as Merleau-Ponty is concerned, as he is, as will be demonstrated, one of the most paradoxically 'scientistic' (in the neutral sense of the term) phenomenologists ever.

9. Merleau-Ponty quotes Valery and his conception of 'chiasmus' (Mearleau-Ponty 1964a: 284).

10. See the chapter entitled 'The Intertwining – The Chiasm', in Merleau-Ponty 1968. In the *Dictionnaire de Merleau-Ponty*, previously cited, the terms of reversibility and chiasm are given as synonyms. The chiasm is the cross which does not literally refer to the figure which rhetoric strictly defines as ABBA. The term chiasm is also often used (Louis Marin; Hubert Damisch) as a cross in space, a painter's technique: see for example, an article entitled 'Le chiasme cézannien', a structuralist study of semiology in painting (Boudon 1981).

11. Two long chapters are devoted to space whereas time is dealt with in only one short chapter.

12. Cassirer (then K. Lewin, Panofsky and Francastel) thought of the topology as more 'concrete' than Euclidian geometry. It is a commonplace in the 1950s. Merleau-Ponty was influenced by this reception of 'new geometry'.

13. TN: 'Sensibly' meaning 'perceptible through the senses'.

14. 'Eye and Mind', trans. by Carleton Dallery, in Edie 1964: 159–190. Revised translation by Michael Smith in *The Merleau-Ponty Aesthetics Reader* (1993), 121–149.

15. Note also 'Yet Descartes would not have been Descartes if he had thought to *eliminate* the enigma of vision' (Merleau-Ponty 1964b: 10); and 'All the inquiries we believed closed have been reopened' (Merleau-Ponty 1964b: 12).

16. Translated by the author.

17. The term is initially used by Cassirer, then taken up by Panofsky.

18. In this regard, Panofsky is not mentioned once in Saint Aubert's three books (published by Vrin) which claim to be an exhaustive list of Merleau-Ponty's influences.

19. For the definition of philosophy as chiasm and encroachment, see, among others, *The Visible and the Invisible*, 'The true philosophy = apprehend what makes the leaving of oneself be a retiring into oneself, and vice versa' (199); and on the extension of the category to think the relations between various fields of knowledge and not only the relation to the proper body, see Thomas-Fogiel 2008: 46–80.

20. It is my thesis in my book *Le concept et le lieu* (Thomas-Fogiel 2008).

21. The *analysis situs* is already the ancestor of topology.

22. Translated by the author.

23. 'As primitive man in the desert is always able to take his bearings immediately without having to cast his mind back and add up distances covered and deviations made since setting off' (Merleau-Ponty [1945] 2002: 115).

24. One has to come back to the 'brute', 'wild' being (1964d: 212), the 'pre-objective', the world where the 'vertical' being of before 'our idealisation and our syntax' (ibid.: 102).
25. For all these expressions, see Merleau-Ponty 1964a: 83–84.
26. We must remember that Damisch is the pupil of Merleau-Ponty. According to Damisch, Merleau-Ponty's project of return to the origin has numerous weaknesses: indeed, can we really say of a perception, which we strive to come back to through various conceptual means, that it is truly 'brute' and 'wild'? Can perception, which will happen after the deconstruction of perspective and which will have therefore required considerable effort of the mind, really be deemed as preceding reason? Let us not forget either, that one of the highest claims of perspective is to make painting able to express a truth never before attained, and therefore to reflect the perception of human vision genuinely. This questioning on the relation between perspective and perception is central in Damisch's text on the origin of perspective, and conditions Damisch's criticism of his master. On Damisch's relation to Merleau-Ponty, see Thomas-Fogiel 2011.

References

Boudon, Pierre. 1981. 'Le chiasme cézannien', *Communications* 34(34): 97–134.
Bouveresse, Jacques. 1999. *Prodiges et vertiges de l'analogie*. Paris: Raisons d'agir.
Bozga, Adina and Ion Coperu (eds). 2003. *Merleau-Ponty, Chiasm and Logos*. Studia phenomenologica, Vol III, N° 3–4.
Descartes, René. 1998. *The World and Other Writings*. Trans. by Stephen Gaukroger. Cambridge: Cambridge University Press.
Damisch, Hubert. 1976. *L'origine de la perspective*. Paris: Seuil.
Dupond, Pascal. 2008. *Dictionnaire Merleau-Ponty*. Paris: Ellipses.
Edie, James (ed.). 1964. *The Primacy of Perception*. Evanston, IL: Northwestern University Press.
Hamrick, W.S. 1999. 'A Process View of the Flesh: Whitehead and Merleau-Ponty', *Process Studies* 28(1–2): 117–29.
Marion, J.L. 2003. *Le Phénomène érotique*. Paris: Grasset.
———. 2007. *La Croisée du visible*. Paris: PUF.
Matos Dias, Isabel. 2001. *Merleau Ponty: une poïétique du sensible*. Toulouse: Presses Universitaires du Mirail Toulouse.
Merleau-Ponty, Maurice. 1942. *La structure du comportement*. Paris: PUF.
———. 1964a. *Signs*. Translated by Richard McCleary. Evanston, IL: Northwestern University Press.
———. 1964b. 'Eye and Mind', in *The Primacy of Perception*. James Edie (ed.). Evanston, IL: Northwestern University Press, pp. 159–90.
———. 1964c. *Sense and Non-Sense*. Translated by Hubert Dreyfus and Patricia Allen Dreyfus. Evanston, IL: Northwestern University Press.
———. 1964d. *Le Visible et l'invisible, suivi de notes de travail*. Paris: Gallimard
———. 1968. *The Visible and the Invisible, Followed by Working Notes*. Translated by Alphonso Lingis. Evanston, IL: Northwestern University Press.

———. 1996. *Notes de cours au Collège de France: 1958–1959 et 1960–1961.* Paris: Gallimard.

———. [1945] 2002. *Phenomenology of Perception.* 2nd edn. London and New York: Routledge.

———. 2003. *L'institution. La passivité. Notes de cours au Collège de France* (1954–1955). Paris: Belin.

Olkowska, D. 2006. 'Intertwining and Objectification', *Phaenex* 1(1).

Panofsky, P. 1976. *La perspective comme forme symbolique.* Paris: Minuit.

Reynolds, J. 2002. 'Merleau-Ponty, Levinas, and the Alterity of the Other', *Symposium* 6(1): 63–78.

Saint Aubert, Emmanuel de. 2004. *Du lien des êtres aux éléments de l'être: Merleau-Ponty au tournant des années 1945–1951.* Paris: Vrin.

———. 2005. *Le Scenario Cartésien.* Paris: Vrin.

———. 2006. *Vers une ontologie indirecte.* Paris: Vrin.

Sebbah, David. 2008. *Usages contemporains de la phénoménologie.* Paris: Sens et Tonka.

Thomas-Fogiel, Isabelle. 2008. *Le concept et le lieu: Figures de la relation entre art et philosophie.* Paris: Cerf.

———. 2011. 'Louis Marin philosophe? La signification à la croisée du langage et de la vision' in *La raison des effets, travailler avec Louis Marin.* P.A. Fabre and B. Rougé (eds). Paris: Presses de l'EHESS.

Wersinger, A.G. and S. Perceau. 2010. 'L'auto-réfutation du sceptique vue de la scène antique', *Revue de métaphysique et de morale* 1: 25–43.

CHAPTER 5

CHIASMI FIGURING DIFFERENCE[1]

Stephen Tyler

■ ■ ■ ■ ■ ■ ■

Every epistemological discourse, whether it be epistemology proper, or one of the pseudo-epistemologies called perception or cognition, begins with an account of the origin of identity – of the mastery of difference that reduces chance and chaos to patterns of recurrence and ordered regularity. One need only reflect on the central role these discourses give to the ideas of category and categorization to get a sense of the absolute necessity of this origination of 'sames', and also to divine the problems it creates. Categories create sames by an act of forgetting – the forgetting of differences. This is so, whether the classificatory mode is directly essentializing in the manner of identifying similarities as shared essences, or consists instead of incompletely distributed properties, as in family resemblance or polytypic classification. Categories are duplicitous. They cannot be the same as what they categorize, and they create sames by a kind of falsification. Plant, for example, categorically includes tree and bush, but is neither a tree nor a bush at the same time as it is both a tree and a bush. As Foucault has said: 'The most tenacious subjection of difference is undoubtedly that maintained by categories. … Categories organize the play of affirmation and negation, establish the legitimacy of resemblance within representation, and guarantee the objectivity and operation of concepts. They suppress the anarchy of difference' (Foucault 1977: 186).

Categorization is the essential essentializing means of the Logos, the instrument by which the Logos 'gathers all present beings into presencing and lets them lie before us' (Heidegger 1975: 76). Still, the desire of philosophy, or of reason generally, has been to track down what is prior to categorization in order to reveal or liberate difference at its source as a kind of a-categorial thought. Difference, according to Foucault 'can only be liberated through the intervention of a-categorial thought' (Foucault 1977: 186) or, as Levinas would have it, we have to think the difference between the said and the saying in order to 'release the *anarchy* of difference which is the discourse of the other' (Levinas 1981: 9–11).[2] A-categorial thought is that middle between the sensible and the intelligible that has been identified as the function of the image, the schema, the phantasm – all of those figuring figurations that are simultaneously both particular and universal, both sensible and intelligible, both de facto and de jure.

A-categorial thought is before identity. All identity is a sham – always an other posing as a same. It cannot be thematized, cannot consist of recurrent sames. Consequently, there can be no 'principle of difference', for the function of principle is to thematize, to make an identity of difference. We cannot construct the unity of difference, a unity within difference, or an identity within difference. Nevertheless, consider now the pyramidology of difference in Thought Picture 1A.

Thought Picture 1A illustrates Hegel's system of dialectic. The plus (+) sign indicates the thesis, the minus (–) sign the antithesis, and the zero-slash (Ø) sign the neutralization or synthesis. In this picture the oppositions, differences and negations between {subject, self, I, first} and {object, other, thou, second} are neutralized by the negation of the negation, the difference of the difference. The neutralization is a unity of differences expressed as {one,

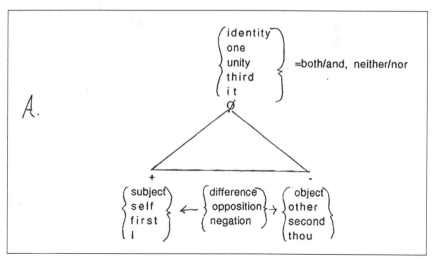

Thought Picture 1A An illustration of the rhythm of Hegelian dialectic.

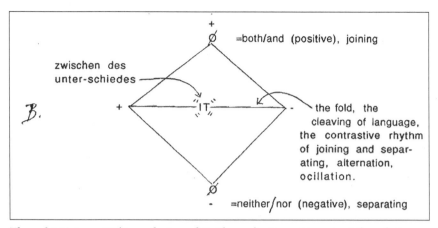

Thought Picture 1B 'A rendering of Heidegger's attempt to orient the relationship between identity and difference'.

identity, unity, it, third}. This neuter is simultaneously 'both/and' and 'neither/nor'. That is to say, this third, this it is both first and second, I and thou, and neither first and second, I and thou. This third is thus a transcendental subject that is constructed through the intentional acts of a subject who constructs the other-as-object and then returns to itself by comprehending its own construction. The rhythm of this projection-reflection establishes the presence of the self to itself in absolute knowledge, and is the means by which consciousness exercises power over itself in simultaneous strangeness and intimacy with itself. Mastery over the self is the consequence of the subject's absolute dominance of the other, which is itself the consequence of the hegemony of representation that enables the ego's intentional act of representing the other to itself. The other – the in-itself, the object – is only a secondary being, a construction of the subject – the for-itself – whose only purpose is to facilitate the subject's self-understanding in the form of the transcendental ego – the in-itself-for-itself. The subject overcomes the difference of the other in the construction of its own identity.

Thought Picture 1B is a rendering of Heidegger's attempt to re-orient the relationship between identity and difference by focusing on the joining and separating acts that establish the unity of the third, and the dominance of identity over difference (Heidegger 1969). He refuses to conflate identity and same, arguing that the same (<*sem- 'single' >'simulacrum,' 'simultaneous,' 'similar') is the simultaneous holding together of what differs and the holding apart of what differs. It contrasts with identity, which always moves towards the absence of difference and is the negation or swallowing-up of otherness. Heidegger's phrasing emphasizes difference. The difference between the 'both/and' and the 'neither/nor' is not reduced to an undifferentiated unity or to a category of shared essence. Where Hegel emphasizes the holding together, Heidegger gives equal emphasis to both holding together and holding apart. Difference, for Heidegger, is the between of subject/Being and object/beings. It is the condition of the possibility of all subjectivity and objectivity, the between that simultaneously joins and separates the irreducible mean that founds the world and everything in it. It is the unifying element of the diaphora, the carrying out and the carrying through (ibid.: 42–44). Difference is never present and cannot be represented. It is before the thought that thinks identity. This before is a time-space where appropriation occurs. Appropriation is a 'neutrale tantum', a neuter it that lies between all differences, oscillating within itself. It gives or sends Being as the unconcealing of presencing, but is not itself revealed in its giving. For Heidegger, language articulates the opening, the between that enables all communication, but it is irreducibly duplicitous. Its poeisis is cleaving, the alternating rhythm of joining and separating that counters the unifying force of the Logos.

A more revealing figuration of Heidegger's solution can be constructed by first inverting the two structures of opposition and then joining them at their apices, rather than at their bases, as was done in Thought Picture 1. This inversion produces a figure of total difference and is illustrated in Thought Picture 2.

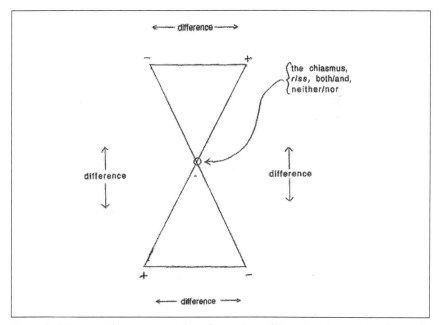

Thought Picture 2 'A more revealing figuration of Hegel's solution' producing 'a figure of total difference'.

In Thought Picture 2, the moment of joining is also the moment of separation, and this simultaneous separation and union of the two structures produces a chiasmus (X), a figure that also symbolizes Siva's drum and the dance of time in the cyclic rhythms of cosmic construction and deconstruction.

Although Heidegger's picture of infinite oscillation between self and other effectively interrupts the *aufhebung* in the Hegelian dialectic, it also eliminates the creative aspect of dialectic. In the back and forth of infinite oscillation there is seemingly no change either in self or other. They remain unchanged in their infinitely indeterminate identities. The pulsational movement of oscillation is not creative. It is only a ceaseless back-and-forth motion that changes nothing and goes nowhere, like an endless irresolvable irony that situates difference within the identity of a fixed and bounded regime of repetitive motion. It does not, in other words, think difference as difference, for it is, after all, only a story of being that tells us nothing about becoming. Heidegger's idea of oscillation accounts for only half of the meaning of difference. Recall that diaphora (<dia-phora) and difference are derived from Indo-European *bhar-, which means not only to 'carry from one side to the other', as in the sense of oscillation, but also means to 'bear', in the sense of giving birth, as in bearing a child, for example. Significantly, this latter sense of *bhar- is the source of the cognate English word 'fertile'. This sense of

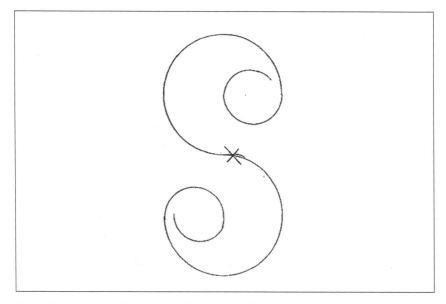

Thought Picture 3 The conjoined triangles of Thought Picture 2 reconfigured as two intersecting spirals.

*bhar- thus implicates change, growth, development and creativity, the very ideas excised from the dialectic in the Heideggerian notion of oscillation.

What is needed in place of the metaphor of oscillation is a figuration that interrupts the *aufhebung* without simultaneously inhibiting the creative work of the dialectic. We need a dialectic that is not just negative in Adorno's sense, but one that allows and accounts for accommodation, growth, decay, change and creativity; a dialectic of becoming that does not necessarily imply the overcoming of difference or a progressive movement towards a final utopian resolution of difference in identity.

Such a figuration can be schematized as the union/separation of continuously intersecting sinistral and dextral spirals, each of which changes at the moment of intersection in the chiasmus that instantaneously joins/separates them. We can thus reconfigure the conjoined triangles of Thought Picture 2 as two intersecting spirals, as depicted in Thought Picture 3.

In Thought Picture 3 the chiasmus is the moment of simultaneous union/separation and represents the 'it' of Heidegger and others. As the spirals continue to unfold and intersect one another they produce the effect illustrated in Thought Picture 4.

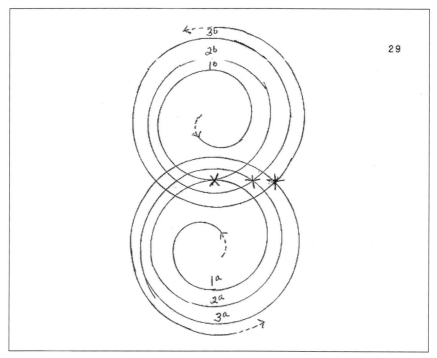

Thought Picture 4 Continuously intersecting spirals transformed by chiasmic crossings.

The individual spirals in Thought Picture 4 are not cycles of identities. The cycles are not repetitions, and this is not a figuration of recurrent identities. Because of the chiasmic crossings, the first spiral is not the same as the second, and the second differs from the third, and so on. Each spiral is transformed in some way by each chiasmic crossing. The whole is a 'phase space', an assembly of symbiotic singularities that is not reducible to a thematization of perduring essence (Guattari 1995: 95). These transformations are represented in Thought Picture 4 as the moving point of the chiasmus.

The aim of these spiral figures is to illustrate the production of difference. Here there is no simple 'back and forth' or oscillation between the components of a single identity, a static figure vibrating ceaselessly between opposite poles. Instead, there is a sequence of momentary heterological singularities that are produced only to be transformed in the next chiasmic encounter with 'them others' in a ceaseless production of 'mutant' subjectivities (Guattari 1995). Thought Picture 4 is a Levinasian infinity, and is not figured by the closure of spirals as in the usual sign of infinity (∞). Since the spirals are figured here as intersecting at a different place each time, we can understand this geometric fact as a kind of metaphoric movement that inscribes a 'life-line' or a 'time-line', or as a Deleuzian 'line of flight', as in Thought Picture 5.

These thought pictures are, of course, over-simplified, for they depict the interaction of only two singularities, and while I can have an intimation of the intersection of multiple singularities, I cannot figure that thought.

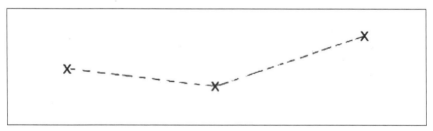

Thought Picture 5 Imaginary 'line of flight' abstracted from the chiasmic intersections in Thought Picture 4.

Notes

1. Excerpt from Tyler 1998.
2. My emphasis.

References

Foucault, Michel. 1977. *Language Counter-memory Practice: Selected Essays and Interviews*. Ithaca, NY: Cornell University Press.

Guattari, Felix. 1995. *Chaosmosis: An Ethico-aesthetic Paradigm*. Bloomington: Indiana University Press.

Heidegger, Martin. 1969. *Identity and Difference*. New York: Harper.

———. 1975. *Early Greek Thinking*. New York: Harper.

Levinas, Emmanuel. 1981. *Otherwise Than Being*. Boston: Martinus Nijhof.

Tyler, Stephen. 1998. 'Them Others – Voices without Mirrors', *Paideuma* 44: 31–50.

CHAPTER 6

Forking

RHETORIC χ *RHETORIC*

(A MEDITATION UPON *RHETORIC* 1354A 1–11, DELEUZE AND JOAN MIRÓ)

IN MEMORIAM GEORGES DUMÉZIL

Philippe-Joseph Salazar

■ ■ ■ ■ ■ ■ ■

ENCOUNTERING THE χ

Rare are the humanistic disciplines that can claim a unique and dramatic foundation, and mention an *Urtext*. Usually such eccentric claims belong to religions, or, less eccentric yet no less stochastic to sudden developments in the sciences. Rhetoric is *Rhetoric*. Or, to replace 'is' with the symbol of chiasmus: Rhetoric χ *Rhetoric*, whereby identity is predicated on marking a *Kreuzung*, a disposition that either binds to fortify (like a bandage or a bond binds the fragments of a broken leg, or two beams), or a rhythmic arrangement of words that binds together meanings into a new, reparative, sequence (Chantraine 2008: 1205).

Whenever I attempt to take in my stride, as a rhetorician or a philosopher, the movement of rhetoric, I am pulled towards the beginning of the Beginning, the first two paragraphs of Aristotle's *Rhetoric*.

Here is a beginning, a *principium* or *arkhē*, that which founds rhetoric as theory and practice. As I begin to find my way into this archeo-logy of democratic persuasion's very Scriptures, the *Rhetoric*, and begin to embark on this walk from, and into the foundation of rhetoric, I find myself twice encumbered: first by 'scruples', as the Latin word says, in my shoes, two little sharp stones in my rhetorical shoes that prevent me from going along at the taken for granted, comfortable pace. They are nagging reminders that, if walking the walk of rhetoric usually follows a trodden path, we carry nevertheless impediments in our shoes. Then comes, as I fidget at the threshold of the *Rhetoric*, and Rhetoric itself, a second impediment: as I am about to retrace the walk (to/into) the foundation, step by step, I am already, albeit not at all ready, at a Heideggerian *Kreuzung*, the χ, a cross that marks the road as it begins; a fork as it were.

Rhetoric's path is crossed here, for ever, in the first two paragraphs of the *Rhetoric*: as we begin, there is a fork, a choice, a dispute, a glance to the right, a glance to the left, a binding too since proceed we must, and as we have since Aristotle. This fork planted at the beginning of, on, Rhetoric/*Rhetoric*'s path has many names: the altercation of good and bad rhetoric, the gendering of manly and womanly persuasion, the disputation between philosophy and practical reason, the foreignness of adulthood and infantile *paideia*, the obsessively generous *cedant arma togae* endlessly replayed throughout Western history in a debate on the realist *ultima ratio* of politics, the game between pathos and logic, logic and ethics, pathos and ethics, the altercation between those who say they alone know how to argue and those who are declared *aneu logou*, 'without deliberative speech', in a long and open-ended series of crossings and criss-crossings, of chiasms which may well be the very destiny of rhetoricians – what I have called, elsewhere, the melancholy of rhetoricians (Salazar 2008).

What are my very own two scruples of *Rhetoric*? How do they perform, each, a crossing at the beginning of the *Urtext*, and, as causes of a rhetorician's melancholy how does each one of them fasten an χ in order to bind or bandage what splintered thought? They are two words: *eikē* (*Rhetoric* 1354a 6) and *hodopoiēin* (1354a 8).

First Scruple of a Crossing: On Random

The first scruple concerns the erratic, yet somewhat consensual rendition of *eikē* by 'spontaneously, without any reasoned process or method' (Aristotle 1980: 3), or 'randomly' (Aristotle 1991: 29), 'au hasard, au petit bonheur' (Chantraine 2008: 302), 'sans aucune méthode' (Aristotle 1931: 70), 'au hasard, sans méthode' (Wartelle 1981: 124), 'au petit bonheur' (Aristotle 2007: 114) while Cope smartly has it qualify a 'use … antecedent to practice' (Aristotle 1877: 4).

I am not taking issue here with philological propriety. I would like to understand what these variances mean. Clearly randomness seems to be the preferred paradigm, but why is 'method' being, even negatively, called upon – Dufour even specifies 'aucune' (without a method whatsoever – which is a way to say that rhetoric is ever the only method)?

As we know, the *Rhetoric* instructs a shift from practice without theory to theory and the practice of the theory, from what Aristotle labels techniques of speaking to rhetoric/*Rhetoric* as the only proper technique: it is this technique by which human beings who live together and practice through debate dissent and assent, with regard to how they can live together as equals, teach each other practical reason and acquire a decorum of civility and perform their human dignity. As Benveniste would say, this tight compact is an 'institution of meaning' (Benveniste 1969). What it highlights is a foundation, which hinges on the invention of the enthymeme, which in turn explains the antistrophic nature of this newly founded theory and practice.

In *Rhetoric* 1406a 17–18 this recurs, concerning the use of poetic epithets in eloquent prose (*eikē legein*). Again, the translation is left floating: 'speaking at random' (Aristotle 1926: 362), 'speaking carelessly', 'Carelessness lacks merit, moderation lacks fault' (Kennedy 1991: 227), 'parole improvisée' (Chiron 2007: 440). Clearly, the options are divergent: 'at random' does not imply an intention from the part of the speaker, except the wish to speak; 'carelessly' is value-laden – it indicates that care ought to be taken, yet what sort of care? Finally 'improvised' may introduce prudence, yet improvisation does not necessarily imply carelessness or even randomness.

Having counted the many granules petrified into my first scruple, let me take another step, however uncomfortable. The first sentence of the founding text provides for its own foundation by enacting what will become the obvious of Rhetoric, yet is proposed as the lack and the absent, the use of enthymematic argument. The foundation is not named (*this* is an enthymeme), it is acted upon. It is a matter of observation indeed: the four species of civil speech (or both genres with their subdivisions: to examine and to maintain, to oppose and to advocate) are merely observed and reported in 1354a 4–6. I take 'species' strictly here, as a recall of *skeptomai*, 'to look at', 'species' being the Ciceronian rendition for *eidos*, which refers, ultimately, to the same idea of vision we find in the celebrated *theōrein* of 1354a 10. Rhetorical genres (*eidē*) are the result of an observation, the spectacle of the agora in its deliberative and judicial operations (see 1358a 36, the opening sentence on the three 'genres'). What is a further matter for observation is how the 'what, how, why, for what' (the causes) produces persuasion and, having been put to the test, becomes the matter of a technique. This layering of observation leads translators to adduce 'method' or 'system'. I will in a moment expand on system and method.

The problem, however, lies in the tension between habit and chance. Habit can be observed both by rhetor and philosopher, and by audience; and its properties can be explicated. Chance can be observed as an event of speech, something that takes place, but, barring a catalogue of events, it cannot be observed for the purpose of an 'antecedent' technique and let alone for the founding *Rhetoric*, as habit does.

Important to note is that *eikē* allows for a direct comparison between the use of civil speech (the one defined here as pre-*Rhetoric*) and the military. Chantraine (2008: 303) exemplifies *eikē* by mentioning *eikoboleō*, 'to speak from the top of our head, to improvise (*parler au hasard*), to throw at random' (on *ballō*, to hit at a distance, by throwing a stone or a javelin). To speak at random is akin to shooting at random, and from the safety of distance. I will return to a similar, military figure later on.

However, when Aristotle does reflect on the possibility to 'theorize' (observe) causes for which some succeed in opposition and advocacy, either randomly or through repetition, this observation of causes, which will transform that which is being founded into a *tekhnē*, rests on an analysis of causes developed in the *Physics*. Indeed, to denote *eikē*, Aristotle had his very own choice of words and concepts, specifically the pair *tukhē/automaton* (Bonitz 1870: 124).

Physics 197b makes it clear that *tukhē* qualifies 'chance and what results from chance are appropriate to agents that are capable of good fortune and of moral action generally' (Aristotle 1952b: 274). Pointedly, 'What is not capable of moral action cannot do anything by chance.' There must be a 'deliberate intention' for an action to fall under *tukhē* and not under *automaton*. The example given by Aristotle (*Physics* 5.196b: 33–35) is about someone who is busy raising funds, goes where the possibility of doing it had not entered his mind, and gets money. He deliberately went there, albeit not to raise funds. It may appear to the contributor that he went there purposefully. *Automaton*, by contrast, is what inanimate objects (or children) do, actions issuing from no deliberate, moral intention.

In this case, how can a rhetor achieve persuasion *automaton*-style? Does it mean that rhetors pre-*Rhetoric* are devoid of deliberate intention? That they are akin to objects or infants? The interesting thing is that, in 1354a 9, when Aristotle acknowledges that the aim (of persuasion) is reached either by *sunētheia* or by *automaton*, the action of 'reaching the mark' (1354a 9) re-activates the verb from which *tukhē* is derived (*tugkhanō*), which means both 'to reach a goal, to succeed' and 'to happen by chance' (on this verb, see

Pucci 2004: 670). In short, what sort of 'careless speaking', to use a standard rendering, is it?

Assuming that *automaton* is not what is meant, it remains that one cannot act by *tukhē*, as one acts by habit (since habit creates some awareness of repetition, it is technique in the making). *Tukhē* defines an event, that which happens. This is the reason why, in 1354a 7–8, Aristotle writes that on the basis of both (habit and chance/carelessness/spontaneity) it is possible to open a road for *Rhetoric*. But, one has to admit, it is a strange observation, or an odd translation: one can, for the sake of the foundation, observe habitual techniques and draw lessons from them; but how can one observe and draw on the experience of singular events, accidents? *Tukhē* and *tekhnē* stand in opposition to each other, while, I believe, *sunētheia* and *tekhnē* are on the same vector. Can we conceive of a theory of rhetoric, today, which would look at practices on such a vector?

A speech (whether it is successfully persuasive or not) has four causes: a material cause, a formal cause, an efficient cause, a final cause. So far, if the material cause (the Greek language as apposite to Logos) is taken for granted, the three others undergo a variety of treatments: the formal cause is, one can say, at the foundation of the *Rhetoric* (how to argue and persuade according to rules that are rational and practical); the efficient cause is analysed negatively in the ethos of the habitual and the casual rhetor, to be surmounted later; the final cause is ambiguous (is the finality of a speech to be practical or is it not to appear to be habitual or casual or to appear as such?).

I wonder if persuasion in a non-rheto-technical culture is not a matter of *tukhē* altogether, which may explain why Aristotle uses *automaton*, a *tukhē* placed under erasure, so to speak. I would like to imagine this scenario: Aristotle, at the moment of foundation, makes a claim that political life must be instructed by what he is about to develop, (the) *Rhetoric*. An educational process is set in motion, which, by the same token, nullifies all that which was 'antecedent'.

As a result, we are being thrown back to what is, for Heidegger, a foundation, an act of *petere principium*: '*Petere principium* … is the one and only step taken by philosophy'. When an audience refuses to accept the principle (*arkhē*) that founds one's demonstration, one has to begin a refutation, a negative demonstration, by letting an opponent state the denial. Hence, a petition of principle is, as the Latin says, a pursuit of the beginning, by proposer, and opponent (*Metaphysics* IV, 4, 1006a 18). Yet, to request a demonstration of a principle when it is obvious this should not happen is a sign of 'want of education' (Aristotle 1952a: 525); to challenge this foundational claim would appear as a sign of 'bad education, lack of formation' (*apaideusia*) (*Metaphysics* IV, 4, 1006a 6), the very proof that rhetorical education has not taken place.

What happens, then, when we are confronted with non-rhetorical audiences, audiences which, today, replicate the pre-*Rhetoric* staging that founds the *Rhetoric*, and when we are affronted by techniques of persuasion that, for lack of being 'antecedent', are nonetheless tangential or incidental to rhetoric, as we know it?

I am thinking of techniques of knowledge management such as storytelling. Regarding audiences, we may consider them as fascinated by persuasion as *thukē* – a game of intentionality (Cassin 2004: 668). The epideictic, performance-value, of the training they offer is highlighted by a commonplace comment: he is a great storyteller. In other words, training resides mainly in being a spectator of the one who performs a 'theory' which remains, by and large, unteachable. This explains why most of the tools of storytelling are freely available: the storyteller is the story. My question is: Is that a practice relevant to rhetoric, or is it not? Or, rather, if it is not, how do we approach that which it is tempting to define as sophistry – provided that, in the first instance, we have considered what an audience that is not rhetorical thinks of persuasion?

I am reminded here of a lecture Leo Strauss gave in 1942 on 'What is political theory?' I think it has some bearing on 'What is rhetorical theory?':

> The term 'political theory' implies that there is such a thing as *theoretical* knowledge of things *political*. This implication is by no means self-evident. Formerly, *all* political knowledge was considered *practical* knowledge ... The term political theory has another important implication. According to present-day usage, theory is essentially asked 'how do you account for this or that event?' His answer: 'I have a theory' ... What is meant by 'theory' in such cases is the essentially *hypothetical* assertion of a *cause* of an observed fact ... This use of the verb *theory* [the original meaning is ... to be an envoy sent to consult an oracle ... to look at, to behold, to inspect, contemplate, consider, compare] does not warrant at all the distinction of theory from observation; it rather excludes it; it certainly does not justify the identification, or almost identification, of theory with an essentially *hypothetical* kind of knowledge. I have some misgivings as regards these two connotations of the term theory; which are, to repeat, (1) the implication that a purely theoretical discussion of political questions is possible, and (2) the view that political knowledge as a whole consists of observation of 'data' and hypothetical explanation of these 'data'; I prefer therefore the term political philosophy which does not imply these assumptions. (Strauss 2007: 515–16)

My question is: can we substitute rhetoric for politics and argue along Straussian lines? Or, what can we draw from such a permutation? The permutation is uneasy as, we would retort, rhetoric is the best instrument we have to intervene in deliberative politics and to observe its workings – to have effects and to observe effects. It is, at foundation, already political.

Can we then make our own Strauss's annoyed remarks and state an analogy, while knowing modern audiences and practitioners of things political – the effected upon and the effecting ones – are no longer rhetorical? Or is it that Strauss is aiming at a difference between method (along the lines: rhetorical/political knowledge is a method to deal with 'data') and system (the diffusion of hypothetical knowledge)?

SECOND SCRUPLE OF A CROSSING: ON PATH

To bring us to that question, I need to retrieve my second 'scruple', where it is question of a way, opened up by the founding gesture and qualified as *hodopoiēin* (1354a 8).

A first set of translations ranges from 'to make a road, to trace out a path' (Grimaldi 1980: 3), to 'by [following] a path' (Kennedy 1991: 29) and 'frayer la route' (Wartelle 1981: 285). Wartelle's version 'to free a road' evokes the standard etymology of French *frayer*, from an older meaning of Latin *fricāre*, 'to open a path by crushing bushes that stand in the way', to free it from natural obstacles. The path is there already, it is just a matter of clearing it or, as Bailly offers (as secondary meaning), 'rendre accessible, praticable' (Bailly 1911: 602). Another set of translations opts for 'tracer une méthode' (Dufour 1931: 70), 'procéder par méthode' (Chiron 2007: 114). Once more, Cope's commentary is a revelator of a translating blur: 'To trace a path to be followed, which will lead you without unnecessary deviations to the place at which you wish to arrive. *Hodos*, therefore, in this metaphorical usage, is not merely *a* way, but *the* way, the *best* way ... Hence it denotes a regular, systematic, or scientific method' (Cope 1877: 4).

This may belong to the same paradigm as *methodos*, nonetheless Aristotle uses the former, not the latter, although, once again, he had, so it seems to translators, a better, ready-made choice. My contention is that the road already exists; it just needs to be cleared and made, as Bailly says, 'practicable', and the clearing instrument is the enthymeme and that which is attached to it – the *Rhetoric itself*. As Grimaldi comments on it, a method is a way set out. By contrast, *hodopoiēsis* is a gesture of discrimination, an act of freeing by contest, a way of 'entering the fray', and on a sure footing. This is a near homonymy: 'fray' (in the expression) comes from French *effrayer* (comp. 'afraid'), while 'to fray' comes from Latin *fricāre*. Homonyms are a form of rhetorical arguments.

However, bearing in mind that *hodos* denotes the path as direction leading to a fixed point ('la direction qui vous mène au but') (Chantraine 2008: 747), is it, in Grimaldi's and others' view, a method? Grimaldi, building upon *methodos* and comparing the two semes, concludes: 'attending to the system … Aristotle implies that what follows in the treatise will be such a road' (Grimaldi 1980: 4).

Method and system are contaminating each other, or casting a ghost, a Derridean spectre, onto *hodopoiēsis*. In Rhetoric 1414b 21, *hodopoiēsis* qualifies the proem of a speech, the prologue of a poem, the prelude of a musical piece. Proems, indeed, respond to rather strict constraints: the way they can open, is marked by the rules of the genre or the species. See how Cope (1877: 162) translates and glosses: 'For all these are *beginnings*, and as it were a paving of the way (preparation, pioneering of the road) for what follows.' However, a proem is an *exordium* in Latin, to recall the technical sense which is that of setting up the threads of a warp on a loom – termed, I may add, in Latin an *ordo*.

I would like to look at how Quintilian paraphrases *methodos: via atque ordo* (*Institutio oratoria*, II, 17.41). The road (*hodos=via*) is supplemented by and equated to order, *methodos=hodos+ordo*, ordo being literally, as mentioned, the threads of the warp.

That, in Latin, *ordo* and *ars* are cognate indicates, indeed, that it is not a matter of method but a matter of technology – a technology of articulation: *ars*, ultimately, refers to the root *ar-* (as in *armus*, arm), or the way in which the arm fits into the socket of the shoulder, providing human beings with an articulation that leads first to grasping material reality, and then to articulating this grasp through *sermo*, which also refers to a technology of articulation (the interlocking of words; comp. *sera*, a lock, where parts are inserted into one another to create an effect, the locking; think also of *series*).

The (late) compact of voice and gesture in persuasive delivery, what is now called embodied rhetoric, is to be first found in this articulation of speech and gesture in the technology of the arm, itself located in *ars* and *ordo*. Quintilian is a good translator in so far as he shows what is inhibited in *hodopoiēsis*: a technology for clearing that which stands in the way. Cordier (2005) provides the elements of an anthropological analysis of the Roman orator's brachial nudity, its des-inhibition, by commenting on an innovation by Gaius Gracchus. Before him orators moved by an aristocratic sense of *pudor* and *decentia* kept their arms wrapped up, often along side their body. The sudden thrust of the tribune's arm, naked and disrobing the shoulder, signalled, in the eyes of historians of Roman oratory, the entry of pathos into eloquence, metaphorically and materially heralding the penetration of populist, democratic and public speaking into aristocratic, republican and near-liturgical oratory. It also introduces in public deliberation, and into the representation of the Republic, that *erōs* Romans saw deleteriously at the heart of the Greek (ineffectual, vitiated) education of its citizens. For them, demagoguery is indeed a sort of erotics of speaking and one just as noxious. Conversely, *via atque ordo* obfuscates an essential meaning of *methodos*, 'pursuit'.

Via typically refers to the road set free for the chariots of combat as opposed to *semita*, the road, for those who have to walk – the walkway. We touch on another aspect of this technology: its agonistic and aristocratic side – after all, this is the site for the art of invective: how to throw words, with deadly accuracy.

Can one refashion oratory as a duality between a high road and a low road, a speech designed for combat and invective, and a speech the design of which is merely made to carry one along?

THE χ STANDS ITS GROUND: METHOD AND SYSTEM

My scruples are intact. The crossing, or chiasmus, that binds and halts holds firm. I actually do not know what the text says, except that, at the very moment of theoretical and practical foundation, a tense bond or an χ between system and method has begun to fasten the beginning of *Rhetoric*/Rhetoric, beyond the call on foundation (and its location in the principle), out of the reach of a demand for further explication, and within the reach of its own petition and claim and call.

The first sentences of the *Rhetoric* are foundational. Aristotle sets the scene for three *dramatis personae*: he projects himself as a founder who creates, names and dismisses from civil deliberation, that which exists as *antistrophos* to Rhetoric, that stands outside and against Rhetoric. And we are cast as his surrogates, as he casts away that which precedes his gesture, the antecedent side of rhetoric, whose practitioners 'are silent, say nothing' (regarding the foundation, enthymemes) (1354a 14). This is possibly the most dramatic moment of Rhetoric's foundation.

How can we interpret this? What is the nature of the attributed silence? The solution, or an indication of a solution, may be traced to the question: What is a foundation? And, once that is resolved, if it is resolved, how do we proceed by method, how do we proceed by system? Clearly, method and system are problematic articulations.

Deleuze, in an early school lecture, and in a classroom where I was to sit some years later, develops an argument about foundation, method and system. His lecture cannot be read in a rarefied atmosphere: it was delivered to students at an elite, meritocratic high school, possibly the brightest of their generation yet equally destined to serve, and possibly to kill or be killed, to torture or be tortured, in the Algerian un-named war. They, and Deleuze, were witnessing the disintegration of a parliamentary republic, the rise of a 'tyrant', and the last significant mass mobilization by the Left, not to mention the probability of a military coup (attempted in 1961); in short, politics at a time when the French Republic was on the brink of an inscrutable re-foundation. The lecture is, by opposition, a scrutiny of foundation.

One cannot read it independently from the philosophical question framed by this historical anchorage – namely, the conditions of possibility of resistance. The underlying question is: as the 4th Republic is grappling with its own discursivity, which underpins Sartre's analysis of political agency (Sartre 1976), what, asks Deleuze of his students, as philosophers attentive to politics-as-events, can we think of it, and do about it?

For Sartre, reflecting on the failure of a popular movement in the face of the Algerian war, *praxis* is 'a passage from objective to objective through internalization ... The subjective contains within itself the objective, which it denies and which it surpasses toward a new objectivity; and this new objectivity by virtue of *objectification* externalizes the internality of the project as an objectified subjectivity' (Sartre 1963: 97–98). This definition acquires the full extent of its meaning in the *Critique* when Sartre positions *praxis* at the centre of his analysis concerning history and 'practical ensembles', or human groupings alienated by labour and in conflict with relations of production. But, when Deleuze lectures his young students, a question is put to them: is the impending political upset by De Gaulle a *kairos*, the occasion to think about foundation and values and eloquence? Will his performance of the Republic, and the extra-ordinary impact of his eloquence, a root of a French 'passion for hyperpolitics', as I have called it (Salazar 2009), provoke him to make the claim of being a founder? What is the nature and energy of his claim? How can we resist?

This being said, here is Deleuze:

> The founder is he who poses and proposes an infinite task. How does he propose it and on what order? To found is to raise nature to the level of history and the mind. All those who propose values call on/back their claim with a foundation. So, when does the question of founding become a philosophical one? From the moment when the founder proposes to us infinite tasks as something that must be realized in this very world. The concept of foundation is now clearer. In the first instance man feels himself as a sentient being, in the second instance as a reasonable being. From one point to the other, foundation becomes self-aware. What is at stake is no longer to found at the level of values, but to interrogate oneself on what is this, to found. One must found the foundation itself. [The founder] is less he who founds than he who calls on a foundation. Literally, to found is to call on a foundation. (Deleuze 1956)

In my view, there are three key ideas: order; infinite, never-ending task; calling on a foundation. The first idea seems an injunction to clear away the sentient, which I interpret, in our own work, as the order to get non-reflective theory out of the way, as belonging to the world of nature – practices Aristotle casts aside into 'saying nothing, being mute' on that which he is calling on (the enthymemes). It posits values, and with them the task, a never-ending task, to reflect on values. This leads to a second idea: to found is to call on a foundation, not to found. The philosophical attitude is then to interrogate the call. This shapes, in turn, the never-ending task to reflect on theory and practice.

I cannot say, at this stage, if our foundation is a call on method (indicated by the clearing, the order of advance, the silencing and the allocation of roles) or a call on system (indicated by the activation of enthymematic thinking right at the outset and that of systemic Aristotelian concepts – *tekhnē, hexis, aitia, ergon*). I cannot even say if the two are inseparable. All I can say is that our rhetorical activity can indeed either call on the infinite task of the method or on the infinite task of the system.

Again, I will resort to Deleuze, and to the very same high school lecture, wherein he asks the young men in his class to consider a dialogue between method and system. Deleuze speaks:

Three Reproaches Made by Method to System:

1. System is man playing God since it carries with it an absolute knowledge. It is a call to find ways to go beyond human condition. Method helps man to assume his own condition. Of course human condition remains, man is part of nature. There always will be a part of passivity in the former. Nonetheless system holds there are ways for man to ward off the inconveniences of human condition. Method actualizes all its virtualities.
2. The second objection is political. Right or wrong, philosophers scent danger for man in system, in relation to tyranny. System is totalitarian. It is not a gross misreading of Hegel to say he has actually seen the moment when his philosophy was being actualized in the Prussian State. Systems and totalitarian regimes are often hand in glove.
3. Third objection: third mystification. System always calls on an a *priori* and seemingly shows disdain toward simple experience. Schelling says that system let experience in through the back door. System seems fit to justify everything. In fact, it sets up factual necessity as rational necessity.

Conversely, system has two reproaches toward method. The latter always maintains a double exteriority with the result that philosophy loses its true goal. Two poles in method. *The Method of Certitude* by Leibniz. He reproaches Descartes for confusing method of invention (one pole) and method of certitude (other pole). The first method claims to recover or reproduce through original means an object which, on the other hand, has already been produced by invention. Man's situation is within a preexistent nature. On the other hand, man invents objects that, in nature, are given him under a different form … First exteriority presupposes nature. Second pole, method of certitude. … The method of invention presupposes nature, so does the method of certitude, or how to recover through artificial means the pure nature of thinking. For Descartes, there is a natural rectitude of thinking but, as thinking beings, we are not able to match it. Method discriminates between us. Method raises the thinking being to the point it can catch up with pure thinking. Therefore, in both cases method always presupposes nature. System has an advantage: it manages to gain access to the interiority of the system and of its object. Thus, the method of invention represents by original means that which is already produced otherwise … The interiority of the system is dual: (1) In [his/its] perspective reproduction or actualization is one with the movement itself of the object; (2) Interiority and reciprocity of thought and object. To each figure of thought corresponds a given type of object. Method always refers to a nature it tries to reproduce or match. Method calls on an exterior nature. System calls on an internal life or an enveloping history. System calls either on a life that runs through it, or on a history that unfolds it. (Deleuze 1956)

I could leave it at that, let the χ stand a second time, and find relief in melancholy. However, to adumbrate the rhetorician's *ergon* or labour (what I call '*roteiro*') (Salazar 2013 in press) and to dramatize how we can 'progress' beyond the double χ, I would like to tell a story, the story of Joan Miró's *Pitchfork*, or *La Fourche* as it is called in French, and that of my dramatic encounter with it.

Story of the *Fourche*

At the Foundation Maeght, above Saint-Paul de Vence, the well-known village in the hinterland of Nice and Cannes, facing the steep valley and the distant Mediterranean Sea, stands a tall metal sculpture by Miró. Propped on a wall of dry stones, the sculpture is set against a luminous backdrop of land-, air-, and seascapes. It is called: *La Fourche*.

What I found attractive, when I saw it for the first time some twenty years ago, was its calculus of serenity, and the meditation borne by numbers. None of the explanations one can read on the Internet is true. Here is mine. True, I hope, to the 'forking' of rhetoric, to return to the initial word of this essay.

Figure 6.1 Miro's Fourche. Philippe-Joseph Salazar, extract from diary, 1987.

Resting on and soldered onto the apex of an elongated pedestal some three meters tall, resembling some primitive column, rests a flat triangular shape with a rounded baseline. The sculptor has paid precise attention to proportions. The triangle is cut out of a metal square that measures a third of the length of the elongated triangular pedestal. A circular hole is punched through the plate, of a diameter slightly wider than the base of the pedestal. This slight difference is a correction to visual distortion as it makes both look equal, although they are not. On the apex of the triangular sheet a pitchfork is balanced, its long handle sloping to the right, its prongs to the left, pointing up and East, towards sky and sea. The whole length of the pitchfork is equal to the height of the metal pedestal plus the base of the triangle up to the hollowed centre of the circle. In fact, I am quite sure the pitchfork, ripped from its support and held upright against the two-tiered plinth, would have the tip of its five prongs draw a horizontal line through the centre of the circle that would connect with sides of the triangle, thus designing a perfect isosceles. But, should the fork loosen its grip and rotate on its axis, it would trace a magnificent circle against the sky, a circle that would divide into two equal segments the height of its pedestal.

A first glance, in the cold light of a black and white winter, with shimmers of sleet on the ledges of the parapet and a veil of frost on its rusted coating, *La Fourche* told me a tale of immutability. This impression was reinforced by the rampart-like stolidity of the rusticated masonry, the serene tallness of the black bark of pines, the impervious landscapes of the lower Alps descending in stable steps towards tabular Mediterranean Sea. Later, as the sun reached its zenith, the sculpture was lit from the front, as if a painter had decided to cast light from another angle. It had lost its razor-sharp definition, which, from afar, made the sculpture resemble a cut-out. Even later, that afternoon, as the winter sun descended rapidly, I went again to look at *La Fourche* before driving back to Nice. It was now feebly lit from the right and the rear. It looked massively sombre, hewn out of funeral marble.

I then realized the obvious. The sculpture was a timepiece, a fantastic grandfather clock with its pendulum, its dial and its asymmetrical hands. Imagine a balance-wheel clock stripped of its inner mechanisms, its cogs and springs turned inside out, soldered, exposed and planted by a fanciful mind in a garden, to resemble the paragon of all timepieces, a standing sundial of the most primitive sort. This eviscerated clock did not 'tell' the time, it was 'told' the time of day by the sun tracing its course around it and casting light on its calculus of shapes.

As I drove back, the Mediterranean had put on violent shades of purple. A storm was gathering over what Italians call the Ligurian Sea. This sculpture is no banal time indicator, I thought, it points to a sea of many names, a mythological sea of course. I began to perceive the less obvious. The hand showing the hours is a five-pronged fisherman fork, Neptune's trident had become a 'quindent'. This timepiece partakes in myth. It does not tell of time hourly, daily or even yearly. *La Fourche* makes manifest time in the everlasting return of the same question in which Nietzsche situated what he called 'superman', in a philosophical conceit that, if the same question is asked repeatedly, it implies that, at some stage, the questioner must rise above the question and be 'superior' to the question itself.

La Fourche tells a Nietzschean tale of questioning our place on earth. It rotates on the purest geometrical forms, as geo-metry is the measuring of earth expressed in its essential forms – circle, square, line. The hands of the clock are a line: the fork handle is a line spliced into five diverging then parallel lines, the prongs. One step further: *La Fourche* is about generating space from a point. Against the backdrop of alleys, and gardens, and trees, this natural and human space, it shows us the kernel of space, the point: the point on which the fork rests on the dial has been elongated into a line, then divided in a variety of lines, then made to rotate, and to create the circle, and in its sweeping scythe to cut out all other geometrical forms. This timepiece is not about time at all. What we witness here is the creation of space, not of time. It is a 'spacepiece', a template, a temple.

As my car found its way through traffic back to *rue des Orangers*, I was mulling over the connection to Neptune, so obvious it seemed shallow. I took the wrong turn-off and got stuck behind a delivery van. I looked at a postcard of *La Fourche*. The 'less obvious' took shape: I had overlooked the low wall on which stands the sculpture. It is a parapet guarding the path that winds downhill, along which I had in fact lost my way – *La Fourche* stands at the edge of a stony maze, a labyrinth.

Aptly enough, the mythical Labyrinth, in which Theseus fought and slew the Minotaur, represented for the Greeks the ultimate human use of geometry, space mastered by numbers, the well-organized Cretan Empire. In Latin, a labyrinth also means inner labour, *labor intus*. The Man-Bull was a monster: half-man, half-bull, a symbol for the political monstrosity of Cretan culture, the first society of control ever known to the Greeks. The Minotaur is the ferocious and voracious passion some of us have for order. Order is animality regained. Only human beings can create disorder. Nature knows nothing else but order. Disorder is what makes human nature so un-natural, so superior to Nature, so un-animal. Read Nietzsche. Theseus' inner labour, beneath Knossos the well-ordered city, was, in killing the Man-Bull and escaping from the geometrical entrapment of the Labyrinth, to thwart monstrosity created by order.

The sun was casting its very last rays, from over the mainland, onto the Baie des Anges. I understood yet another meaning to the 'quindent', the five-pronged pitchfork. It is indeed Neptune's redoubled trident, and does tell us of space made human, and time softening space, for, as you know without time, space would remain just that, immobile and sturdy – time makes space take on new shapes. I say that a five-pronged pitchfork is a trident redoubled because, if you take a trident and you slew it round, pivoting it on the hinge of an outer prong, what you get is not a 'sexdent' but a 'quindent'. *La Fourche* is two tridents fastened in one – two pitchforks, not one.

The original title, in French, is *La Fourche*. 'Fourche' translates as 'pitch-fork', in addition to which it also means a spliced road, our rhetorical χ. That pitchfork is also a fork on a road, a forking. In his walk out of the buried Labyrinth, after he slew the Bull, Theseus had to master the geometry of his path to freedom by deciding, at each fork, which way to slew his walk. Each time he chose right. Road fork after road fork, slewing along, he reduced the forking path to a simpler division until he emerged into the sun. Thanks to his *labor intus*, the underground labour of choosing the right path, guided by the thread Ariadne gave him, he reduced the twisted twine to a point, the ball of thread he now held in his hand, in the open air, in radiant light. Myth has it, that Theseus' slaying of the Bull founded Athens' freedom, democracy. Mythical times came then and there to an end, and Athens entered historical times and rhetorical space. Theseus had gained control over a monstrous organization. Deliberation upon deliberation, he moved on, along that simple line, symbolized by Ariadne's red fleece thread. He got out. When he emerged, the Labyrinth was now inhabited with the sound of deliberation and the echo of human choices, no longer with the roars and the lust of a monstrous institution. What did Theseus do? He played method against system, the χ against the labyrinth, and, perhaps, showed us one way to handle the *Rhetoric*: to assume that method, like Ariadne's thread, is a given; that persuasive, artful and effective democratic speech has to grasp that which is beyond itself – in our case, *hic et nunc*, the absence of a civil, rhetorical culture.

References

Aristotle. 1877. *The Rhetoric of Aristotle, with a Commentary*. Ed. E.M. Cope. Cambridge: Cambridge University Press.
——. 1926. *The 'Art' of Rhetoric*. Ed. J.H. Freese. London: W. Heinemann, Loeb Classical Library.
——. 1931. *Rhétorique I*. Ed. (in French) M. Dufour. Paris: Les Belles Lettres, collection des Universités de France.
——. 1952a. *Metaphysics*, in *The Works of Aristotle, I*. Ed. W.D. Ross. Translated by W.D. Ross. Chicago: The University Press of Chicago.
——. 1952b. *Physics*, in *The Works of Aristotle, I*. Ed. W.D. Ross. Translated by R.P. Hardie and R.K. Gaye. Chicago: The University Press of Chicago.
——. 1980. *Rhetoric I, A Commentary*. Ed. W.M. Grimaldi. New York: Fordham University Press.
——. 1991. *On Rhetoric*. Ed. G.A. Kennedy. New York and Oxford: Oxford University Press.
——. 2007. *Rhétorique*. Ed. (in French) P. Chiron. Paris: Garnier-Flammarion.
Bailly, Anatole. 1911. *Abrégé du Dictionnaire Grec-Français*. Paris: Hachette.
Benveniste, Émile. 1969. *Le Vocabulaire des institutions indo-européennes*. Paris: Minuit.
Bonitz, Hermann. 1870. *Index Aristotelicus*, in *Aristotelis Opera 5*. Eds Immanuel Bekker and Christian Brandis. Berlin: Georg Reimer.
Cassin, Barbara. 2004. '"Thukê" et "automaton" chez Aristote', in *Vocabulaire européen des philosophies*, Paris: Le Robert/Seuil, p. 668 (insert 2).
Chantraine, Pierre. 2008. *Dictionnaire étymologique de la langue grecque*. Paris: Klinscksieck.
Chiron. See Aristotle 2007.

Cope. See Aristotle 1877.

Cordier, Pierre. 2005. *Nudités romaines. Un problème d'histoire et d'anthropologie.* Paris: Les Belles Lettres.

Deleuze, Gilles. 1956. *Qu'est-ce que fonder?* Cours hypokhâgne, Lycée Louis le Grand 1956-1957-00/00/1956 (notes taken by Pierre Lefebvre) http://www.webdeleuze.com/php/texte.php?cle=218&groupe=Conférences&langue=1

Dufour. See Aristotle 1931.

Freese. See Aristotle 1926.

Grimaldi. See Aristotle 1980.

Kennedy. See Aristotle 1991.

Pucci, Pietro. 2004. 'Kêr, Moira, Aisa, Heimarmenê, Anagkê, Peprômenê, Tukhê', in *Vocabulaire européen des philosophies.* Paris: Le Robert/Seuil, pp. 665–71.

Salazar, Philippe-Joseph. 2014 in press. 'Midnight Rhetor, ou le roteiro de Joe Buck l'indomptable', *Cahiers Michel Leiris* 4.

———. 2008. 'Rhetoric on the Bleachers or, The Rhetorician as Melancholiac', *Philosophy & Rhetoric* 41(4): 356–74.

———. 2009. *L'Hyperpolitique, une passion française.* Paris: Klincksieck.

Sartre, Jean-Paul. 1963. *Search for a Method.* Trans. Hazel E. Barnes. New York: Knopf.

———. 1976. *Critique of Dialectical Reason: Theory of Practical Ensembles.* Trans. Alan Sheridan-Smith. Ed. Jonathan Rée. London: NLB.

Strauss, Leo. 2007. 'What Can We Learn From Political Theory?' *The Review of Politics* 69: 515–29.

Wartelle, André. 1981. *Lexique de la Rhétorique d'Aristote.* Paris: Les Belles Lettres.

I acknowledge support received from the Research Committee of the University of Cape Town and the National Research Foundation of South Africa (IRR grant). Views expressed are not those of the NRF.

■ ■ ■ ■ ■ ■ ■

PART III

SENSUOUS EXPERIENCE MEDIATED BY CHIASMUS

CHAPTER 7

CHIASM IN SUSPENSE IN PSYCHOANALYSIS

Alain Vanier

■ ■ ■ ■ ■ ■ ■

Dictionaries provide two or three definitions of the word chiasm, depending on whether or not they distinguish between 'chiasm' and 'chiasmus'. In trying to think its possible relevance to psychoanalysis,[1] it is the first definition – 'a sign in the form of the Greek letter χ (chi) on the margin of a manuscript, indicating a rejected passage'[2] – that immediately fits the bill. This mark can function as a figure of one of the basic operations of censorship in the psyche: the rejected passage remains latent, only appearing in the manifest text in distorted form, and must be deciphered in order to be rediscovered.

Not infrequently this distortion takes the shape of a chiasm in the rhetorical sense of a 'figure, by which the order of words in one clause is inverted in a second clause',[3] an inversion distinguishing it from 'parallelism', where no such inter-crossing between the two clauses appears. Freud thus tells us that when a patient, following an account of a dream in which a woman appears, says 'this woman is not my mother', we should understand 'my mother is this woman'. Certainly this is a slight forcing, because the formula could also be expressed as: 'this woman is not my mother, this woman is my mother', that is to say, in the form of a parallelism. Yet we see that the chiastic form, which in the second clause puts 'my mother' in the subject position, emphasizes the operation more strongly. I have come to think that in the field of psychoanalysis, chiasm is virtually omnipresent and at the same time curtailed because one of the two clauses is repressed and therefore not enunciated. This specific type of chiasm accentuates the split between the two clauses, which cannot both be spoken at the same time: as the split between the unconscious and consciousness. The general formula of the chiasm in psychoanalysis could be expressed in the terms Lacan claimed to have got from Claude Levi-Strauss: 'The subject receives from the Other his own message in an inverted form'.[4] The repressed clause, in relation to which the manifest utterance stands in a chiastic relationship, shows that the two registers of knowledge (*savoir*) separated by this split coexist in a paradox: on the one hand, knowledge which is known, which functions as a reference and includes theoretical elaboration; on the other hand, unknown, textual knowledge, the product of the unconscious within the analytic course of treatment. As Octave Mannoni has shown, the censorship operating between these two orders of knowledge is inevitable and demonstrates the connection between theoretical knowledge and resistance (Mannoni 1968).

The third definition of a chiasm sometimes refers to it as a 'chiasma'. This is an anatomical term, denoting the inter-crossing of the optic nerves on the body of the sphenoid bone. It was probably this anatomical meaning that prompted Maurice Merleau-Ponty to turn chiasm into a concept in his book *The Visible and the Invisible* (1964), but, since this work was left unfinished, without specifying or developing it in any way, the concept has remained obscure, reflecting a system of intertwining notions in which various heterogeneous elements can coexist. The first appearance of the work in 1964 led Lacan to develop the link between heterogeneity and chiasm further, firstly by bringing our attention to a type of chiasm corresponding to the function of the eye as an organ (Lacan 1964). Lacan's argument has to do with the specificity of human vision and its characteristic of not being identical over the whole surface of the retina. The central part of the retina allows us to see only if there is sufficient light, while the peripheral part provides a vision which is less clear yet remains possible even under diminished lighting. Similarly, in the so-called Arago phenomenon, in which one wants to observe a star of fourth or fifth magnitude at night, it is necessary not to look straight at the object, but rather a little to the side.[5] Nevertheless, Lacan's preoccupation is not with this particular characteristic of human vision per se; rather, he insists on a 'cleavage' (*schize*) between the eye and the gaze as two heterogeneous levels. Here too we find the fundamental split of all chiasm in the field of psychoanalysis. The distinction between seeing and looking has to do with this split: 'I can only see from a certain point but, in my existence, I am being looked at from everywhere' (Lacan 1964: 69).[6] This can be expressed as a chiasm: things are looking at me, I see things. In a normal situation, there is an elision of the gaze. This separative elision can disappear for example in psychosis, where the gaze can become manifest, such as in delusions of being watched. Without going as far as psychosis, it is clear that we are always, more or less unawares, being looked at. We are the object of this external gaze, a fact which organizes our way of being in the world. I present myself differently according to the situation. It is in relation to this outside gaze that I organize the appearance that I want to offer the Other in order to cheat him or seduce him. We find here again what was originally constituted as a matrix during the mirror stage. Facing the mirror, the child is held by his mother, who is looking at him. This first gaze will be lost, yet preserved on another level. It takes on the form of a drive, in the case of the scopic drive, '*qua* object *a*', which may 'come to symbolize the central lack of castration ... leaving the subject in ignorance as to what there is beyond appearance' (ibid.: 73). Finally, due to this gaze, the 'subject is presented as other than he is' but 'what one shows him is never what he wishes to see'. This split can be expressed as follows: 'You never look at me from where I see you, what I look at is never what I want to see' (ibid.: 94–95). Painting allows Lacan to develop this theme further, especially around the notion of perspective, as symmetry between, on the one hand, the gaze as an object and, on the other hand, the geometric point as the place of the subject of representation. This scheme appears as a crossing formed around a split represented by the surface of the painting.

There is a link between this split and desire, which itself is a split. Desire is not a predicate of the body but the body itself. It is connected to those bits and pieces, including the gaze, which were lost in the history of the subject. Pleasure, on the other hand, exists in the register of the senses. Here we find a chiastic dimension, because pleasure is not satisfaction of desire but rather desire's turning back on and interlacing with itself. In this way, the surface of the body as a site of perception is where, in the mirror, desire is reflected. The question of desire is posed in this very reflection. Thus we see again the crucial dimension of a split between consciousness and the unconscious.

This becomes a starting point for Lacan's effort to bring back the Cartesian cogito; in his various readings, the emphasis is always on this split. He will suggest that we write: 'I am thinking: "therefore I am"' (Lacan 1966: 517). Thought founds being by situating it where there is no thought. This disjunction between thought and being can be articulated as follows: 'I am not, in the place where I am the plaything of my thought; I think of what I am, in the place where I do not think I am thinking' (ibid.). Or, more simply, in an explicitly chiastic form: I am not where I think; I do not think where I am. Indeed, 'psychoanalysis posits that the unconscious, where the subject's "I am not" has its substance can be derived from the "I do not think", inasmuch as he imagines himself to be the master of his being, that is to say, not to be language' (Lacan 1967). Psychoanalysis thus reestablishes a chiasm – a split and an inter-crossing – which sutures the Cartesian utterance. Lacan is then right to say that psychoanalysis operates upon the subject of science, which demonstrates the Cartesian cogito.

However, this restitution does not cancel out the split, leaving the chiasm as if unaccomplished. The chiasm Lacan finds at the heart of the Cartesian cogito is the same one which he unearths between science and psychoanalysis. While science forecloses the truth of the subject as its own cause, a cause of which it wants to know nothing, psychoanalysis on the other hand 'reintroduces the Name of the Father into scientific thinking', in this way bringing back the question of truth as a cause. Yet, since truth can never be completely totalized, never completely made into knowledge, the chiasm reaches an impasse.

Lacan discovers this dimension, which he calls 'suspense', in sexual *jouissance*. A certain form of *jouissance* – that of the Other – remains suspended.

> It is because the inter-crossing, the chiasm one would expect, would rightly make of each of the bodies a signifying metaphor of the *jouissance* of the Other, it is because this chiasm remains suspended that we can, from whichever side we look at it, see the displacement which really makes one *jouissance* dependent on the body of an other and thanks to which the *jouissance* of the Other remains, as I have said, far adrift. (Lacan 1966–67)

Indeed, *jouissance* is only possible for the subject as partial and limited, as based upon its original partial loss. Nevertheless, this first *jouissance* is one which the subject had to give up in order to come into existence, a subtraction represented for Freud by the incest prohibition and meaning that an absolute, full, total *jouissance*, which would be the *jouissance* of the primal Other, becomes impossible.

The chiasm which we find in these different approaches is a correlation of this split. As an effect of the separation from the Other, which gives rise to the subject in the split between consciousness and the unconscious, this division radicalizes the chiasm and leaves it suspended because it literally cannot be completed, its two sides belonging to different registers and remaining radically heterogeneous: a split which not even psychoanalytic experience itself is able to resolve. Finally, does not the importance of this paradoxical trope in the psychoanalytic field, which always belongs simultaneously to different registers, confirm Lacan's argument that 'the psychoanalyst is the presence of the sophist in our time, yet with a different status' (Lacan 1964–65) or, as he says even more radically in 1977, that 'the psychoanalyst is a rhetor' (Lacan 1977–78). He adds: 'One tries to tell the truth', but truth is not all, it can only be half said, and the second part of the chiasm remains suppressed – subjected to the split between the two clauses, which leaves them insolubly heterogeneous.

Trans. Kristina Valendinova

Notes

1. Chiasm is not a psychoanalytic concept. We do not find it either in Freud or later authors, and only rarely in Lacan.
2. Dictionary of the *Centre National de Ressources Textuelles et Lexicales*, CNRS Paris.
3. *The Shorter O.E.D.*, 1983 (3rd edition) 'We eat to live, not live to eat' is an example most commonly used.
4. Boris Wiseman has judiciously shown this formula to be the generalized form of the chiasm between the unconscious and consciousness, the Other being the site of the unconscious.
5. We could make a connection between this phenomenon and the way in which the analyst should listen to the analysand, by not paying special attention to any single discursive element. Freud calls this distanced listening 'suspended attention' (*gleich-schwebende Aufmerksamkeit*).
6. All translations from the French are by the translator.

References

Lacan, Jacques. 1964. *Les Quatre concepts fondamentaux de la psychanalyse*. Le Séminaire, Livre XI. Paris: Seuil.

———. 1966. *Écrits*. Paris: Seuil.

———. 1967. *Résumé du Séminaire La Logique du fantasme*. Paris: Annuaire de l'École pratique des Hautes Études.

———. [1964–65]. *Problèmes cruciaux pour la psychanalyse*. Le Séminaire, Livre XV. Unpublished.

———. [1966–67]. *La Logique du fantasme*. Le Séminaire, Livre XIV. Unpublished.

———. [1977–78]. *Le Moment de conclure*. Le Séminaire, Livre XXV. Unpublished.

Mannoni, Octave. 1968. *Freud*. Paris: Seuil.

Merleau-Ponty, Maurice. 1964. *Le Visible et l'invisible*. Paris: Gallimard.

CHAPTER 8

Quotidian Chiasmus in Montaigne
Arguing Impotence and Suicide

Phillip John Usher

■ ■ ■ ■ ■ ■ ■

Rather than aiming to make a given point of view memorable or afford it public appeal, the rhetoric that Montaigne deploys throughout his *Essais* (1580–92) generally functions anti-rhetorically – to unseat knowledge, to generate and to confer doubt, and to position human judgement in the fray of contradictory arguments. As Lawrence D. Kritzman has summarized, Montaigne is, above all, 'un rhétoricien qui s'intéresse plus au fonctionnement de son texte qu'à une vérité absolue' (a rhetorician more interested in his text's functioning than in absolute truth) (Kritzman 1980: 162). It is not that Montaigne, marshalling rhetoric antithetically, is *only* interested in his text, nor that he is not interested in truth. It is rather that the deployment of rhetoric serves to argue against dogmatism and to underline the active nature of human judgement. In reference to essay I.5, Kritzman concludes that 'L'intérêt du texte vient du refus de la part du rhétoriqueur d'installer une morale inébranlable' (The text's interest comes from the rhetorician's refusal to install a fixed moral system) (Kritzman 1980: 40). The topics that Montaigne submits to the anti-rhetorical mêlée of Ancient authors and contemporary anecdotes are frequently those of daily life.[1] Indeed, 'Montaigne's effort is not a determined onslaught on the web of belief but a subtle regimen for the consideration of claims of believability and acts of believing, in their intrusions into and compromises with quotidian reality' (Struever 1992: 226). Essential to Montaigne's arsenal of anti-rhetorical rhetoric as he battles to make sense of the quotidian is the figure of chiasmus, on the levels of local word order and long-range structure.

It is worth noting, before we look at several ways in which chiasmus collides with the everyday in Montaigne, that Medieval and Renaissance writers did not speak of 'chiasmus'. Rhetorical treatises, such as the pseudo-Ciceronian *Rhetorica ad Herennium*, known to writers of Montaigne's generation, did speak of *antimetabole* (ἀντιμεταβολή) and other texts spoke of *commutatio*, but there is, strictly speaking, a difference. Whereas chiasmus refers to the inversion of structural elements (as in 'We knowingly lied and we followed blindly' – adverb, verb; verb, adverb), *antimetabole* or *commutatio* also imply the exact reprise of terms in that reversal (as in 'I know what I like and I like what I know'). To approach chiasmus in Montaigne means that we are using a term he himself did not use in this sense. Yet chiasmus is quite obviously ubiquitous throughout the *Essais* (Gray 1958: 46), beginning with the very first essay of Book One, 'Par divers moyens on arrive à pareille fin' (We Reach the Same Ends by Discrepant Means), wherein the words *fortis* (strong) and *mollis* (soft) are woven into a complex chiastic structure that sets the opening text as an essay on method as much as an essay about a specific topic (Cottrell 1982: 65–71). As well as structuring the collection's first essay, chiastic reversal also undergirds what are most likely Montaigne's most read essays, which have inscribed him in literary history as the inventor of cultural relativism, namely 'Des Coches' and 'Des Cannibales'.[2] As Edwin Duval has shown, the structure of 'Des Coches', for example, is that of a chiastic disposition of major themes which can be summarized as: Roman coaches → Roman pomp → age of world || age of world → New World pomp → New World coaches (Duval 1983). Many other essays could be (and have been) analysed for their inherently chiastic nature.

As the present volume invites us, the present pages will focus on two aspects of how Montaigne's use of chiasmus relates to the dramas of everyday life. In particular, it will be examined how self-regulation through chiasmus in two aspects of daily life – impotence and suicide – are treated respectively by Montaigne in essays I.21, 'De la force de l'imagination' (On the Power of the Imagination) and II.3, 'Coustume de l'isle de Cea' (A Custom of the Isle of Cea). Before approaching these two essays, it is worth noting the (rather obvious, but important) connection between chiasmus and Montaigne's debt to the scepticism of Sextus Empiricus with whose words Montaigne decorated the wooden beams of his study (Legros 2000: 377–79). Returning to Sextus Empiricus' *Outlines of Pyrrhonism*, we recall that scepticism is zetetic (in its form of inequity), ephectic (in its suspensive state of mind), and aporetic (from its habit of doubting) (Sextus Empiricus 1992: I.7) and that the ultimate goal is to attain a state of unperturbedness or quietude (i.e. ataraxia [Ἀταραξία]), and that the means employed is, in a nutshell, the opposing of 'appearances [objects of sense-perception] to judgments [objects of thought], with the result that, owing to the equipollence of the objects and reasons thus opposed, we are brought firstly to a state of [ataraxia]' (Sextus Empiricus 1992: I.8). In particular, Montaigne learned from the *Outlines of Pyrrhonism* that the most fundamental principle of the Sceptic system is 'that of opposing to every proposition [λόγος] an equal proposition' (Sextus Empiricus 1992: I.12).· As John O'Brien (2004: 14) has noted,[3] Montaigne translates this central principle about balancing proposition and counter-proposition,[4] at the beginning of II.15, as 'Il n'y a raison qui n'en aye une contraire' (No reason but has its contrary), a precept to which Montaigne refers here as a 'beau mot' (fine saying) that recently, and seemingly not for the first time, he has been in the process of 'remash[er]' (chewing over) (Montaigne 1962: 596; Montaigne 1991: 694) (Screech's translations have been modified as necessary).

Montaigne's Chiastic Cure for Impotence

'Fortis imaginatio generat casum' (a powerful imagination generates the event), begins essay I.21, 'De la force de l'imagination' (On the Power of the Imagination) (Montaigne 1962: 95; 1991: 109). Montaigne, who tells us in his initial address to the reader that, after all, he is writing about himself – 'c'est moy que je peins' (Montaigne 1962: 9; 1991: lviv) – notes that he is particularly susceptible to his imagination's sway and empire; his own art, he says, 'est de luy eschapper, non pas de luy resister' (is escaping it, not resisting it) (Montaigne 1962: 95; 1991: 109). Various examples are adduced as to the imagination's great sinew: the possibility of bringing fevers and other maladies upon oneself merely through the sight of others who suffer; how the 'jeunesse bouillante' (fiery young men) may ejaculate as they dream about sex (an example borrowed from Lucretius) (Montaigne 1962: 96; 1991: 110); or how a man might grow horns after watching a bullfight and dreaming about it overnight. The imagination is blamed for miracles, visions and various other forms of enchantment. Montaigne develops one particular victim of the imagination: the male member and its surrender to imagination-imposed impotence.

In approaching such an issue, Montaigne is reacting to contemporary popular beliefs, according to which impotence was caused by demons and witches. The same year that Montaigne's first book of *Essais* was published, Jean Bodin's *La Démonomanie des sorciers* (1580) appeared. In its preface,

Bodin acknowledges that the topic of *sorciers* (witches, male or female) 'semble à toutes personnes estrange à merueilles, & à plusieurs incroyable' (appear to everyone marvellously strange – and to some, unbelievable). His goal was to break down the strangeness and incredibility of the topic, by discussing the nature of demons (book 1), the traps they use (book 2), the means by which to undertake a witch-hunt (book 3), the inquisitions and trials against those accused of such magic, etc.[5] Impotence was most often considered one of the *malefici's* ways of interfering with the correct functioning of human society, as categorized, for example, by Johannes Nider in his *Fornicarius: De Visionibus et Revelationibus* (1435–37) (Culianu 1987: 152). It was a malady much discussed in the sixteenth century, generally referred to by expressions such as *noueries d'aiguillettes, avoir l'esguillette nouée.* Cotgrave (1611) defines the latter as 'The charming of a mans codpiece point so, as he shall not be able to use his owne wife, or woman (though he may use any other)', highlighting both the etymology of the word (the *esguillette* refers to the closing mechanism of breeches, the precursor of the button and the zip) and the fact that impotence most often referred to impotence between man and wife. Bodin (1580) himself spoke of the *noueries d'aiguillettes*, calling it a 'méchanceté damnable' (damnable wickedness) and the demons responsible for it murderers, 'car celuy n'est pas moins homicide qui empesche la procreation des enfans que s'il leur coupoit la gorge' (because anyone who interferes with the procreation of children is just as much a murderer as someone who cuts children's throats).[6] And indeed, men and women would be condemned for such a crime, as can be seen in Jaubert's *Glossaire du centre de la France* (1584) which mentions a shepherd named Blaise Leduc condemned as a *noueur d'aiguillette* and sentenced to beatings and flaying by birch branch (Gelin 1910: 125–27).

Montaigne, in reaction to widespread superstition, thus proposes to relate the ailment rather to each man's own mind. The essayist speaks, he says, 'par experience' (out of experience) by first discussing the case of someone about whom he can 'respondre comme de [lui-]mesme' (vouch for, as if himself) and about whom 'il ne pouvoit choir soupcon aucune de foiblesse' (there could be not the slightest suspicion of sexual inadequacy) who, having heard another man discuss the issue, fell victim to it (Montaigne 1962: 97; 1991: 112). From that point on, 'ce villain souvenir de son inconvenient le gourmand[ait] et tyrannis[ait]' (the ugly memory of his failure taunted and tyrannized him) (Montaigne 1962: 97; 1991: 112). The rhetorical gesture – that Montaigne can *vouch* for this other man as if for *himself* – is, of course, most likely a mask allowing Montaigne to talk of his own condition without specifically admitting it[7] – an echo of the opening *Au lecteur's* slight hesitancy over self-portraiture.[8] Of interest here is not the identification between the author and the man for whom he can vouch, but the cure that Montaigne sketches out via this exemplum. The cure that the impotent man finds is described as follows: 'Il trouva quelque remede à cette resverie par une autre resverie' (He found a remedy to this vain imagining by means of another vain imagining) (Montaigne 1962: 97; 1991: 112). The sceptical trading of λόγος for λόγος is here recast as trading *resverie* for *resverie*. Montaigne explains the cure as follows: 'C'est que, advouant luy mesme et preschant avant la main cette sienne subjection, la contention de son ame se soulageoit sur ce, qu'apportant ce mal comme attendu, son obligation en amoindrissoit et luy en poisoit moins' (He admitted beforehand that he was subject to this infirmity and spoke openly about it, so relieving the tensions within his soul; by bearing the malady as something to be expected, his sense of constriction grew less and weighed less heavily upon him) (Montaigne 1962: 97; 1991: 112). Not only this, but when a propitious occasion arose, his body was now ready to respond and the man's body 's'est guari tout net à l'endroit de ce subjet' (clean cured itself of that condition) (Montaigne 1962: 98; 1991: 112). Impotence, argues Montaigne *contra* Bodin and popular belief, is caused by the imagination (Non-impotent state → Talking about impotence → Imagining impotence → Impotence); it can be cured, he advances, through a chiastic reversal of terms (Impotence → Imagining impotence → Talking about impotence → Non-impotent state). Alan Boase has referred to Montaigne's explanation as 'psychological', in that it stands in opposition to the period's more widely accepted explanation put forward by demonologists (Boase 1970: 5). The rhetorical emphasis – the man must invert his thinking by trading *resveries* – allows a controlling of one's own psychology.

As is often the case in the *Essais*, a subsequent example is provided by the essayist to remind the reader that it is less the specifics of the *autre resverie* which counts than the very fact of chiastic reversal. The new example concerns another supposed friend of Montaigne's, this time a 'conte de très bon lieu' (a highly placed count) who was getting married to a beautiful woman (Montaigne 1962: 98; 1991: 113). Fearing that his friend might suffer impotence upon arrival at the marriage bed, Montaigne gives his friend 'certaine pièce d'or platte, où estoient gravées quelques figures celestes, contre le coup de soleil et oster la douleur de teste, la logeant à point sur la cousture du test' (a certain little flat piece of gold on which were engraved celestial symbols, protecting against sunstroke and relieving headaches when correctly applied to the cranial suture) (Montaigne 1962: 98; 1991: 113), an object which had been given to Montaigne by fellow writer and translator Jacques Peletier du Mans. On handing the golden coin to the groom, Montaigne instructed him that, should he be troubled, he was to dismiss the wedding guests and playfully seize yet another amulet – this time, Montaigne's own 'robbe de nuict' (nightshirt) (Montaigne 1962: 98; 1991: 113). Following this, the man was to repeat specific prayers three times while placing the lucky medal 'sur ses roignons' (over his loins) (Montaigne 1962: 99; 1991: 113). This, said Montaigne, would solve the problem – and, apparently, it did. As the essayist concludes, '[c]es singeries sont le principal de l'effect, nostre pensée ne se pouvant desmesler que moyens si estranges ne viennnent de quelqu'abstruse science. Leur inanité leur donne poids et reverence' (It is such monkeyings-about which mainly provide results: our thoughts cannot free themselves from the convictions that such strange actions must derive from some secret lore) (Montaigne 1962: 99; 1991: 114). What should also be acknowledged here is that the medallion and the nightshirt serve as articulators of chiastic reversal, objects that allow the individual who falls victim to his imagination to locate his excess of thought within something tangible and thus to set about carefully undoing its power over the body. The objects function as markers for the rhetorical centre of symmetry in chiasmus.

Montaigne subsequently offers somewhat more practical advice, namely that men and women getting married have plenty of time to work on the sexual side of their relationship, but the essayist's emphasis is rather on the out-tricking of the imagination by bringing thought under the control of language. Moreover, it is not just the male member whose good functioning depends on such trickery or control: all parts of the human body have 'des passions propres, qui les esveillent et endorment, sans nostre conge' (have their own passions, which arouse them or send them to sleep, without leave from us) (Montaigne 1962: 100; 1991: 115). Selected for special mention are the face, heart, lungs, pulse, hair (in regard of it standing on end when we are frightened), hands, tongue and bowels: 'Les utils qui servent à discharger le ventre ont leurs propres dilatations et compressions, outre et contre nostre advis, comme ceux-cy destinez à discharger nos roignons' (The sphincter which serves to discharge our stomachs has dilations and contractions proper to itself, independent of our wishes or even opposed to them; so do those members which are destined to discharge the kidneys) (Montaigne 1962: 101; 1991: 115). Further examples are included: first, a Swiss man who suffered from the stone and who found relief only in enemas that his doctors never actually performed (allowing the mind to reverse its attachment to its ailment); second, a woman who feared she had swallowed a pin and whose choking was cured when, after vomiting, she saw a bent-up pin in the vomit, which had been placed there by someone else; and several others. 'On the Power of the Imagination', then, can be read as a mini-treatise on how to harness the power of rhetoric in general and of chiastic reversal in particular in order to self-regulate, in order to establish the true cause of certain bodily ailments and set the terms in a reverse order, so as to free the body. Montaigne was not the first to put forward psychological explanations of this kind or to discuss the role that imagination might play in cures of bodily afflictions. The physician Girolamo Cardano (1501–76) spoke of an ill woman cured 'vel daemone ... vel imaginatione, fideque' (by the demon ... or by imagination and faith) (Siraisi 1997: 166). One can think more specifically of Queen Isabelle of Castille who, in discussion with the Dominican Diego de Deza regarding the impotence of her niece's husband, affirmed that 'such things are more due to discord among humans than to interference by powerful demons' (Stephens 2002: 314; see also Stephens 1998).

The power of the impotent man's mind to operate chiastic reversal, thus effectuating a cure, was however not generally accepted in Montaigne's time. It is hardly surprising, then, that several Early Modern readers, beginning with the Jesuit Martin Del Rio, a vague cousin of Montaigne's, reacted directly to Montaigne's explanation in order to reassert the power of the demonic. Slightly later, Pierre de Lancre would take up Del Rio's commentaries. The latter's tone is one of pure mockery: 'Lecteur, tu peux entendre comme bien témérairement Michel de Montaigne ... oste ce genre de malefices au Diable pour l'attribuer à la force de l'imagination' (Reader, you can hear how rashly Michel de Montaigne ... steals this kind of *maleficium* from the Devil to attribute it to the force of the imagination) (Villey 1935: 103). The rashness of such a move is underscored when de Lancre notes that 'rapporter tant et de si divers effets à l'imagination seule, Oreste mesme n'en seroit d'avis aux plus claires pauses de sa fureur' (to relate so many and such varied effects to nothing but the imagination – even Orestes would disagree in the clearest interruptions of his madness) (ibid.). For Montaigne, the psychological rather than demonic explanation allows the individual to turn the situation on its head by means of reversing the terms first used to express it.

SEX AND SUICIDE

From chiasmus' role in taking control of one's own mind, we move now to one example of how Montaigne harnesses the power of chiasmus in relation to forms of external authority over individual choices. In essay II.3, 'Coustume de l'isle de Cea' (A Custom of the Isle of Cea), an essay which Marcel Tetel (1990: 11) called 'a typical case of [Montaignian] ambiguity', Montaigne collects together arguments for and against suicide, not a minor undertaking given the Catholic Church's utter condemnation of all suicide as morally wrong, an attitude with a long history (see Bayet 1922: 556–58). The Synod in Antisidor in 590 first systematized the condemnation of suicide and the Synod in Nîmes in 1096 had established that suicides could not be buried in consecrated soil; in the thirteenth century, Thomas Aquinas voiced the Church's official stance: suicide was wrong because it was unnatural, anti-social, and because life was a gift from God (Retterstøl 1993: 17–18).[9] Such a view filters into the seventh circle of Dante's *Inferno* (canto XIII) where suicides are transformed into bushes and trees, and torn at by the Harpies, never again to inhabit their bodies, 'non è giusto aver ciò ch'uom si toglie' (it is not right for any man to have what he himself has cast aside) (Dante, *Inferno* 2004, XIII: 105). Dante's real-life example is that of Pier delle Vigne, chancellor for Frederick II, whose description reworks Virgil's Polydorus in *Aeneid* III (Lindheim 1990: 1). Although suicide became a topic of philosophical debate in the sixteenth century, the condemnatory Catholic point of view remained largely unchanged.[10] Montaigne's essay on the topic, then, must be seen against such a background. Just as chiasmus can reverse the direction of an impotent man's thoughts, so here chiasmus can function to question societal beliefs. Patrick Henry has called this essay a 'rhetorical masterpiece' (Henry 1984: 278) and noted how it is 'dialogically woven together' by carefully demonstrating Montaigne's reliance on Seneca, Augustine, and numerous other sources, to form not merely an anthology, but a carefully balanced construction. Here, I should like to pursue Henry's reading by putting specific emphasis on how the essay's dialogic balancing relies heavily on chiasmus.

As Henry notes, the essay first offers eight arguments for suicide (largely drawn from Seneca's *Ad Lucilium Epistulae Morales*), then, following the announcement that 'Cecy ne s'en va pas sans contraste' (That does not go by without opposition) (Montaigne 1962: 332; 1991: 394) and drawing heavily (although not exclusively) on Augustine's *De Civitate Dei*, eight arguments against it, and finally a discussion of the cases when suicide might be justifiable. The pro and contra arguments in respect of suicide are not set out in direct opposition to each other, so the essay as a whole is, while chiasmus-like, not strictly so. For example, the first argument for suicide, drawn from Seneca – 'le sage vit tant qu'il doit, non pas tant qu'il peut' (a wise man lives not as long as he can but as long as he should) (Montaigne 1962: 331; 1991: 393)[11] – is only somewhat vaguely reversed by the final argument against suicide – 'La securité, l'indolence, l'impassibilité, la privation des maux de cette vie, que nous achetons au pris de la mort, ne nous apporte aucune commodité. Pour neant evite la guerre celuy qui ne peut jouyr de la paix; et pour neant fuit la peine, qui n'a dequoy savourer le repos' (Freedom from care, from pain and from emotion, together with freedom from the evils of this life, if purchased by our deaths can bring no advantage to us. Avoiding war means nothing if you cannot enjoy the peace: fleeing pain means nothing to a man who has no means of savouring the respite) (Montaigne 1962:

334; 1991: 397). On the other hand, another early pro argument – 'le present que nature nous ait fait le plus favorable, et qui nous oste tout moyen
de nous pleindre de nostre condition, c'est de nous avoir laissé la clef des
champs. Elle n'a ordonné qu'une entrée à la vie, et cent mille issues' (the
greatest favour that Nature has bestowed on us, and the one which removes
all ground for lamenting over our human condition, is the one which gives
us the key to the garden gate; Nature has ordained only one entrance to
life but a hundred thousand exits) (Montaigne 1962: 331; 1991: 393) – is
taken up somewhat more directly by later contra arguments (via Lucan and
Lucretius – 'c'est contre nature que nous nous mesprisons et mettons nous
mesmes à nonchaloir' (it is against nature that we should despise ourselves
or care little for ourselves) (Montaigne 1962: 334; 1991: 397). Still, the main
presence of chiasmus in this essay and its discussion of self-regulation by
means of suicide is in the texture of individual arguments, not in overall
structure.

The essay's opening pages are particularly rich in chiastic structures,
deployed in such a way – anything but ornamental – as to uproot a number of
hard-held beliefs about suicide. Having paraphrased Cicero (in the 1580 text)
regarding the fact that Nature offers the individual only one entrance into life
but many exits, Montaigne intercalates (in the 1588 reworking) a statement
made by Boiocalus to the Romans: 'Nous pouvons avoir faute de terre pour y
vivre, mais de terre pour y mourir, nous n'en pouvons avoir faute' (We may
lack land for living, but land for dying will never lack) (Montaigne 1962: 331;
1991: 393). The structure is grammatically chiastic – *faute de terre pour y vivre*
is traded for *de terre pour y mourir, nous n'en pouvons avoir faute* – but, in
addition, Montaigne also swaps *vivre* (to live) for *mourir* (to die). Similarly,
moving to the outer edges of the original sentence, Montaigne negates *nous
pouvons*, which becomes *nous n'en pouvons*. Montaigne's source is Tacitus'
Annals 13:56: 'deesse nobis terra in vitam, in qua moriamur, non potest' (We
may lack a land to live in; we cannot lack one to die in). (Tacitus, ed. Fisher,
1906, and ed. Church, 1942). The Latin, while chiastic in what it expresses, is
not so syntactically. Montaigne's rendering undoes surface dissymmetries by
essentially repeating the infinitive *deesse* (in *avoir faute de*) and by regulariz-
ing the noun (*vitam*) and verb (*moriamur*) into two infinitives (*vivre, mourir*).
Latin's economy in matters of what can be grammatically left out is swapped
for a fuller and more obviously chiastic structure in Montaigne's French. If
we accept the comparison with a source text as a means to judge the intention and impact of the final text, then Montaigne's text here clearly stages the
chiasmus in such a way that the reader cannot miss it.

Returning to the 1580 text after this reworking of Tacitus, Montaigne
quickly moves to his next quote, this time from Seneca's *Phoenissae*. This

time, however, Montaigne quotes the text in Latin, rather than paraphrasing:

Ubique mors est: optime hoc cavit Deus,
Eripere vitam nemo non homini potest;
At nemo mortem: mille ad hanc aditus patent.

(Death can be found everywhere. It is a great favour from God that no man can wrest death from you, though he can take your life; a thousand open roads lead to it.) (Montaigne 1962: 331; 1991: 393)

The pairing of *vitam nemo* ... and *nemo mortem*, positioned in a horizontal mirror that doubles the reversal of word order, makes the chiasmus perfectly clear and functions to bring home the same message as the chiasmus paraphrased from Tacitus. The following paragraphs are equally textured by chiasmus, even when word order is not reversed: 'La vie despend de la volonté d'autruy; la mort, de la nostre' (Our lives depend on the will of others; our death depends on our own) (Montaigne 1962: 331; 1991: 393); 'Le vivre, c'est servir, si la liberté de mourir en est à dire' (Living is slavery is freedom to die is wanting) (Montaigne 1962: 331–32; 1991: 393), etc. The reader, then, is invited to reconsider suicide from new perspectives by reorganizing the terms used by various authorities to state their opinion. Chiastic reversal allows Montaigne and his reader to break down received knowledge and evaluate other ways of interpreting situations.

CONCLUSIONS

Chiasmus – alongside, although distinguishable from, paradox,[12] oxymoron, contradiction, and irony – is an operative figure throughout the *Essais*, part of a '(dis)organizing principle' (see Regosin 1996: 176) that allows Ancient authorities and the drama of daily life to be put into dialogue. Although we have only seen several examples here, it is fair to say already that purposeful disorganization and contradiction are not, in the *Essais*, 'bluff' (Bowen 1972):[13] Montaigne's purpose is never to lie, never to merely tease or joke; his goal is rather to feel out truth on a philosophical level and in daily life, allowing him to shed light on such questions as how to cure male impotence or how a woman can enjoy sex. In her study about one of Montaigne's contemporaries, Giordano Bruno, Arielle Saiber has defined chiasmus as 'an invitation to assess new angles of meaning in a text' (Saiber 2005: 96) and it is precisely this searching out of new angles via reversals of terms suggestive of chiasmus that we find in Montaigne. Such structures do not always fit the strictest AB-BA or ABC-CBA definition; the reader is invited to explore not just bilateral symmetries, but to engage in a more vigorous and open movement. In this, Montaigne echoes earlier models of chiasmus, such as Plato in his *Timaeus* where chiasmus is set to reveal truths about cosmic structures, unlike the superficial use of chiasmus by sophists (Harvey 2001: 14–18). Chiasmus and chiasmus-like movements perform a mimetic function, revealing – or 'inventing', as a Renaissance writer might more likely have put it – the inherent multiplicities and uncertainties in the world around us, not only in matters of great historical or philosophical import, but in daily life. But Montaigne not only reveals or invents, he also seeks to situate himself and the reader at the point of chiastic reversal, an empowering gesture that sketches out a rhetorical taking control that refuses dogmatism or sophistry while also promoting certain cures.

Notes

1. As well as the scholarly writing that focuses on those of Montaigne's *Essais* that focus on daily life, it is worth noting that in a recent guide for students, Peter Král situated Montaigne at the origins of French literature's considerations of the 'routines and paraphernalia of everyday life' (Král 2009: 105). Montaigne, as an early point in French literature's emphasis on the drama of daily life, is also treated (in respect of Philippe Sollers and others) by Marchi 1994, esp. 278–320.
2. For a recent point of view on this New World diptych, see Conley 2005: 74–95.
3. The volume as a whole offers a useful overview of varied (sometimes opposing) views on Montaigne's scepticism.
4. On Montaigne's art of balancing and counter-balancing, see Gray 1982 and O'Brien 2001: 107–22.
5. A useful introduction to Bodin's treatise is provided by Pierre Mesnard (1965: 333–56).
6. Jean Bodin, *Le Fléau des démons et sorciers* (1579), quoted in Gelin (1910: 125–26).
7. As Thibaudet suggests in a footnote to his 1946 edition of the *Essais*, Montaigne is most likely referring to his own condition (Lee R. Entin-Bates, 'Montaigne's Remarks on Impotence', p. 642, n. 9). See also Strowski 1938, p. 42.
8. 'Que si j'eusse esté entre ces nations qu'on dict vivre encore sous la douce liberté des premieres loix de nature, je t'asseure que je m'y fusse très-volontiers peint tout entier, et tout nud.' (Had I found myself among those peoples who are said still to live under the sweet liberty of Nature's primal laws, I can assure you that I would most willingly have portrayed myself whole, and wholly naked) (Montaigne, *Essais*, 'Au lecteur' [To the Reader], 1962, p. 9 / lviv).
9. For further review of medieval attitudes to suicide, see Murray 2000.
10. For Renaissance views, see Georges Minois' (1995) useful *Histoire du suicide*.
11. Montaigne here translates (without acknowledging it) Seneca (1917): 'Itaque sapiens vivit, quantum debet, non quantum potest'.
12. On Montaigne's epistemological paradoxes, see Colie 1966, part III.
13. Montaigne is discussed in Ch. 3, 103–61. Bowen detects (and, in this author's opinion, overly conflates) 'deliberate untruth, ambiguity, irony, paradox, and contradiction' (103).

References

Bayet, Albert. 1922. *Le suicide et la morale*. Paris.

Boase, Alan Martin. 1970. *The Fortunes of Montaigne*. New York: Octagon Books.

Bodin, Jean. 1580. *La Démonomanie des sorciers*. Paris: Chez Iacques du Puys, preface.

Bowen, Barbara C. 1972. *The Age of Bluff: Paradox and Ambiguity in Rabelais and Montaigne*. Chicago: University of Illinois Press.

Colie, Rosalie L. 1966. *Paradoxia Epidemica: The Renaissance Tradition of Paradox*. Part III. Princeton: Princeton University Press.

Conley, Tom. 2005. 'The Essays and the New World', in Ullrich Langer, *The Cambridge Companion to Montaigne*. Cambridge: Cambridge University Press.

Cotgrave, Randle. 1611. *A Dictionarie of the French and English Tongues*. London: Adam Islip.

Cottrell, Robert D. 1982. 'Croisement chiasmique dans le premier *essai* de Montaigne', *Bulletin de la Société des Amis de Montaigne*, sixième série, n° 11-12, juillet-décembre 1982: 65–71.

Culianu, Ioan P. 1987. *Eros and Magic in the Renaissance*, trans. Margaret Cook. Chicago: University of Chicago Press.

Dante, *Inferno*, trans. Allen Mandelbaum 2004. New York: Bantam Classics.

Demonet, Marie-Luce and Alain Legros (eds). 2004. *L'Ecriture du scepticisme*. Geneva: Droz.

Duval, Edwin. 1983. 'Lessons of the New World: Design and Meaning in Montaigne's "Des cannibals" (I:31) and "Des coches" (III.6)', in *Yale French Studies* 64: 95–112.

Gelin, Henri. 1910. 'Les noueries d'aiguillette en Poitou', in *Revue des Etudes Rabelaisiennes* 8: 122–33.

Gray, Floyd. 1958. *Le Style de Montaigne*. Paris, Nizet.

———. 1982. *La Balance de Montaigne*. Paris: Nizet.

Harvey, Andrew James. 2001. 'Chiasmus in English Renaissance Literature'. Ph. D. Thesis, The University of North Carolina at Chapel Hill.

Henry, Patrick. 1984. 'The Dialectic of Suicide in Montaigne's "Coustume de l'Isle de Cea"', in *The Modern Language Review* 79(2).

Král, Peter. 2009. 'Comprehending the Quotidian', in John Taylor (ed.), *Paths to Contemporary French Literature*. New Brunswick: Transaction Publishers, p. 105.

Kritzman, Lawrence D. 1980. *Destruction/Découverte: Le fonctionnement de la rhétorique dans les Essais de Montaigne*. Lexington, KY: French Forum.

———. 1987. 'My Body, My Text: Montaigne and the Rhetoric of Sexuality', in Harold Bloom (ed.), *Michel de Montaigne's Essays*. New York: Chelsea House Publishers, pp. 81–95.

———. 1991. *The Rhetoric of Sexuality and the Literature of the French Renaissance*. Cambridge: Cambridge University Press.

Legros, Alain. 2000. *Essais sur poutres: peintures et inscriptions chez Montaigne*. Paris: Klincksieck.

Lindheim, Nancy. 1990. 'Body, Soul, and Immortality: Some Readings in Dante's *Commedia*', *MLN* 105: 1.

Marchi, M. 1994. *Montaigne among the Moderns: Receptions of the Essais*. New York: Berghahn Books.

Mesnard, Pierre. 1965. 'La Démonomanie de Jean Bodin', in *L'Opera et il pensiero di Giovanni Pico della Mirandola nella storia dell'umanesimo*. Florence, vol. 2, pp. 333–56.

Minois, Georges. 1995. *Histoire du suicide: la société occidentale face à la mort volontaire*. Paris: Fayard.

Montaigne. ed. Albert Thibaudet and Maurice Rat. 1962. *Œuvres Complètes*. Paris: Pléaide.

———. 1991. *The Complete Essays*, trans. M.A. Screech. London: Penguin.

Murray, Alexander. 2000. *Suicide in the Middle Ages: The Curse on Self-murder*. Oxford: Oxford University Press.

O'Brien, John. 2001. 'Question(s) d'équilibre', in J. Supple and N. Peacock (eds), *Lire les Essais de Montaigne*. Paris: Champion.

———. 2004. 'Si nous avons une très-douce médecine que la philosophie', in Marie-Luce Demonet and Alain Legros (eds), *L'Ecriture du scepticisme*. Geneva: Dros.

Regosin, Richard L. 1996. *Montaigne's Unruly Brood: Textual Engendering and the Challenge to Paternal Authority*. Berkeley: University of California Press.

Retterstøl, Nils. 1993. *Suicide*. Cambridge: Cambridge University Press.

Saiber, Arielle. 2005. *Giordano Bruno and the Geometry of Language*. Aldershot: Ashgate.

Seneca. 1917. *As Lucilium Epistulae Morales*. Cambridge: HUP (Loeb), II. LXX. 58.

Sextus Empiricus. 1992. *Outlines of Pyrrhonism*, trans. R.G. Bury. Cambridge, MA: Loeb Classical Library.

Siraisi, Nancy G. 1997. *The Clock and the Mirror: Girolamo Cardano and Renaissance Medicine*. Princeton, NJ: Princeton University Press.

Stephens, Walter. 1998. 'Witches Who Steal Penises: Impotence and Illusion in *Malleus Maleficarum*', in *Journal of Medieval and Early Modern Studies* 28: 495–529.

———. 2002. *Demon Lovers: Witchcraft, Sex, and the Crisis of Belief*. Chicago: University of Chicago Press.

Strowski, Fortunat. 1938. *Montaigne: sa vie publique et privée*. Paris: Éditions de la Nouvelle Revue Critique.

Struever, Nancy S. 1992. *Theory as Practice: Ethical Inquiry in the Renaissance*. Chicago: University of Chicago Press.

Tacitus, ed. Alfred John Church. 1942. *Complete Works of Tacitus*. New York: Random House, 1942.

Tacitus, ed. Charles Dennis Fisher. 1906. *Annales ab excessu divi Augusti*. Oxford: Clarendon Press.

Tetel, Marcel. 1990. *Montaigne*. Boston: Twayne Publishers.

Villey, Pierre. 1935. *Montaigne devant la postérité*. Paris: Boivin.

CHAPTER 9

TRAVESTIS, MICHÊS AND CHIASMUS

CROSSING AND CROSS-DRESSING IN THE WORK OF NÉSTOR PERLONGHER

Ben Bollig

■ ■ ■ ■ ■ ■ ■

Néstor Perlongher (1949–92) is best known in his native Argentina as a poet and as an anthropologist in Brazil, where he lived for much of the 1980s.[1] His border-crossing life is reflected by the importance of the chiasmus and crossing in his work. This piece aims to trace the development of the chiasmus and chiastic thought in Perlongher's poetry and related anthropological works, and to demonstrate through his works the great importance of chiasmus as a literary and cultural driving force in a number of contexts, in particular the lived experiences of sex and mysticism. His earliest poems, written in the 1970s, deal with border-crossing and the inter-penetrability of national frontiers, and a discussion of chiasmus is necessary in order to address Perlongher's perception of the nation and the border. In subsequent works, Perlongher uses chiastic aspects of the *travesti* or transvestite to put into question the stability of received perceptions of sex and gender. The aesthetic of chiasmus, for example, whereby accentuated physicality crosses between pre-established boundaries, and chiasmus as a poetic trope, are both key to his presentation of the *travesti*. The *travesti* dresses up, disguises him/herself, and then defies expectations through potential active-insertive sexual participation, thus committing a double crime of being excessively female for a male and excessively male for a female. Perlongher's early work uses the dressing up and sex-changing of the *travesti* and the *marica*, or effeminate male homosexual, to create a radical political position.

In his anthropological work from the 1980s, Perlongher conducted an extensive and detailed investigation of the circuits and practices of male prostitution in São Paulo. In his Masters thesis on the business of male prostitution (Perlongher 1987), he outlined the ways in which prostitutes and clients both accentuate racial, class, age and gender differences and simultaneously cross and contradict such distinctions. Here, chiastic movements destabilize the assumptions of structural anthropology. With the onset of AIDS and the increased penetration of transvestite figures into the public sphere and the mass media, Perlongher abandoned the theme, having presented in poems a new, fatal stability in relation to the *travesti*. Rather than questioning received gender structures and engaging in constant, unstable crossing between genders, In these poems Perlongher sees the transvestite as aiming at simply being a woman.

By the end of the 1980s, Perlongher's anthropological work had shifted in focus from sex and gender issues to mystical matters. While this would lead one to expect the abandonment of the chiastic *travesti* and the gender-crossing chiasmus, the aesthetic of crossing survives in his last, mystical poems from the early 1990s. Here chiasmus persists as a destabilizing tool; Perlongher crosses between traditional Spanish verse forms, such as the *silva* (a verse form of seven- and eleven-syllable lines popularized by Luis de Góngora in the 1600s) and the sonnet, between set line lengths, and between the physical and mystical world. Throughout his work, then, the chiasmus is an important rhetorical and political tool for destabilizing perceived molar identities and stable divisions.

Some explanation of terms is required at this juncture. I choose the term *travesti*, which appears frequently in Perlongher's poetry and essays, as an umbrella word to describe and connect a number of different but closely related themes and aesthetics: cross-dressing, or wearing the clothes socially appropriate for the opposite sex to one's own; drag, or the performance of dressing up as a member of the opposite sex, often as part of a theatrical show; and transvestism, the medical term for those who feel compelled to wear clothes more appropriate to the opposite sex. Ben. [*sic*] Sifuentes-Jáuregui states that 'transvestism is about the raw touching, gentle tampering, and, literally, fucking up of any fixed notion of genders', a 'performance of genders'. It is, he continues, 'an operating strategy that deconstructs a specific "normality" in a gender binary hierarchy'. The word has its origins not only in the Latin *trans-vestire*, to dress across, to cross a gender space but, also, via the French, *travesti*, to the English *travesty*, a lie. 'By representing the other's "realness", transvestism also reveals the "falseness" (that is, the construction) of the other' (Sifuentes-Jaúregui 2002: 2). The *travesti* in Perlongher's work, and more generally in Argentina, is a figure closely related not only to local sexual practices and identity politics, but also economic necessity and class issues. Thus I am not discussing here the transvestite as described by Lesley Gordon in his/her *Aspects of Gender*:[2] 'Homosexuals are rarely transvestites and only the rare transvestite is homosexual. Homosexuals, after all, are men looking for other men as love objects, not women, or ersatz women.' The difficulty of such an essentialist approach is apparent in Gordon's assertion that transvestites 'in general terms ... are genuine males who function as such, are generally heterosexual and do not necessarily or inevitably or are even likely to want to abandon their male lifestyle' (Gordon 1995: 4–7).

Another important term for this piece is *michê*, a Brazilian Portuguese word used to describe male prostitutes who accentuate their masculine attributes, frequently claim to be heterosexual, and offer overtly 'active' or 'insertive' sexual services to supposedly effeminate, 'passive' clients. In practice, the *michê* may also adopt the 'passive' or 'recipient' role, often for an increased fee. The American English 'hustler' or the Spanish 'taxiboy' might be considered rough equivalents. Both the *travesti* and the *michê* were key concepts in Perlongher's anthropological and poetic work.

Three further terms feature prominently in the analysis to follow: 'thematics', 'aesthetics' and 'poetics'. I use these in a way close to their Greek derivations. 'Thematic', from the Greek *tithenai*, to lay down, is my way of describing what is 'laid down' in Perlongher's poetry, in vulgar terms, what his poetry does or contains, or how the work connects with the world. This term does not deny the possibility that many of Perlongher's poems are frequently, and deliberately, 'about' nothing, and may even attack the notion of about-ness. However, it forces close attention to the words on the page, to what they might mean. This attention is vital in reading poetry that is as allusive and suggestive as Perlongher's. 'Aesthetic', from the Greek *aisthanesthai*, deals with feeling and perception, and therefore the shapes, movements and patterns in Perlongher's works. Finally, 'poetics', from the Greek *poiein*, to make, encompasses the techniques Perlongher uses in his poems, and deals with the small-scale, perhaps traditional, analysis of the poem. In addition, a working definition of chiasmus is important for my investigations. As Harald Horvei suggests, the meaning of chiasmus has changed considerably since the appearance of its Greek etymon: 'Chiasmus has changed between antiquity and the early Renaissance and today' (Horvei 1985: iv). Horvei states that the term has expanded 'to include a wide range of structural varieties, in which the basic idea is of a crosswise positioning of equivalent parts' (ibid.). The term now includes the inverted repetition of phonetic elements and an artistic principle of composition based on the inverted recurrence of corresponding 'leitmotifs', ideas and similar (ibid.). Horvei goes on to identify the 'chiasmus of identity' (x is y; y is x), as well as sound patterns and grammatical patterning as worthy of the name chiasmus (Horvei 1985: 4–5). While proposing that neither structural nor conceptual chiasmus is more deserving of the name than the other, Horvei does insist on the need for what he calls a 'proper reversal' (ibid.: 2). This distinction is useful, as we shall see, in assessing some of Perlongher's earlier works, in which crossing and parallelism occur, without what may be called a strict chiasmus. This follows debate in recent years over the specificity of the use of the term. Paul R. Olson, a rare Hispanist working on chiasmus, adopts the broad *OED* definition, itself close to the Greek origins of the word: 'a grammatical figure by which the order of works in one of two parallel clauses is inverted in the other' (Olson 2003). Its roots are of course found in the Greek letter chi, and thus the x shape of a cross. Similarly broad in his conception is John Welch, who states that 'the objective criteria alone do not tell the whole story. Evidence of chiasmus is not entirely objective and quantifiable' (Welch 1993: 13). Thus I feel compelled to oppose John Breck's rather rigid conception in his exposition of Biblical chiasmus, in which he insists that chiasmus requires a central point to its x shape, and that 'authentic chiasmus produces balanced statements, in direct, inverted or antithetical parallelism, constructed about a central idea' (Breck 1994: 18). While I understand chiasmus in the broad sense of a crossing of ideas or words with reversal, in contrast to simple parallelism, it is my aim in this piece to assess a number of examples of both simple crossing and more strict chiasmus in order to assess the development of Perlongher's poetics and aesthetics alongside the importance of this poetic and rhetorical trope as a driving force in his work, while demonstrating chiasmus's vital role as a destabilization agent against conservative stabilities.

Early Crossing

The opening poem of Perlongher's first collection, *Austria-Hungría* (Perlongher 1997a), details various movements in territory:

> Es una murga, marcha en la noche de Varsovia, hace milagros
> con las máscaras, confunde
> a un público polaco
> Los estudiantes de Cracovia miran desconcertados:
> nunca han visto
> nada igual en sus libros
> No es carnaval, no es sábado

no es una murga, no se marcha, nadie ve
no hay niebla, es una murga
no hay serpentinas, es papel picado, el éter frío
como la nieve de una calle de una ciudad de una Polonia
                                        que no es
                                        que no es
lo que no es decir que no haya sido, o aún
que ya no sea, o incluso no esté siendo en este instante
Varsovia con sus murgas, sus disfraces
sus arlequines y osos carolina
con su célebre paz – hablamos de la misma
la que reina
recostada en el Vístula
el proceloso río donde cae
la murga con sus pitos, sus colores, sus chachachás carnosos
produciendo en las aguas erizadas un ruido a salpicón
que nadie atiende
puesto que no hay tal murga, y aunque hubiérala
no estaría en Varsovia, y eso todos
los polacos lo saben
(Perlongher [1980] 1997a: 23)

[It's a murga, it marches in the Warsaw night, makes miracles
with masks, confounds
a Polish public
The Krakow students look on disconcerted:
they've never seen
anything like this in their books
It's not Carnival, it's not Saturday
it's not a murga, it doesn't march, no one sees
there's no fog, it's a murga
they're not streamers, it's tickertape, the cold ether
like the snow on a street in a city in a Poland
                                        that isn't
                                        that isn't
which is not to say it may not have been, or still
may not be, or even it may not be being right now
Warsaw with its murgas, its disguises
its harlequins and Carolina bears[3]
with its famous peace – we're talking of the very same
the Queen[4]

lying on the Vistula
the torturous[5] river where the murga
falls with its whistles,[6] its colours, its carnal cha-cha-chas
producing in the bristling waters a splashing noise
that no one notices
given that there's no such murga and even if there were
it wouldn't be in Warsaw and that's something all
the Poles know][7]

Visually, the poem offers a number of chiastic characteristics: the short lines 5 and 19 separate two sections which then reverse around the central axis of lines 12 and 13, 'que no es | que no es'. This highlights the central, paradoxical negation of the poem: the *murga*, in Argentina a rowdy musical procession and the style of singing and chanting that accompany it, that at once *is* and *is not*. However, on closer inspection, both this and other smaller textual elements are examples of parallel negation rather than chiasmus: 'es una murga'; 'no es una murga', echoed on the macro-scale by the transition from the opening positive proposition of the *murga's* existence and the final denial, 'no estaría en Varsovia, y eso todos | los polacos lo saben'.

While chiasmus is not directly present here, crossing takes place at the thematic and poetic level. Perlongher creates two horizons: Warsaw, and Buenos Aires, the home of the *murga*, and then throws the reader between the two, talking of one as the other, distracting the reader's attention with one while talking about the other, and thus creating two spaces and crossing between them. This effect of shuttle, where the reader is thrown forwards and backwards in the text, is achieved particularly through the use of proparoxytone words ('hubiérala', 'máscaras', 'Vístula') and alliteration ('murga ... marcha ... papel picado'), or by the juxtaposition of two disparate elements ('murga', 'Varsovia'). Other techniques that create this effect of shuttle are phonic and visual, for example the repetition of the 'es' / 'no es' formula, as in lines 1 and 7 ('Es una murga ... / ... No es carnaval'). This is aided by the form and rhythm, for example the absence of full stops and the use of capital letters without any accompanying punctuation.

Perlongher's poem immediately demands unconventional logical agility from its reader. Logical contradictions placed closely together ('no es una murga ... / ... es una murga') deny conventional logic in favour of connections and contradiction, as in statements such as 'en la noche de Varsovia / ... no esté siendo en este instante ... / ... Varsovia'. Once either Poland or Buenos Aires is established as a coordinate, the negation takes us to another space, the other space being by a process of elimination Buenos Aires or Poland. These logic-defying negations and the complex web of connections allow two different discourses and spaces to overlap. Although a number of logical propositions and rhetorical formulas are used, for example 'no es', 'hablamos', 'puesto que' or 'aunque', the prevalence given to enumerative descriptions such as 'con sus' with four nouns ('murgas', 'disfraces', 'arlequines', 'osos carolina') and then again with three ('pitos', 'colores', 'chachachás') suggests a poem that is sensuous rather than rational. This is further emphasized by the self-contradictory grammar and syntax of the poem. The repetition of 'que no es' in lines twelve and thirteen could be a double negative or a refrain. The reader is again left in an undecided shuttle. Buenos Aires and Warsaw are separated in space; Perlongher's poem, however, leaves the reader in a position of not being able to distinguish between the two owing to the rapid movement traced in the poem. Thus in answer to the question, 'are we in Buenos Aires or Warsaw?', a question that demands the limitation of two exclusive spaces, Perlongher's reader must affirm that he or she is in a space that is at the same time either Buenos Aires or Warsaw. Perlongher's poem thus reveals the difficulties masked by attempts to fix the nation to a given space, and attempts to create an alternative form of nation, where national borders do not disguise their penetrability, and seems to propose an Argentina more open to Latin America, at odds with stable identities, called into question by his crossing movements. Furthermore, he does this through a call to Carnival, a sociocultural phenomenon based on chiasmus, whereby the master becomes the slave and the slave the master in an archetypal chiastic reversal. At the same time, the instability present responds to a characteristic of chiasmus identified by Ralf Norrman in his work on Samuel Butler, specifically the importance of inconsistency in chiasticism: 'the opposite is always true', thesis and antithesis but never synthesis (Norrman 1986: 18); in Perlongher's case, if we are in Buenos Aires, and not Warsaw, we are also in Warsaw and not in Buenos Aires. Thus while chiasmus is not present in this early work, chiastic thought is clearly an important part of his attempts to destabilize the nation.

THE *TRAVESTI* AND CHIASMUS

One can find in Perlongher's first collection, *Austria-Hungría*, a poem that combines *travesti* aesthetics and chiastic elements to deconstruct binary gender divisions in language, 'El polvo'.

> En esta encantadora soledad
> – oh claro, estabas sola! –
> en este enhiesta, insoportable inercia
> es ella, es él, siempre de a uno, lo que esplende

[...]
esos destrozos recurrentes de un espejo en la cabeza de otro
   espejo
o esos diálogos:
'Ya no seré la última marica de tu vida', dice él
que dice ella, o dice ella, o él
que hubiera dicho ella, o si él le hubiera dicho:
'Seré tu último chongo
[...]' (Perlongher 1997a: 31)

[In this enchanting solitude
– oh sure, you were alone! –
in this erect, unbearable inertia
is she, is he, always one at a time, that which splendours
[...]
those recurrent ruins of a mirror in the head of another
   mirror
or those dialogues:
'I won't be the last pansy in your life', says he
that she says, or she says, or he
that she would have said, or if he had said it:
'I'll be your last stud
[...]'

The chiasmus is clearly identifiable: 'dice él | que dice ella, o dice ella, o él'
(AB: B'A'); the effect is to cross between male and female personal pronouns
and thus throw into doubt the gendered identity of the implied speaker. Just
as earlier crossings had destabilized the nation, here chiasmus throws divisions between genders into doubt. This chiasmus is accompanied by two other
important, related elements: firstly, the parallelisms that we discussed above,
for example the repeated and often uncertain 'ella – él' dyad; and secondly,
the thematic suggestion of chiasmus in the image of the double mirror: 'un
espejo en la cabeza de otro | espejo'. The double or recessed mirror suggests a
permanent and unstable movement of crossing.

The poem challenges the normalization of gender through grammar,
what the theorist Brian Massumi calls 'standardized contexts within which
every word spoken echoes those spoken in all others' (Massumi 1999: 33),
with the chiasmus being one of a number of poetic techniques. Perlongher
adopts ambiguous vocabulary, for example, the title 'El Polvo' – *polvo*: dust,
powder, sexual intercourse, ejaculation, cocaine and makeup, or *marica*: a
male homosexual and a type of magpie. Perlongher also uses ambiguous

pronouns. 'Él' and 'ella', taken simply, are the binary opposites on which gender is stratified and functions in language. However, through chiasmus, juxtapositions and undecided alternatives ('ella, o dice ella, o él / que hubiera dicho ella, o si él le hubiera dicho') this binary is stretched into movements and tensions between genders. Furthermore, Perlongher uses dialogue to problematize stable gender; in the 'diálogos' section, the 'él' voice is at times a 'marica' and at others a 'chongo', at once a homosexual man and a stud in the circuits of cruising and prostitution. Similarly, subjunctive verbs amongst the masculine and feminine pronouns ('hubiera dicho') suggest degrees of possibility rather than stable being, movement rather than fixed positions. These techniques unite to create the effect of messing up grammatically stable gender, one of the tenets of correctly written Spanish, as well the basis for many legal aspects of identity, for example the use of identity cards specifying sex. As the theorist Judith Butler suggests in her book *Gender Trouble*, '[i]f gender itself is naturalised through grammatical norms ... then the alteration of gender at the most fundamental epistemic level will be conducted, in part, through contesting the grammar in which gender is given' (Butler 1999: xix). Thus we can detect in Perlongher's poem an attack on the type of divide detected by Hélène Cixous and Catherine Clément: 'activity/passivity, sun/ moon, culture/nature, day/night, father/mother, mind/heart, intelligible/palpable, logos/pathos, man/woman' (Cixous and Clément 1993: 43). This early poem then continues the use of a *travesti* aesthetic alongside the chiasmus as a grammatical attack on gender divisions, and links chiasmus to the lived experience of gender.

In the collection *Alambres*, published in 1987 but containing poems that were published elsewhere as early as 1981, Perlongher does not use the chiasmus at a textual level but, rather, adopts three *travesti* techniques to question received gender structures which in turn lead to chiastic effects: naming, a 'boudoir' effect, and cutting. The first technique is exemplified in the titles of some of his poems, such as 'Ethel' or 'Daisy'. Both are feminine names. However, not only do the poems clearly describe *travesti* characters, but their titles are neutral in grammatical gender and are the types of name used by *travestis*, being imported, exotic, and not Spanish. The names and titles of Perlongher's poems thus cross geographical borders, and also cross the boundary between the sexes on two counts.

The boudoir effect is traced in *Alambres* in *details*, the paraphernalia of feminine adornment on the body:

Como en ese zaguán de azulejos leonados
donde ella se ata el pelo con un paño a lunares – y sobresale un pinche
como un punto: en el bretel donde el mendigo gira

las huellas de los hombros embarrados en la gasa desnuda
('Ethel', Perlongher [1981] 1997a: 84)

[As in that hallway of tawny tiles
where she ties up her hair with a polka-dot cloth – and a hairpin sticks out
like a point: in the strap where the beggar tramps
the marks of muddy shoulders on the naked gauze]

si al follaje ebrio lames, no es ese rouge que dejas pringar
en el pescuezo, como una boa nacarada?
('Daisy', Perlongher [1983] 1997a: 85)

[if the inebriated foliage you lick, is it not that rouge you let smear
on the neckscruff, like a nacred boa?]

Three processes contribute to the poem's boudoir effect: firstly, the juxtaposition of items, such as fabrics ('paño'), hairpieces ('pelo'), straps ('bretel') and make-up ('rouge'), that, in almost cubist fashion, unites the elements required for the *travesti* performance, and places us in an environment of adornment and disguise. Secondly, the poems stress performance and dressing up through the many body parts, poses and positions that occur, at the expense of individual characters. The person is not stable but instead is dependant on context, specifically what he or she is doing and how he or she is dressed. Finally, 'Daisy' and 'Ethel' make unexpected physical and vocal demands of the reader. The use of half-sets of question marks (as opposed to the correct practice in Spanish of preceding and following a question, thus: ¿...?) questions the way we read: the reader can either skim ahead, realize there is a question mark and then alter tone accordingly, see the question mark and then turn back, suddenly raise pitch, or ignore it altogether. Either way, the poem insists on shuttle movements backwards and forwards not in keeping with the normal direction in which one reads, and directly affects the reader's body. The rich sound of the poem, full of /s/, /r/ and /l/ phonemes, creates a text that is almost sticky to read, particularly with the Buenos Aires accent demanding many /zh/ or /sh/ sounds. These two effects demand a parsimonious, luxuriant reading that moves in directions not expected in poetry. The ensuing luxuriant slowness is similar in its non-productive pleasure to the dressing-up aesthetic of the *travestis* present in the poems. Perlongher's poem thus utilizes *travesti* performance in order to call into question received gender structures.

The third element of Perlongher's early *travesti* poetics is found in the notion of the cut. In 'Daisy' we read of 'tajos del corte', 'el tajo', 'un corte' (all terms for cuts), 'navaja' (a clasp/pen knife), 'la "heridilla"', 'llagas', and 'heridillas' (types of wound). This density of cutting has two effects: firstly, it calls to mind the very real process of cutting involved in what Deleuze and Guattari call 'the prodigious attempts at a real transformation on the part of certain transvestites' (Deleuze and Guattari 1999: 275). As a subset to this form of cutting, we must also remember the sartorial efforts above, whereby cutting fabric, particularly in the alteration of clothes, forms a central part of the *travesti* performance. Both surgical operations, such as breast implants or gender reassignment (extremely rare in Argentina in the late 1970s and early 80s), and the use of clothes and adornment, show how the link between the body, the individual, sex and identity is socially constituted, and also how it can be questioned by the *travesti*. Secondly, the poem displays the cut as an attack on the individual and the limits of the body; Judith Butler talks of 'the boundary and surface of the body as politically constructed' (Butler 1999: xxxi). That is to say that what constitutes the limits of one's body, where the individual starts and ends, is a political matter. Butler goes on to suggest, in keeping with what we read in Perlongher's poem, that the questioning of such natural limits can have radical potential for questioning the political status quo: 'just as bodily surfaces are enacted as the natural,' she states, 'so these surfaces can become the site of a dissonant and denaturalised performance that reveals the status of the natural itself' (ibid.: 186). *Travesti* techniques form a radical attack on received gender and identity structures.

Furthermore, whilst the chiasmus does not appear directly in these poems, the *travesti* aesthetic is one closely related to chiastic forms; as Butler suggests, the outside says female – women's clothes and make-up – with the body inside being male; conversely, this outside also proclaims its masculinity – broad shoulders, large hands – with a feminine inside, a 'woman trapped in a man's body' in vulgar terms (Butler 1999: 174). The *travesti* dresses up, disguises him/herself, and then, as Perlongher states, defies expectations through potential active-insertive sexual participation, thus committing a double crime (Perlongher 1993: 49). The *travesti* thus reveals the instability of binary divides between both sex and gender, and that performance is a key element not only of the *travesti* but also of the construction of gender within society. As Butler would have it, '"the normal", the "original", is revealed to be a copy, and an inevitably failed one, an ideal that no one can embody' (Butler 1999: 175). Horvei (1985: 43), meanwhile, underlines 'an almost osmotic function [which] seems visualized through chiasmus', similar one might suggest to the osmotic penetration and dissolution of gender divides. Ralf Norrman stresses the importance of a lack of fixed or fixable limits in chiasmus. In the case Norrman examines, that of Samuel Butler, he suggests that chiasmus proposes that even perceived opposites must possess something of each other, rather like the alternate coloured spots in the yin-yang symbol (Norrman 1986: 16). Hence chiastic thinking in relation to the *travesti* forms an important part of Perlongher's assault on fixed or binary perceptions of sex and gender, and their effects on the everyday lives of people, and, as we shall see, develops in his anthropological work.

ANTHROPOLOGICAL CHIASMUS

In addition to the polar reversals of pairs of terms we have examined so far, Ian Thomson suggests another type of chiasmus, closer perhaps to the palindrome, which he calls the 'chiasmus of intermediate length' (Thomson 1995: 23). Although Thomson suggests that such a chiasmus may contain between ten and twenty elements stretched over seven to fifteen verses, his term is useful to refer to chiastic patterns that run beyond the common four element AB: B'A' pattern. In Perlongher's anthropological work on male prostitution in São Paulo, such chiastic patterns appear.

Much of his study (Perlongher 1999) consists of analyses of interviews with clients, prostitutes and other figures in the circuits of male prostitution, which often highlight the instability of identity classifications and taxonomies:

> Llegué a una fiesta con un cliente con el que yo transaba, ahí había *boys* (chongos, *michês*) y maricones. Pero bebí demasiado y comencé a soltarme, a tener gestos femeninos, y me volví marica. Entonces la marica que estaba conmigo se volvió macho y comenzó a disputarme con otros michês que me querían coger. (Perlongher 1999: 22)

> [I got to a party with a client who I was going with, there were *boys* (studs, *michês*) and queers. But I drank too much and started to let go, to have feminine gestures, and I turned into a pansy. Then the pansy who was with me turned all macho and started arguing over me with the other prostitutes who wanted to fuck me.]

Here the micro chiasmus is evident in the second and third sentences: 'michê – marica: marica – michê' (masculine – feminine: feminine – masculine). With the Dionysian effects of alcohol, in the charged and desiring atmosphere of the *fiesta*, the macho becomes effeminate and the effeminate gay man becomes macho. Such crossings are typical of the subjects of Perlongher's anthropology, where *travestis*, *maricas* and *michês* often alternate and switch roles, before, during and after sexual commerce.

The intermediate chiasmus becomes important as we assess Perlongher's attempts to identify the broader generic structures of male prostitution. As he states in a companion article:

Las relaciones de la prostitución viril están marcadas por una exacerbación de la diferencias. Diferencia de edad, ... de clase, ... Las grandes oposiciones binarias que codifican el *socius* aparecen siendo ellas mismas deseadas; revelan así su reverso intensivo. (Perlongher 1997b: 52)

[The relationships in virile prostitution are marked by an exacerbation of differences. Difference in age, ... in class, ... The great binary oppositions that encode the *socius* appear themselves as objects of desire; thus they reveal that intensive reverse.]

Perlongher goes on to list further differences which may be classified thus:

| **Client:** | More Effeminate | Older | Richer | Higher class | Whiter | Suburban-dwelling |
| **Michê:** | More *Macho* | Younger | Poorer | Lower class | Darker | Working in Centre |

Thus the process of prostitution unchains a number of complex movements: client and *michê* both accentuate their attributes, as in the above list (a client has to appear rich to be valued; a *michê* has to look as macho as possible to achieve selection). This accentuation would appeal to structural anthropological readings of *O negócio do michê*, yet at the same time, Perlongher is at pains to stress the instability of these distinctions, with, as in the example above, identities alternating and changing. Another chiastic process is at work: the macho prostitute becomes effeminate; the effeminate client becomes macho, for example, or the suburban dweller comes to the centre and takes the urban worker to the suburbs. In each case the chiastic crossing between previously opposed elements underlines the instability of such social-identitarian labels. Thus Perlongher's work exhibits a shift from the structural anthropology of Lévi-Strauss to the post-structural readings of Félix Guattari, in which instability is the norm, as well as identifying a chiastic aspect in the everyday practice of prostitution.

Curiously, Perlongher's poetry from the same period, as collected in *Parque Lezama*, seems to underline the predominance of certain stereotypes within the *michê* community – a form of reterritorialization of identity at odds with much of his anthropological work. The poem 'Al deshollinador' deals with some of these stereotypes:

el suplente es un moreno aceitunado
que tiene tiznados los resortes
por la bruma de un madero que se reaviva
y clava sus estocadas gelatinosas
en la brillantina de las sombras.
(Perlongher 1997a: 196 [1990, Buenos Aires])

[the replacement is an olive-skinned dark guy
whose springs are smeared with soot
from the mist of a timber that's revived
and nails its gelatinous thrusts
in the brilliantine of the shade]

The poem creates a relationship between a client and a chimney sweep. The relationship is couched in terms from his anthropological work: class (higher to lower), skin colour (lighter to darker), wealth (richer to poorer) and gender (feminine to masculine). This is reinforced by the repeated references to 'hollín' (soot), a word used throughout *Parque Lezama*, for example in 'Pavón' (Perlongher 1997a: 229), associated with excrement and thus the anus. The sweep, a replacement, is just another of the dark, lower-class masses, capable of adopting the required pose and hardness. Practically then, the *michê* is both labelled and carries out a process of self-labelling. Such a set of clichés, or stereotypes, applies to the sexual partners observed in almost all the poems in *Parque Lezama*. Dirtiness, hardness, strength, erectility, and violent energy are all constants in these poems. This would suggest that reterritorialization dominates in the circuits of male prostitution, not just in the adoption of certain territories, but also in settling down to certain roles, at least in terms of the technique for picking up work. Perlongher insisted that the *michês* offered the possibility of a break with the social order through beginning a process of becoming-woman (Perlongher 1997b: 50). However, the space of the *boca* (a term Perlongher preferred to *gueto* or ghetto) is also one of reterritorialization and striation, with its own codes and regulations. Thus an important and revealing contrast can be identified between Perlongher's chiastic anthropology and his stable poetry from the same period which suggests a greater stability present in his work.

AN END TO CROSSINGS? AIDS IN PERLONGHER'S WORK

In Perlongher's later work, the role of the *travesti* and the other sexual marginals of his earlier poetry changes. The poem 'Devenir Marta', for example, from the collection *Hule*, is much less optimistic than earlier poems about the *travesti* as a politically and sexually provocative figure:

A lacios oropeles enyedrada
la toga que flaneando las ligas, las ampula
para que flote en el deambuleo la ceniza, impregnando
de lanas la atmósfera cerrada y fría del boudoir.

A través de los años, esa lívida
mujereidad enroscándose, bizca,
en laberintos de maquillaje, el velador de los aduares
incendiaba al volcarse la arena, vacilar

en un trazo que sutil cubriese
las hendiduras del revoque
y, más abajo, ligas, lilas, revuelo
de la mampostería por la presión ceñida y fina que al ajustar

los valles microscópicos del tul
sofocase las riendas del calambre, irguiendo
levemente el pezcuello que tornando
mujer se echa al diván
(Perlongher 1997a: 139 [1989, Buenos Aires])

[To the wither'd tinsels ivy'd
the toga that flaneuring the straps, ampulates them
so the ash may float in the wandering, impregnating
with wool the closed and cold atmosphere of the boudoir.

In the course of the years, that livid
womanliness encoiling itself, squinting,
in labyrinths of make-up, the nightlight in the encampment[8]
caught light as the sand spills, to hesitate

in a trace that subtly would cover
the cracks in the plaster
and, further down, straps, stalks, fluttering
of masonry by the snug and fine pressure that on tightening

the microscopic valleys of tulle
would suffocate the reins of cramp, raising
lightly the fishneck that turned
woman lays on the divan.]

While the great amount of detail – for example the fabrics, make-up, cutting and stitching that we also saw in 'Dolly' and 'Ethel' above, the focus on the body and its adornment, the clothes, the fabrics and interiors – are all characteristic of Perlongher's earlier *travesti* poems, and while the title itself ('Devenir Marta') describes that process as 'becoming-woman', there are a number of discordant elements. Whereas the earlier *travesti* poems showed the body connecting and defying limits, here the body is stuck in the 'atmósfera cerrada y fría'; age is signalled 'a través de los años' as the aged *travesti* becomes less provocative and dynamic than the youthful counterpart of the earlier poems; and the 'maquillaje' is also a potentially fatal 'laberinto': rather than dynamic crossing, instead the possible dead end of the maze. While the final verse traces a proud movement up, 'irguiendo / levemente el pezcuello', and the becoming-woman reaches a form of completion in the past participle, 'tornado / mujer', the movement down, onto the 'diván', further closed off by the oxytone stress, suggests another dead end. Rather than crossing or chiasmus, here Perlongher sees a straight change from male to female; thus the poem suggests misgivings about a possibly identitarian *travesti* model by which, rather than provocative movements and changes, the *travesti* offers the possibility of a stable female identity.

Alongside this pessimistic view of identitarian transvestism, 'Dolly', also from *Hule*, offers a clear portrayal of the eruption of AIDS amongst River Plate homosexuals, and demonstrates how AIDS violently shut off the possibility of sex as an attack on patriarchal stratification:

> La telaraña de jeringas
> diestros cintazos pernoctaba
> el *pernod* junto al jarabe .
> que en el vaho de alcohol
> cierne la pierna,
> [...]
> La cantarera, a pedacitos.
> Desabrochada en la camilla,
> atada a la máquina de ojear
> que regula las disfunciones
> de los órganos, en el
> dolor arqueante de ese vieja
> [...]
> Pues desplegando el nervio herido, hendido
> aullaba el cocoliche los fastos de una regia
> victoria en el canal, cisco tortuoso
> reducido al vidráceo por la faca
> de dos filos, legumbre
> sanguinolenta lentejuela tuesta
> a su rispidez el estertor de un chancro religioso [...]
> (Perlongher 1997a: 146–47 [1989, Buenos Aires])

> [The spiderweb of syringes
> dexterous sashcracks spend the night
> the pernod next to the syrup

that in the vapour of alcohol
covers a leg
[...]
The potter-lady, in shards.
Undone in the little bed
tied to the watching machine
that regulates the malfunctions
of the organs, in the
arching pain of that old lady
[...]
For unfurling the wracked, cracked nerve,
howled the *cocoliche* the annals of a regal
victory on the canal, tortuous dross
reduced to glassiness by the double-edged
knife, vegetable
bloodied toasted sequin
in its roughness the death rattle of a religious chancre [...]

The body, apparently that of a *travesti*, given the use of the name 'Dolly', is still shown defying the binary divisions of gender, as in the confusingly gendered phrase 'ese vieja' ('ese' is a masculine pronoun; 'vieja' is a feminine noun). Rather than crossing or moving, though, Dolly is trapped and still. The new element in the poem is the medicalization of the body, which is shown full of syringes and tied to machines. These are not positive connections when compared to the physical connections between people and organs presented in earlier poems; the poem mentions 'opilaciones', an illness whereby menstrual fluid does not flow. This has a double significance; firstly it identifies Dolly by analogy as a *travesti*; secondly it shows the ways out of the individual body being shut off, as AIDS blocks these flows and connections. The reference to River Plate slang ('cocoliche', a theatrical Italianate style of Spanish from Buenos Aires) sets this within an Argentine context. Thus the poem shows the chiastic sexual attacks on patriarchal stratification of Perlongher's earlier poems being violently shut off as the body is tied to machines and enclosed in the clinic. This reflects the new aesthetics of gay rights politics in response to AIDS: as many older homosexual men very visibly died of AIDS, an occurrence portrayed in the mass media as evidence of the dangers of promiscuity and lack of self-control, the 'gay-gay' couple became a symbol of sexual responsibility and individual self-control in Brazil (and, to a lesser extent Argentina) while the *michês, chongos, maricas escandalosas* and *travestis* continued to be harassed not only by the forces of law and order but also by fashion and the mass media in both countries. As Perlongher stated elsewhere, 'a partir de la irrupción del SIDA, un dispositivo mucho más potente

está montándose en el creciene medicalización higienista de la existencia'
(Perlongher 1997b: 56) [With the emergence of AIDS, a more powerful model
is being created with the increasing hygienist medicalization of existence].
Perlongher reacted against the new climate of fear and repression found in
popular opinion, politics and medicine, brought about by AIDS, by rejecting
the new stable model of the (respectable, monogamous) 'gay-gay' couple and
by appearing to turn away from the *travesti* as a theme in his writing.

MYSTICISM: A RETURN OF CHIASMUS?

Perlongher's response to the emergence of AIDS, safe sex and the ensuing
end of widespread orgiastic sexual practices, worked out with reference to
the French philosopher Georges Bataille's work, *Eroticism*, is another line of
flight: the mystical. The first poem from the collection *Aguas aéreas* illustrates
the poetics of this new line of flight:

> [...]
> Recio el cantor, bruñidas las guedejas,
> dejo de mambo inflige al modular
> intensidades en el cieno,
> > plástica
> porosidad de la materia espesa.
> En el dejo de un espasmo
> contorsionaba los ligámenes
> y transmitía a los encajes
> la untuosidad del nylon
> rayándolos
> en una delicada precipitación.
> (Perlongher 1997a: 247–48 [1991, Buenos Aires])

> [Strong the singer, burnished the locks,
> aftertaste of mambo inflects as it modulates
> intensities in the mire,
> > plastic
> porosity of the thick matter.
> In the aftertaste a spasm
> contorting the ligaments
> and transmitting to the lace
> the unctuousness of nylon
> striping it
> in a delicate precipitation.]

The poem was 'inspired' by the Santo Daime church in São Paulo (Perlongher 1997a: 293), a religion that believes that a vision of the divine can be achieved through ritually imbibing the hallucinogen *ayahuasca* or *yagé*, and accompanying the ensuing visions and physical purging of the body with ceremonies, songs, prayers and dances. In Perlongher's poetry, the *ayahuasca* ceremony seems to offer a way out of individuation. In the first poem of Aguas aéreas, Perlongher describes the ceremony through the depiction of four areas. Firstly, he describes a quasi-spastic Dionysian dance ('el dejo de un espasmo'); secondly, he describes the song that accompanies the ceremony and its singer ('el cantor'); thirdly, Perlongher details the sickness induced by the drug, the 'purge' that *ayahuasca* users experience, closely related to the dance ('contorsionaba los ligámenes'); and, finally, the mystical experience itself, the visions of lights and flashes that precede the appearance of the divine, are described ('una delicada precipitación'). Thus Perlongher details an experience that appears to offer a way out of individuation and the division between persons, instead creating a communal intensity within the religious framework of the ceremony that allows the subject to stretch beyond itself and join with others and the divinity. This is in keeping with Perlongher's writings on the subject of São Daime: 'la experiencia dionisíaco ... asegura, en lugar de la individualización, justamente una ruptura con el *principium individuationis*' (Perlongher 1997b: 153) [The Dionysian experience ... assures, in place of individualization, precisely a rupture with the *principium individuationis*].

However, even as Perlongher attempts to write poetry that captures the *ayahuasca* ceremony, a spiritual experience, he seems drawn to the physical side of the ceremony. This is manifested in two areas. Firstly, Perlongher focuses formally on the corporeal, for example the rhyme that moves down from 'nylon' to 'precipitación', or the line-end focus on 'encajes' and 'ligámenes', both drawing attention to the body and its adornment, or 'precipitación', which could be a dive into the unknown, a stream of lights, a gush of vomit, or simply a ladder in one's nylons. Secondly, and vitally, we have elements drawn from the portrayal of the *travesti* of earlier poems: 'encajes' and 'nylon', both part of the *travesti* aesthetic of dressing-up we saw above. What this reveals is that Perlongher's mystical line of flight is still very much linked to the vocabulary and aesthetics of his earlier *devenir mujer* or becoming-woman poems, and that to deal with the force of the spiritual – exemplified by the bodily contortions and hallucinogenic lights above – without falling into the abyss of madness or death, Perlongher is reliant on forms from these earlier poems. The intensity of the *travesti's* becoming-woman is both a starting point and a source of vocabulary for his mystical writings. Thus the spiritual is physical and the physical is spiritual: a perfect ontological chiasmus.

The importance of physical elements drawn from his earlier *travesti* poems is further drawn out in Perlongher's other attempts to present the *aya-huasca* experience. In an essay published posthumously but similar in theme and content to a number of essays written around 1990, Perlongher draws on the ideas of Deleuze and Guattari in his attempt to theorize *ayahuasca* usage, describing the ceremony as exhibiting a 'plano de los cuerpos' and a 'plano de expresión' (Perlongher 1997b: 163) [plane of bodies; place of expression]. The former consists of the lights, visions, and physical experiences of the ceremony, as described in the poem (the contortions or lights, for example); the latter contains the songs and dances of the ceremony, echoed in the poem through formal tropes and repetitions. What is interesting is the curious oversimplification that Perlongher commits, whereby he replaces Deleuze and Guattari's terms in *A Thousand Plateaus*, drawn from the linguist Louis Hjelmslev, 'plane of content' and 'plane of expression' (Deleuze and Guattari 1999: 43, 88), with 'cuerpos' and 'expresión'. While Deleuze and Guattari's plane of content does include the body, it is not just that, but also actions and passions. So it would seem that even as Perlongher attempts to theorize intellectually a spiritual experience, he is drawn again to the very physicality of the ceremony.

The fifth poem in the series is thus formally intriguing, as it clearly adopts an aesthetic of crossing thematically linked to Perlongher's chiastic *travestis*:

SI LA DIVINIDAD LIQUIDA AHÓGASE
o bulla, en el calor carnal,
su playa látex – antes
que promontorios, grutas –

gránulos de negrura
oh noctiluca enardecida yergue
en la onda de conchas y cangrejos
el anillo de espuma

en la piel tensa y tenue
muelle el despeñadero en remolinos
el simulacro de su frenesí

huecos estampa en el alud coral
para que halague su volcán el ala
de un camoatí libélulas libando.
(Perlongher 1997a: 255 [1991, Buenos Aires])

[If the liquid divinity drowns
or din in the carnal warmth,

its latex beach – rather
than promontories, grottos –

grains of blackness
oh enflamed firefly erects
in the wave of shells and crabs
the ring of spume

in the tense and tenuous skin
soft the clifftop in swirls
the simulacrum of its frenzy

holes stamps in the coral slide
so that its volcano finds the wing
of a camoati supping dragonflies.]

The poem is obviously a sonnet (fourteen lines). Traditionally sonnets have uniform line lengths. However a syllable count here reveals another important verse form: the seven and eleven syllable lines of the *silva*, the form used by the Golden Age poet Luis de Góngora in his *Soledades*. There are other clear Góngoran elements: the 'si' opening, the comparison form 'antes que x, y', and its vocabulary ('promontorios', 'grutas') in lines three and four.

Before we can classify this poem as an attempt to marry two of the most important verse forms for innovation in Hispanic poetry, the sonnet and the *silva*, there is an element that does not fit. The oxytone ending of line two, 'carnal', leaves us with a line length of nine syllables rather than seven or eleven. Thus Perlongher performs an attempt to be both *silva* and sonnet at the same time, the becoming-sonnet of the *silva* and the becoming-*silva* of the sonnet, but with the awareness of corporality and physicality, embodied in the two syllable oxytone of 'carnal', that does not fit received forms such as the sonnet or the *silva*. Thus on the macro-scale the whole poem is between a *silva* and a sonnet, whilst on the micro-scale, line two is between a heptasyllable and a hendecasyllable. This contradictory aesthetic of chiasmus, whereby accentuated physicality ('carnal') crosses between pre-established boundaries, is the same as that demonstrated above by the *travesti*. The sonnet is becoming *silva* and the *silva* is becoming sonnet, while the physical becomes spiritual and the spiritual becomes physical. Thus Perlongher's mystical poetry still draws on the *travesti* aesthetic and the chiastic techniques used in his earlier poetry.

In conclusion, the chiasmus is a subtle yet often important presence in Perlongher's work. Chiasmus emerges alongside the presentation of the *travesti* and *travesti* thematics, and in Perlongher's investigation of the *michê*. Both chiasmus and the *travesti* are tools for destabilizing conservative notions of identity and gender, and for questioning the structures of anthro-pological theory. While chiastic thought rather than chiasmus proper tends to dominate in Perlongher's *oeuvre*, analysis of the development of chiasmus in his work is an important tool for understanding the complex evolution and fluctuations of his sexual politics. More importantly, Perlongher's work offers another example the role of chiasmus as a potent force that drives and enriches literary and cultural production, and is central to its engagement with everyday life.

Notes

1. I have dealt with the subject of the *travesti* in Perlongher's work in the essay 'Perlonger, Poetics and Transvestism', *Journal of Latin American Cultural Studies* vol. 12, no. 1, and in Chapter 4 of my book, *Néstor Perlongher: The Poetic Search for an Argentine Marginal Voice* (University of Wales Press, 2008). The research for this chapter was facilitated by grants from the AHRB, King's College, London, and the University of London.
2. Gordon maintains a certain ambiguity in self-identification in *Aspects of Gender*, hence I maintain his/her personal pronoun usage.
3. *Oso Carolina* (n), a traditional Southern Cone carnival costume, consisting of a man dressed up in brown rice sacks to look roughly like a bear.
4. *Reina, reinar* (v), to reign; although this is a verb, to translate thus would lose the pun on 'reina' (n), queen, and with it 'reina'/'queen' in the slang sense.
5. There is, I would argue, a pun in 'proceloso' on 'proceso', a shortened form of the dictatorship of 1976–83's term for itself, the 'Process of National Reorganization'; more literal translations of 'proceloso' do not capture this.
6. *Pito* (n), whistle; also colloquial for penis.
7. All translations from Spanish and Portuguese are my own unless otherwise indi-cated in the bibliography; some of the translations from Perlongher's poetry first appeared in *Calque* 5 (Spring 2009).
8. *Aduar* (n), gypsy or Bedouin encampment, from Arabic.

References

Breck, John. 1994. *The Shape of Biblical Language: Chiasmus in the Scriptures and Beyond.* Crestwood, NY: St Vladimir's Seminary Press.

Butler, Judith. 1999. *Gender Trouble: Feminism and the Subversion of Identity.* London: Routledge.

Cixous, Helène, and Catherine Clément. 1993. *The Newly-Born Woman.* Minneapolis: University of Minnesota Press.

Deleuze, Gilles, and Félix Guattari. 1999. *A Thousand Plateaus: Capitalism and Schizophrenia.* London: Athlone.

Gordon, Lesley. 1995. *Aspects of Gender: A Study of Crossdressing Behaviour.* Waltham, MA: IFGE Publications.

Horvei, Harald. 1985. *The Changing Fortunes of a Rhetorical Term: The History of Chiasmus*. Bergen (Author's edition).

Massumi, Brian. 1999. *A User's Guide to Capitalism and Schizophrenia: Deviations from Deleuze and Guattari*. Cambridge, MA: MIT Press.

Norrman, Ralf. 1986. *Samuel Butler and the Meaning of Chiasmus*. Basingstoke: Macmillan.

Olson, Paul R. 2003. *The Great Chiasmus: Words and Flesh in the Novels of Unamuno*. West Lafayette, IN: Purdue University Press.

Perlongher, Néstor. 1987. *O negócio de michê*. São Paulo: Editorial Brasiliense.

———. 1993. *La prostitución masculina*. Buenos Aires: Ediciones de la Urraca.

———. 1997a. *Poemas completos*. Buenos Aires: Seix Barral.

———. 1997b. *Prosa plebeya*. Buenos Aires: Colihue.

———. 1999. *El negocio del deseo*. Buenos Aires: Paidós.

Sifuentes-Jaúregui, Ben. [sic]. 2002. *Transvestism, Masculinity and Latin American Literature*. New York: Palgrave.

Thomson, Ian H. 1995. *Chiasmus in the Pauline Letters*. Sheffield: Sheffield Academic Press.

Welch, John W. (ed.). 1993. *Chiasmus in Antiquity: Structures, Analyses, Exegesis*. Hildesheim: Gerstenberg Verlag.

■ ■ ■ ■ ■ ■

PART IV

CHIASTIC STRUCTURES IN RITUAL AND MYTHO-POETIC TEXTS

Parallelism and Chiasmus in Ritual Oration and Ostension in Tana Wai Brama, Eastern Indonesia

E. Douglas Lewis

■ ■ ■ ■ ■ ■

As part of the International Rhetoric Culture Project, Strecker and Tyler begin the first volume of the series 'Studies in Rhetoric and Culture' (Strecker and Tyler 2009) with the thesis that 'rhetoric … is the decisive factor in the emergence of cultural diversity past and present. … there is no "zero degree rhetoric" in any of the patterns of culture' (Strecker and Tyler 2009: 1), meaning 'there is no "zero degree" rhetoric in any utterance because there would be no utterance without a rhetorical impulse' (Kennedy 1997: 4–5). By Strecker's and Tyler's account, one of the original foci of the rhetoric culture project was the 'chiastic relationship between rhetoric and culture' (Strecker and Tyler 2009: 5) by which 'rhetoric is founded in culture and culture is founded in rhetoric' (ibid.: 4, 21). *Rhetoric* and *culture* are concepts of a high order of generality and abstraction. That said, chiasmi are common in the dramas of life-as-lived socially in human communities. In addition to relating abstractions, chiasmi are observable in the flow of quotidian discourse in which all human beings, including ethnographers, are immersed. With speech, we project thought into the world and condense the world into thought; the real becomes ideas, and ideas, real. With chiasmus, the subject becomes object and the object becomes subject.

This aptitude for shifting perspective, which is built into the syntaxes of languages, lies near the heart of human creativity.

In conversation in 2009, Strecker suggested (or Strecker and I agreed; memory fails) that the concept of chiasmus might be usefully extended to include 'chiasmus phenomena' such as inversions in ritual of the kind I know from mortuary rites in the domain of Wai Brama in the Tana 'Ai region of Flores, eastern Indonesia, where I have done ethnographic research (Strecker, personal communication, May 2009, Melbourne; Paul and Wiseman, 'Introduction', this volume). Thinking about such inversions led immediately to a search for chiasmic constructions and other devices of rhetoric in the ritual speech that is an element of all ritual performances in Wai Brama. The search led to a surprising result (the best kind), a feature of ritual speech and the poetical ritual language in which it is spoken by Wai Brama ritualists that I had not noticed before.

In this chapter I will experiment with the extension of the idea of rhetoric and its devices to the analysis of ritual by treating two events in Tana Wai Brama as occasions on which chiasmus has played a role. The first was the death of a ritual specialist during the performance of a large-scale ritual in 1980, a death which other ritualists attributed to a chiasmus unintentionally inserted into a narration of myth in ritual speech. Although accidental and contingent, surviving ritualists subsequently defined it categorically as *hura hugar* (STA 'sequence' or 'pattern' 'reversed' or 'inverted'),[1] a turning upside-down or a crossing over. The second is a rite performed at the foot of the grave of a newly interred corpse, an exigent event that is part of the liturgical order of funerary rites in Wai Brama. The first occurred in speech during an oratorical performance. The second is not, strictly speaking, oratorical, but is ostensible, to employ a distinction made by Fox (1979) in a discussion of rituals on the eastern Indonesian islands of Roti and Savu.

Apart from analysing these two cases of inversion, my larger aim is to see what might be discovered about the culture of the people of Wai Brama by extending the concept of chiasmus beyond that of a device of rhetoric to the analysis of occurrences in the most dramatic events in their lives.

RITUAL AND RITUAL LANGUAGE IN TANA WAI BRAMA

Tana Wai Brama (SS the 'domain' of Wai Brama) is the largest and, according to the mythic histories of its people, the oldest of the seven ceremonial domains of the Tana 'Ai (SS 'land' 'forest', that is, 'forest land' or 'forested land') region of Kabupaten (BI 'regency' of) Sikka in east central Flores, eastern Indonesia. The liturgy of all ritual in Tana Wai Brama consists of two rites, each with its own mode of action. The first rite is the invocation of ancestors, spirits or the deity, or the chanting of the mythic histories of the clans of Wai Brama in ritual language (*bleka hura* STA 'patterned' or 'ordered speech'). Invocations and clan histories, and the chanting in which they are embedded, are oratorical and rhetorical in character.

The second rite consists of sacrifices of rice and coconut water or rice and animals whose blood is sprinkled and smeared on an altar.

In all rituals, invocation occurs prior to sacrifice and, in large-scale rituals, the two rites are carried out by different ritualists or groups of ritualists. In very small-scale rituals, such as the 'cooling' of forest materials used for the construction of a new house, the construction of a protective sign for a fruit tree or areca palm and in offerings made at the edge of a forest in which a man intends to hunt game, a single man performs both rites, but always with the offering or sacrifice following an invocation.

The temporal sequence in which the two rites are performed provides a clue to the logic which gives form to ritual in Tana Wai Brama. The sequence can be completed in a few minutes, as in an offering for a hunt, but may require a number of days, as in the performance of large-scale rituals such as the *gren mahé* (STA 'celebration of the *mahé*', the culminal rites of the ceremonial system of the domain)[2] or the third stage mortuary ritual of a clan (STA *'lo'é 'unur*, 'forelock and fingernails' [of clan ancestors]). It can also require several months, as in the rituals of the garden, for which invocations are performed at the time of planting and sacrifices are performed months later at the time of harvest. Invocation initiates ritual and sacrifice ends ritual.[3]

In the time required to complete the two rites, ritualists and those on whose behalf a ritual is performed are subject to certain restrictions, as is the place in which a ritual is enacted. Thus, following the planting rite, in which spirits of the land and ancestral spirits are invoked to watch over the garden, and until the sacrifices following the harvest, spirits are present in the garden, which is subject to strict rules governing, for example, who can enter the garden and the paths that one can take through it while rice is growing.

In a comparison of ritual on Roti and Savu in eastern Indonesia, Fox (1979: 147–51) has usefully distinguished oration and ostension as 'contrasting modes of ritual orientation' – perhaps better distinguished as contrasting media of ritual action or performance. The Rotinese are 'indifferent ritualists' who 'have preserved their culture verbally' (ibid.: 148) and, '[o]n Roti, rituals are primarily acts of oration' (ibid.: 149). In contrast, '[o]n Savu ... ceremonies are not the occasion for elaborate oratory'[4] (ibid.: 149–50). Rather, '[c]eremonies, on Savu, require ritual action and ... need little verbal accompaniment ... rituals are primarily acts of ostension' (ibid.: 150). In Tana Wai Brama, ritual consists of both oration and ostension, but the verbal acts of chanting the mythic histories and invoking ancestors and the deity are separated from ostensible acts of sacrifice, a separation of events in time which is reflected in a sociologically revealing division of ritual performers such that chanters do not sacrifice and sacrificers do not chant. Fox's distinction thus accords with the thought and practice of the people of Wai Brama and is useful for the analysis of the ceremonial system of the domain.

Oration is prior to ostension and, in terms of the values which animate the two rites, more care is devoted to the chanting of invocations and the mythic histories of the domain than to sacrifice. Indeed, the ritualists of Wai Brama say that, in the most important rituals, an error in chanting ritual language can be fatal for the chanter or, at least, will adversely affect those for whom the ritual is performed. Just as oration takes precedence over ostension in the performance of ritual, chanters are usually drawn from the corps of senior ritualists in the domain, who delegate to junior ritualists or even non-ritualists the tasks of sacrifice.[5]

In Tana Wai Brama, the sacrifice of animals and the offering of rice are ostensible acts by which things or persons are 'cooled' and by which the ancestors and deity are 'fed'. The two rites, the oratorical rite of invocation and the sacrifice, which is signalled by the rite of 'cooling' with the blood of animals or coconut water, are so closely interconnected, both in the thought of the Ata Tana 'Ai and in the performance of rituals, that they can be taken as indices of one another and, together, define action as ritual.

Whereas the Ata (SS 'people' of) Wai Brama are occasionally diffident in the conduct of the ostensible acts which partly make up ritual, they are exceedingly meticulous chanters of the invocations and mythic histories which are the oratorical elements of ritual performance. The main exceptions to this observation are the 'lo'é 'unur (third stage mortuary rituals) and the rarely performed celebration of the domain's origins, the gren mahé, in which considerable care is taken in the ordering of sacrifices which make up these events and in the techniques the acts employ.

In the thought of the Ata Tana 'Ai, human acts have as their consequences in time necessary states of affairs in the future. Proper speech in ritual language, in contrast, recounts the history of past events. More than simply recounting history, ritual language allows a ritualist to reconstruct states of affairs in the past. The logic which binds together word and act, oration and ostension, is based on implicit assumptions about the nature of causality and intention. In the thought of the Ata Tana 'Ai, that which is past is not immutable, except that past actions and their consequences are in accord with hadat (SS, a polysemous word encompassing custom, tradition, propriety, fitting, true to nature, decorous).

Figure 10.1 The *mahé* Tana Wai Brama before the *gren mahé* in 1980. The ceremonial ground in the *mahé* forest has been cleared, but three ritual huts have not yet been constructed. The altar consists of a branched tree trunk surrounded by menhirs representing the clans of the domain. A second, shorter branched tree trunk behind the larger one still stands from when it was replaced in 1960. The trunks of a banyan tree are in the background. The flat and spherical stones at the front and base of the *mahé* are receptacles for the blood of sacrificed animals (see Lewis, Asch and Asch 1993). (Photograph by E.D. Lewis)

Hadat is the classificatory order encoded in the poiesis and parallelisms of ritual language. Acts not in accord with *hadat*, the immanent order of the world, lead to confoundings of categories with consequences detrimental both to human beings and to the world itself. Such acts may be unintentional on the part of individuals. Unintentional acts contrary to *hadat* are signalled by their injurious consequences. Through the words of ritual language the chain of causality, which begins with an act and engenders subsequent events, can be reconstructed and understood, and the particular act which has resulted in a specific consequence can be identified. The words – the oratorical act – of the ritualist take him backwards through the historical chain of causally connected events initiated by a single act.

The *Gren Mahé* of Tana Wai Brama

Most rituals in Tana Wai Brama[6] include invocations of ancestral spirits (STA *nitu* 'spirit' or *nitu maten* 'spirit of the dead') or the aboriginal spirits of the land, forests and springs of Tana 'Ai (STA *guna déwa*). These rituals are conducted on such occasions as funerals, the sanctification of newly constructed houses and granaries, the protection of fruit and palm trees, and before hunters enter forests in pursuit of game. In contrast to other rituals, which can take place in (or under) houses, in gardens, on the edge of forests, or indeed anywhere in the domain, invocations of the deity only take place in a clearing in a patch of primary forest in which is located the *mahé*, the domain's central altar for sacrifices to the deity. Rituals of the *mahé* include those conducted by a small corps of ritual specialists twice a year, once to secure the start of the rainy season and once to ensure its end. These rituals are part of the horticultural cycle of the domain's people. Only infrequently does the whole of the community gather at the *mahé* for the *gren mahé*, the feast or celebration of the *mahé*.

The *gren mahé* occurs according to no fixed calendar. In 1980 it had last been done in 1960. Circumstantial evidence suggests the *gren* is conducted only when the community is experiencing stress or a crisis of some kind. 1980 followed two years of crop failures and the death of the old *tana pu'an* (STA 'source of the domain', the leader of the domain's ceremonial system) in August 1979. While the 1980 harvest was better than those of the previous two years, no new leader of the domain had yet been recognized by the community's corps of ritualists when, in early November, the ritualists of the domain gathered to commence the *gren* which had been announced by the old source of the domain shortly before he died. In anticipation of the 1980 *gren*, I returned to Tana Wai Brama in July with Professor Timothy and Mrs Patsy Asch to film the *mahé* rituals and the community's preparations for them.

The rites of the *gren mahé* are invocations of the deity performed by the domain's leading ritual specialists, and entail sacrifices of pigs and goats. In addition to the invocation of the deity, the histories, that is, the origin myths, of the domain's five clans are spoken. The invocation and the histories are performances in ritual language, the special poetical genre of Sara Tana 'Ai distinguished from ordinary language by a rigorous semantic parallelism, a couplet structure, and syntactical elision. While all members of the community understand ritual language to a greater or lesser degree, fluent masters of the genre are small in number and all are ritualists in the domain's ceremonial system. The public invocation of the deity of Wai Brama is an event of such gravity and celebration that, in 1980, practically every member of the domain attended, along with expatriate kin, visitors from other domains of east central Flores, a number of students from the island's Catholic seminary (all writing *skripsi*, BA undergraduate theses), three anthropologists and film-makers,[7] and a district government official who wished he was elsewhere. The event lasted four days and three nights. The two central days were raucous, chaotic and undirected, but punctuated by intervals of profound quiet when the domain's small corps of ritual specialists summoned the deity, the land's spirits, and, through the second night whilst the revellers slept, chanted the mythic histories of the domain's clans.

A Death by Mischant

They are tendentious, contentious, capricious, malicious and too often men-dacious, and summoning those -*ishus* entities men call deities is a hazardous business. Seeking converse with a god is like prodding a dozing kraken into wakefulness: one cannot know what will happen.

In Wai Brama, as in most places, even before one places before it the meal one has prepared and with which one hopes to entice the deity into accepting a covenant, making a promise or agreeing to a contract, one sum-mons the deity – or, if it is ubiquitous, catches its attention – with speech. In Wai Brama, the business of dealing with the deity begins with the word and, should the deity respond at all, it is the words of human speech of a particular kind that awaken it.

In the *gren mahé* of 1980, the invocations of the deity and spirits were achieved without incident, although there were long discussions – argu-ments, really – about some of the pigs and goats to be sacrificed before the invocations and who should provide them.

Among the ritualists of the domain, however, there was a shortage of senior chanters to chant the history of clan Ipir Wai Brama. Ipir's ancestors – the brothers Hading Dai Dor and Uher La'i Atan – were the first to come to the land of Wai Brama. In the history, they discovered the land empty, set up the *mahé*, and established the domain. As other ancestors found the domain, the Ipir brothers delegated to them rights to land and responsibilities in the domain's ceremonial system. Each arriving ancestor founded a clan. After Ipir came Tapo, Mau, Magé and Liwu. The order of the clans' ancestors' arriv-als established the *oda* (STA), the 'precedence' of the domain's clans.

Because the two Ipir brothers became separated on their journey to the land that became Wai Brama, one arrived before the other. The first to arrive was Hading Dai Dor, the 'elder' brother. Thus, his descendants are *pu'an*, (STA: source, trunk, centre, central, first in precedence) and it is from them that the community's source of the domain, the holder of precedence who is paramount among the domain's ritualists, must come.

On the second night of the *gren*, Mo'an[8] Rénu of clan Tapo (the second rank clan of the domain's order of precedence), a senior ritualist, was co-opted to help two other men chant Hading Dai Dor's part of the history of clan Ipir. The chanting of Ipir's history lasted from late evening of the second day to early morning of the third. The chanting alternated between those chanters telling the history of the elder brother and those who told the history of the

Figure 10.2 Mo'an Rénu Tapo, the principal chanter and ritualist of clan Tapo, at home in his *lepo* (STA clan house), Hila Klo'ang, Tana Wai Brama, 1978. Mo'an Rénu was one of the author's informants in matters of ritual during his first season of fieldwork in Tana 'Ai (1978–1979). (Photograph by E.D. Lewis)

younger brother. It was, for chanters, the rapidly dwindled audience, the government official denied sleep by his place of honour in the proceedings, and the anthropologist-filmmakers, an exhausting night.

During the night, Mo'an Rénu made an error in chanting. A short while later, he left the *mahé* and set out for his clan house, about a kilometre from the *mahé*. We in the *mahé* received word early the next morning that Rénu had reached his house, where he had died before dawn. As everyone participating in the *gren* was under restrictions, no one was allowed to help to organize or attend his burial. I was told that his burial would be immediate but that funeral rites would be delayed.

Rénu had been indisposed, but not seriously, and no one expected his death, which was much discussed once the *gren* was completed. No one I spoke to attributed his death to the deity and no one spoke of divine retribution, nor suggested that Rénu's error of speech was displeasing to the deity or to any of the other noumenal entities whom the ritual specialists of the community addressed during the *gren mahé* of 1980. In any case, the deity works more subtly than by simple retribution. Nor did he die from some preternatural power of words. No one among the people of Wai Brama knows why he died, and nor do I. But the death of a senior ritualist during a major ritual was a notable and worrying event. Afterwards, the ritual specialists of the domain attributed his death to an error in ritual speech, by which language itself was misrepresented, *misspoken*, mismanifested in speech, in an *act* that was an error. Their comments, in 1980 and in following years, imply that they thought his death resulted from his misrepresenting the order of the world and humans in it. He spoke an untruth in the sacred language of ritual, a violation of cosmological axioms. This was his fellows' reading of his death.

The language of daily discourse is fragmentary and unpredictable. Quotidian speech is thus at once unaesthetic and more useful than ritual speech, at least in the business of making a living in the world and getting other people to do what you want them to do while getting along with them. Ordinary language and speech are for the vicissitudes of life and the vagaries of fate. Creativity, innovation and change come from and require quotidian speech. It is the language of adaptation to changing environmental and social conditions; the language for conceiving, discussing, imagining innovation and adopting new ways of doing things, and then doing them. Quotidian speech is in the language of those 'alternatives' (Rappaport 1999: 17–22) to the current state of affairs and ways of doing things to which syntax and metaphor give us access and among which, once given voice, a community chooses its future.[9] With respect to literature, George Steiner is aware of the paradox of creativity arising from syntax and innovation from conventionally defined words:

Figure 10.3 Mo'an Rénu Tapo and E.D. Lewis near Watuwolon, Tana Wai Brama, 1980. (Photograph by Timothy Asch)

> Literature is language, whether oral or written. It is, as Mallarmé reminded Degas, made of nothing but words. Its components are arbitrary phonetic units pre- and over-determined by consensual usage, by precedent meanings and connotations. Its major themes appear to conform to the laws of *ricorso*, of the 'riverrun' upstream invoked by Vico and by Joyce. Originality would, indeed, signify a return to origins. Could it be, therefore, that literature is the most inventive but least creative of artefacts? Could it be that the principal congruence is that between fiction, which is the substance of literature, and invention (we have, already, noted the crucial affinities between the fictive and the invented)? This paradox merits closer study. (Steiner 2001: 159)

The problem with quotidian speech is that, having begun an utterance, one is never certain in advance how it will end, whether it is that of an interlocutor or one's own. And, half the time, it seems that what people say to one makes no sense at all or leads to dispute, even violence. This is never the case in the properly spoken ritual language of Wai Brama.

Unlike everyday speech, in ritual speech every word is inexorably and ineluctably bound to another word, indeed, to all the words that precede and follow it. In the semiotician's jargon, each word of ritual speech is an index – a synecdoche, to be precise – of all the others. The chanter of an invocation or of a clan history is not free to innovate, that is, to make up and speak a world alternative to that of the-way-things-were-and-how-they-came-to-be narratives that make up myth and the religion of Tana Wai Brama. A chanter's words are true because they are the same ones spoken by the ancestors, who first lived, and then told, the tale he is vouchsafed to tell. True, the deity may become disturbed at mistakes in the narrative, but it is more likely long bored by its creatures' clumsiness, talentlessness and errors, and so cannot be bothered.

Ritual speech articulates ideas about the universe and its order that Rappaport called 'cosmological axioms'. If not explicitly, the poetry of ritual language sets out the structure of the cosmos and the essential system of categories by which the Ata Tana 'Ai describe their conceptions of the nature of the universe. The people of Wai Brama take these cosmological axioms to be unchanging and unchangeable.

Pius Ipir Wai Brama comments in Bahasa Indonesia on the nature of ritual speech, translated as a subtitle in the film, *A Celebration of Origins* (Lewis, Asch and Asch 1993, shot 90). 'Everyday language', he says, 'we call "speaking ourselves". It can be about important things or just random speech. But ritual speech is different: it employs the language of the true core of things. We must speak the truth. Speaking falsely [in error] can kill us'. (See also the shot list to the film [Lewis n.d.].)

Ritual language, the narratives and poiesis of ritual in Wai Brama, is true. It indexes the world as it is by telling truly how the world – and the people in it – came to be as it is. Truth lies in origins, and in myths of origins the structure and logic of the world are set out for all to hear. Thus the relation between ritual language and the world is also indexical, powerfully so.

Rénu was killed by the inevitable mismatch between language and speech. In particular, he died from a chiasmus, a verbal catastrophe by which he inverted the order of the world. The error placed the feminine element of the deity in the firmament and the deity's masculine part on the earth. The deity, perhaps distracted by the feast it would soon be given, did not seem to mind. But language and the world did, and Rénu died.

Rénu's speech miscast what Rappaport calls a 'cosmological axiom'. Rappaport proposed that the liturgical order of a society's religion (generally taken by anthropologists to be manifest in ritual and myth, religion's phenomenal side) is hierarchically ordered and the hierarchy has certain formal properties (Rappaport 1999: 263). Among the levels of the liturgical order are cosmological axioms. Cosmological axioms are 'assumptions concerning the fundamental structure of the universe or ... the paradigmatic relationships in accordance with which the cosmos is constructed' (ibid.: 264). The axioms are rarely articulated explicitly by those who live in a cosmos so constructed, but 'they are manifested in social and physical phenomena'.[10] The expression of cosmological axioms is implicit in much of daily life (ibid.: 265), but also in myth and ritual, which is the confine of what Rappaport calls Ultimate Sacred Postulates – the highest level of a liturgical order. Cosmological axioms serve as the basis from which rules for conduct and the proprieties of social life derive: 'they *sanctify*, which is to say, *certify*, the entire system of understandings in accordance with which people conduct their lives' (ibid.: 265).

Rénu's was a mistake that any chanter could make; indeed, there were many such mistakes made during the chanting of clan histories during the *gren* of 1980. It happened that Rénu died from his. The surviving ritual specialists of the *gren* discussed Rénu's death among themselves after the *gren*; and they spoke about it to me during the years that followed and in which I pursued them with questions about the matter.

Of course, ritual language does change, through time, as can the liturgy of ostensible ritual (Lewis 1989a). It is rare for a full complement of chanters to gather in Wai Brama for any ritual. Indeed, the chanters themselves recognize the vagaries of performers and performance. Couplets and entire episodes of a history may be omitted from a narration of the domain's mythic histories. Such omissions may be intentional on the part of a chanter, but they can also arise from forgetfulness. In the turn taking of chanting, a chanter who thinks something has been left out of a narration or an error has been made may, upon taking up the chant, begin with the following couplet:

Ha lupa ha heron   If one forgets, another will speak,
Ha hulir ha donen   If one lapses [errs, forgets], another will point the way [instruct].

This commonly spoken couplet shows both that omissions are possible and that they can be corrected. However that may be, the people of Wai Brama conceive (and represent) their 'histories' as the unaltered words of the ancestors. To stand the semantic pairs of a couplet of ritual language upside down in speech is to turn the world upside down. Changing the cosmos in words can be fatal.

The Lethal Sanction of Words and Rénu's Error

'Sticks and stones can break my bones but words can never hurt me', as countless anglophone children in countless schoolyards have chanted for generations. Children know this simple line in trochaic septameter to be false; hence the need for the mantra, to ward off the damage, the hurt, of false and ugly words. So, too, we adults and the Ata Tana 'Ai know the power and dangers of words.

The questions that arise from Rénu's death are not whether or not words can kill, but why the people of Wai Brama think that some words carry lethal sanction, and why the sanctioned words are those spoken in ritual while not those of quotidian discourse.

Ritual speech is in the language of the 'true core of things', said Pius Ipir Wai Brama when commenting on the *gren mahé* and after he became Wai Brama's *tana pu'an* (source of the domain), the paramount ritual leader of the domain. Speech in ritual language, he meant, is true speech, that which employs true words, words whose truth, their match to the way things were and are, cannot be gainsaid.

I have searched through the transcripts of all of the recordings made during filming of the *gren mahé* and have examined those of Rénu's chanting on the second night of the rituals most intensively. My memory tells me of Rénu's sudden pause in the flow of ritual speech, a moment's startled look, a momentary confusion, a stumble or stutter in the scansion of performance, when he recorded his dismay at having said something wrong. But the camera may have been off when the moment occurred and I find no indication of the event in the transcripts of film sound.[11] Thus, the moment is in my memory, but not only there since it was recalled and discussed by ritualists with whom I spoke after the *gren* was completed. Indeed, Rénu's error and his death were subjects of discussion initiated both by myself and others when I returned to the Tana 'Ai valley eighteen months after the *gren* to document our footage and in subsequent field seasons to 1985.

Rénu died in the middle of the *gren mahé*, when the community and, most especially, the community's ritual leaders, were under restrictions. They could not become involved in a burial whilst the *gren* was undertaken. I fell under those restrictions and, in any case, I was unable to visit Rénu's *lepo* (STA clan or ritual house) for his burial or to speak to people there about his death, as a practical matter during the filming.

But informants were later emphatic and unanimous. Rénu had died as a result of an error he made in ritual speech, whereby he inverted one or more semantically paired words in the ritual idiom. The inversion was of a crucial relationship that follows from one among the cosmological axioms of the community's religion.

Because I cannot pinpoint the error in the transcripts of the event, I must rely on the testimony of my informants, who agreed that Rénu's error was to speak of:

Ina nian tana réta   Mother land and earth above
Ama lero wulan wawa   Father sun and moon below

rather than the canonically – and cosmologically – correct sequence of words denoting the quadripartite deity of Tana 'Ai:

Ina nian tana wawa	Mother land and earth below,
Ama lero wulan réta	Father sun and moon above.

In the cosmology and classifications of the people of Wai Brama, the land and earth, as 'mother', are feminine, while the sun and moon, as 'father', are masculine.[12] The land is below the sun and the moon is above the earth. While not in the form we would normally expect of a chiasmus, Rénu spoke, in other words, chiasmatically and turned the world upside down.

Errors in ritual speech (the chanting of 'histories' in ritual language) are relatively rare. Few are to be found in several hundred pages of transcripts of ritual language from Tana 'Ai and the central region of Kabupaten Sikka. The most common 'errors', that is, mistakes recognized by other chanters present on an occasion of ritual speech, are omissions of couplets or episodes in a clan history. Few if any errors in the sequence of semantically paired words are to be found in my recordings and texts. A chanter may occasionally repeat a four-word line of a couplet while recalling or composing its parallel line, and lines occasionally are spoken without their following parallel. The kind of error ritualists attributed to Rénu in the *gren* is very rare. It may well be that, as rhymes – that is, phonetic parallelism – in English poetry may provide a mnemonic for a reciter, so, too, may semantic parallelism make it less likely that a chanter will err in speaking a history or an invocation.

There are a number of problems with the accounts I received. To begin with, when his error was putatively made, Rénu was chanting a history of the journey of clan ancestors to Tana Wai Brama. The couplet which Rénu bungled is not normally spoken in the course of chanting clan histories, but more commonly in invocations of the deity. Still, he may have inserted an invocation of this kind into his history, although I find no evidence for that in the transcripts of his chanting.[13]

Still, it was this *kind* of error which, people agreed, Rénu had made, and the kind of error they used as an example when speaking to me about the event.

Speech in Ritual and Ritual Language as Anti-Rhetoric

When speech becomes part of the liturgy of ritual – as it inevitably must – ritual itself becomes vulnerable to the errors of ritualists and the 'vices of language'. Foremost among language's vices is the lie.

In what must be one of the most important books in the library of twentieth century anglophone anthropology, Roy Rappaport suggested that ritual ameliorates the vice of language, with its innate capacity for prevarication, deceit and misrepresentation which follows from its symbolicity and its protean capacity for metaphorical replacement. With language, we humans acquired the negative. As symbol-using animals, Kenneth Burke wrote, we are the inventors of 'that peculiarly human marvel, the negative' (Burke 1968: 9): there are no negatives in nature; the negative is a product of human symbol systems. And we acquired a means to express the counter-factual, the that-which-is-not, in multifarious ways – all of them fictional.

So, what happens when speech, with which we effortlessly toss off contradictions, paradoxes, counter-factuals and lies, is itself a crucial part of liturgy? How can speech be made invulnerable to the vagaries of language, to its omnipresent inclination to change itself? The answer is by building into what is said an anti-rhetorical force of invariance. This is done in the ritual languages of eastern Indonesia by constructing what is said in accord with a built-in way of signalling when something has been changed in the verbal liturgy, when an error has been made or a change intentionally introduced by a speaker. In the case of these special genres of language in eastern Indonesia, the device for the preservation of proper speech is semantic parallelism.

Change, even to sacred strings of words, cannot be avoided in time, but its likelihood can be reduced. In ritual language, one wants no new metaphors, no new tropes, no rhetorical flourishes, no individual poiesis, no brilliant, egoistical expression of the self. Continuity is what is needed. In Wai Brama, the mind of a novice chanter is a vessel to be filled, not a flame to be lit.

A.F.C. Wallace once observed that, in terms of information theory, ritual (by which he meant what Rappaport calls 'canon') is 'a very peculiar form of communication because it is devoid of information'. As Wallace put it, a ritual is 'a particular sequence of signals which … allows no uncertainty, no choice, and hence in the statistical sense of information theory, conveys no information from sender to receiver. It is … a system of perfect order and any deviation from this order is a mistake' (Wallace 1966: 233).

The idea from information theory that Wallace invokes is that the informational content of a message is inversely proportional to the expectability of that message's receipt. It can be captured succinctly in the following representation: $I \sim 1 \mathbin{/} E_m$, where I is the amount of information contained in a message (or utterance) and E_m is the expectability of the message being received (a measure of the probability of its receipt). On this basis, Wallace proposed that 'Ritual may … most succinctly be classified as communication without information' (Wallace 1966: 233).

But Wallace goes on to point out that information and meaning are not the same thing. 'Not all meaningful messages', he writes, 'are informational' and not all informational messages are meaningful. In other words, a sequence of meaningful signals whose order is fixed, so that the receiver always knows what signal will follow the preceding one, will have no information value because there is no uncertainty to be reduced by the outcome of each successive event. Conversely, a message may be meaningless either because its information value is too high or because the component signals are arbitrary. (Wallace 1966: 236)

This idea is useful for understanding the fundamental nature of ritual language.

One may suggest that the effect of a chiasmus – whether verbal or literary – is, at least in part, the result of surprise. According to information theory, surprising messages are informational. While elegance and suitability in context may contribute to a chiasmus's impact, unexpected information may be the source of the chiasmatic effect. In ritual language and its manifestation in ritual performances in Wai Brama as ritual speech, new information, surprises and innovations of any sort are what one does not want if one is charged with the preservation of the fertility of the land, the abundance of crops, the fecundity of animals and, indeed, that of humans themselves – in short, the prosperity of the community – through the conduct of ritual.

If there is to be no change to the verbal liturgy, no plays on words and no new tropes, there can be no chiasmi and no antimetaboles, except those that may be handed down incidentally in the poetical tradition. Since the essence of chiasmus includes an element of surprise, and since there should be no surprises in ritual speech, then there is no place, no need, for chiasmus. Indeed, the requirements of strict semantic parallelism, which is the essential poiesis of eastern Indonesian ritual languages, denies chiasmus. Put simply, the semantic pairs of ritual language encode classifications of a sacred kind, and in ritual speech can be read the cosmological axioms of Wai Brama thought and religion. Parallelism guards these axioms from alteration. The reason for this will become clear in what follows.

RHETORIC, CHIASMUS, ANTIMETABOLE AND PARALLELISM

'So let rhetoric be defined', wrote Aristotle, 'as the faculty [power] of discovering in the particular case what are the available means of persuasion. This is the function of no other art [save Dialectic]' (Cooper 1932: 7).

As I was taught in school, rhetoric is the art of persuasion with oratory marked by eloquence and elegance of expression. Because it was published in the year I finished school, neither I nor my teachers enjoyed the benefit of Corbett's *Classical Rhetoric for the Modern Student*. There, on page 3, we would have found: 'Rhetoric is the art or discipline that deals with the use of discourse, either spoken or written, to inform or persuade or move an audience, whether that audience is made up of a single person or a group of persons' (Corbett [1965] 1971: 3).

According to *Webster's Third New International Dictionary* (1971), rhetoric is, firstly, 'the art of expressive speech[14] or discourse'. It is then 'verbal communication : DISCOURSE' and, further, 'persuasive or moving power'. Rhetoric is related to oratory, which is: 'the art of an orator : the art of speaking in public eloquently or effectively : the exercise of rhetorical skill in discourse : ELOQUENCE ... an example or instance of rhetorical speech or art : the substance of such speech' (Gove 1971).

The definitions of rhetoric that Corbett cites in the introduction to his book all invoke the relationship between speaker and audience. They include that of Kenneth Burke: 'For rhetoric as such is not rooted in any past condition of human society. It is rooted in an essential function of language itself, a function that is wholly realistic, and is continually born anew; the use of language as a symbolic means of inducing cooperation in beings that by nature respond to symbols' (Burke [1950] 1969: 43). The shift here is a subtle one from persuasion, even coercion, to cooperation, by which all of language and its use in speech is rhetorical. And it implies there is something peculiar about symbolization.

'That's just rhetoric', says the cynic of a shifty politician or an argument to which he is not drawn. 'That's all just myth' he says in another context. These are usages which abuse the concepts of rhetoric and myth. Rhetoric is discourse which, consisting of speech and writing (or, broadly, communication), is mainly what human beings do in each other's presence. For an anthropologist, myth comprises the narratives upon which humans build cultures, societies and religions. We would do well not to misuse these concepts.

It was also Burke, perhaps the most important rhetorician since Aristotle and Quintilianus (who, some rhetoricians reckon, was not all that important),[15] who closed *Permanence and Change* by adjuring us to remember that 'men build their cultures by huddling together, nervously loquacious, at the edge of an abyss' (Burke [1935] 1984: 272).[16] The key phrase for us who make arguments for an intimate relationship between rhetoric and culture is 'nervously loquacious'.

A few months before I first learned about rhetoric during my first or second year of high school, John F. Kennedy was inaugurated as president of the United States. Thus his inaugural address was available for consideration when one of my teachers spoke about rhetoric. Kennedy exhorted the nation:

> And so, my fellow Americans, ask not what your country can do for you;
> ask what you can do for your country.

And again, in the same speech:

> My fellow citizens of the world, ask not what America will do for you, but
> what together we can do for the freedom of man.

I do not remember clearly, but it is possible that my teacher identified chiasmus as a rhetorical device and pointed out the chiasmi in Kennedy's speech. Kennedy had won the 1960 election by one of the smallest margins of the popular vote in United States history. He and Theodore Sorenson, who drafted the speech, knew its importance. The speech mobilized broad support for the new president. The larger message, that words change the world, was not lost on one fifteen-year-old boy.

Chiasmus is the 'inversion of the order of syntactical elements in the second of two juxtaposed and syntactically parallel phrases or clauses (as *a superman in physique but in intellect a fool*)' (Gove 1971, italics in the original); and antimetabole is a special form of chiasmus in which the words, inflections or meanings in one phrase are the same in the other, but are reversed in order. Kennedy's 'ask not' speech, while chiasmatic, employed antimetabole. 'Time flies when you're having fun', it is said, but a nervously loquacious amphibian (Kermit the Frog) rendered the idea as 'Time's fun when you're having flies'.

The idea I wish to pursue here is that the parallelism of semantic dyads in Tana 'Ai ritual language ensures that chiasmic reversals cannot occur. In my work, I have always transcribed ritual speech in Sara Sikka and Sara Tana 'Ai as couplets, generally of four words per line since the four-word line is the ideal. The earliest literary transcriptions of Sikkanese ritual language by literate Ata Sikka themselves are by A.P. Boer and D.D.P. Kondi, two among the first generation of literate Sikkanese (see Lewis and Mandalangi 2008 and Lewis 2010). They also wrote down ritual language in couplet form, as in

Ina nian tana wawa,
Ama lero wulan réta.

That said, ritual speech can also be recorded as one complete thought per line:

Ina	nian	tana	wawa,	Ama	lero	wulan	réta
A	B	C	D	A'	B'	C'	D'

The order of the first four words determines absolutely the order of the subsequent four words, since

ina //[17] ama	mother // father
nian tana // lero wulan	land earth // sun moon
wawa // réta	below // above

are semantic dyads whose order in speech cannot be reversed.

There is an implicit hierarchical order in the expression, that is, the utterance, of the elements of the dyads. The order may find expression in a hierarchy of value (moral, social or otherwise) but is in all instances a temporal (or metonymical) hierarchy by which, if in ritual language one speaks of mothers and fathers, the word *ina* (mother) must be spoken first, then the word *ama* (father). This temporal or metonymical hierarchy is not a grammatical rule, but is a syntagmatic imperative. It is deeply ingrained in speakers of Sara Tana 'Ai in both its ritual and quotidian registers. It touches on the Ultimate Sacred Postulates (Rappaport 1999: 262–76) of the community. Reversal of the order is even deeply dissonant to me, a speaker of Sara Tana 'Ai as a second language. *Ina ama* and *wawa réta* are simply right; *ama ina* and *réta wawa* are not simply incorrect, these word orders are unsettlingly wrong. And so there is a right and wrong with all of the semantic dyads of ritual language in Tana Wai Brama.

Antimetabole is a species of chiasmus. Whereas chiasmus employs different words in its reversed phrases or clauses, an antimetabole is a chiasmus that employs the same words in its second clause as in its first, but in reversed order. Thus, whereas 'a superman in physique but a fool in intellect' employs simple parallelism (ABAB or AB // 1/A 1/B; a fool is the opposite of a superman and intellect is the opposite of physique), 'a superman in physique but in intellect a fool' (ABBA or A B // 1/B 1/A) is a chiasmus in which the order of syntactical elements is inverted in the second of the two parallel phrases whose words differ. In contrast, President John F. Kennedy's 'ask not what your country can do for you; ask what you can do for your country' (ABBA) is an antimetabole, a formation that employs the chiasmic inversion, but with the same words in both phrases.

One of my favorite antimetaboles comes from T.K. Whipple's essay 'The Myth of the Old West' in a collection of his critical essays on the American character. Whipple sets out a key idea about the relationship of the pioneers of the American West to their descendants that parallels themes of Tana 'Ai myth. Indeed, Whipple's paragraph could as well be about the people of Wai Brama as about my own Texian and Oklahoman ancestors and others of the Old West since, as it happens, his pairings of ideas are identical to dualistic themes in Wai Brama ritual language and the thought of the Ata Tana 'Ai. His paragraph reads thus:

Our forefathers had civilization inside themselves, the wild outside. We live
in the civilization they created, but within us the wilderness still lingers.
What they dreamed, we live; and what they lived, we dream. (Whipple
1943: 65)[18]

The force of Whipple's paragraph depends upon a number of semantic relationships between key words and a final transformation of those relationships
in an effective antimetabole. The first sentence is constructed upon semantic
parallelism:

civilization // wild, inside // outside.

The second sentence adds a further semantic parallelism:

we [the living] // they [ancestors].

A	B	C	A	1/B	1/C
Our forefathers had	civilization	inside	themselves,	the wild	outside.

1/A	B	A	D	C	1/A	1/B	1/D
We live in	the civilization	they	created,	but within	us	the wilderness	still lingers.

A	E	1/A	F	A	F	1/A	E
What they	dreamed,	we	live;	and what they	lived,	we	dream.

Together, the first two sentences set up a number of paired elements linked by
semantic opposition or, depending upon one's viewpoint, complementarity:

forefathers // we
civilization // wild, wilderness
inside // outside
created // lingers (that which lingers is not a new creation)

E is a transform of B and C (dreaming of something occurs inside, within the
mind of a person); F is a transform of 1/B and 1/C (wilderness is lived in and
is outside the person), themselves inversions of prior terms. Ancestors create
(A and D); their descendants maintain (1/A and 1/D).[19]

The oppositions prepare the reader for what in speech writing is called
the reveal (or the punchline in writing a joke), in which the oppositions are
resolved in a perfect antimetabole. And this, I think, is why Whipple's is a
dramatic and effective paragraph. As a species of chiasmus, Whipple's line
is an antimetabole because in the second phrase it inverts the order of two
words in the first phrase. It is a powerful example of the creativity of language

that cannot happen, except as an error, without sanction in Tana 'Ai ritual speech, given that ritual language is governed by semantic parallelism.

PARALLELISM AND MO'AN RÉNU'S FATAL CHIASMUS

The phrase *nian tana lero wulan* (STA land earth sun moon), the words that come closest to the idea of 'deity' in the cosmology of the Ata Tana 'Ai, occurred nowhere in chanting for the *gren mahé* in 1980. Indeed, these words are spoken as a single phrase only rarely and not in ritual speech because the four-word phrase itself consists of two semantic dyads (*nian // tana* and *lero // wulan*) that pair only with each other as *nian tana // lero wulan*. The complete phrase thus cannot be the first four words of a couplet in ritual language. In other words, *nian tana* form a dyad only with *lero wulan*. However, the long phrase can be broken into two, and one half can be a phrase in the first line and the other half a phrase in the second line of a couplet. This happens in invocations in ritual speech and occurred frequently during chanting in the *gren mahé*. Two invocatory couplets drawn from transcripts of ritualists' invocations of the deity in the 1980 rites were:

1	*Topo ora nian tana,* *Hawon ora lero wulan.*	[We] summon the land and earth, [We] ask of the sun and moon

and

2	*Marin ora nian tana* *Heron ora lero wulan*	Speak with the land and earth, Converse with the sun and moon.

The strict form of semantic parallelism prevents chiasmus and chiastic innovation in ritual speech. The restriction is a consequence of the conventions of semantic dyads, which also produce the couplet structure of ritual speech:

marin // heron (speak // talk to, converse)
ora // ora (with)
nian tana // lero wulan (land and earth // sun and moon)

The elements of a semantic dyad can be synonyms (*marin* to talk about, to speak with; and *heron* to discuss, to converse), antonyms (*wawa* below, under; and *réta* above, atop), or complementary taxa in a simple classification system (*ina* mother and *ama* father, *bliro* brahminy kite and *gak* [or *glak*] black hawk) – that is, words for things related as species of a genus. The parallel and dyadic structure can be represented with the terms A//A', B//B', wherein // means 'forms a semantic dyad with'.

A	B	C	
Ina	nian tana	wawa	Mother land and earth below
A'	B'	C'	
Ama	lero wulan	réta	Father sun and moon above

To say:

Ama nian tana wawa,   Father land and earth below,

as Rénu did, would be a profound error in ritual speech, as would:

Ina nian tana réta,   Mother land and earth above.

To obtain an ABBA chiasmus in ritual speech, one would have to say:

A	B		
Ina	nian tana	wawa	Mother land and earth below
B'	A'		
Lero wulan	ama	réta	Sun and moon father above

or

	A	B	
Ina	nian tana	wawa	Mother land and earth below
	B'	A'	
Ama	réta	lero wulan	Father above sun and moon

Both of these constructions, indeed all such chiasmi, violate the parallelism of semantic dyads dictated by the structure of recurrence in the syntax of ritual language. Because of the compulsion of the formula of parallelism, this does not happen because it cannot happen, except by misspeaking or mischanting.

Both 'eat to live' and 'live to eat' (an antimetabole which, if I recall correctly, comes from Socrates by way of Plato) are syntactically correct and make sense in English. In Sara Tana 'Ai, neither *nian tana réta, lero wulan wawa* (land and earth above, sun and moon below) nor *ama nian tana, ina lero wulan* (father land and earth, mother sun and moon) makes sense. Both are out of accord with cosmology. Not only do these solecisms violate the logic of semantic dyads and parallelism, they are also violations of cosmological axioms. These axioms are deeply embedded in the structure of ritual language. To misspeak them can only happen in the way that Spoonerisms happen, as neurolinguistic glitches in the flow of speech, when the vocal apparatus fails to obey the intending mind. Thus,

'Ask not what your country can do for you

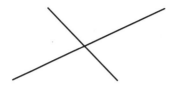

Ask what you can do for your country.'

is a memorable chiasmus (actually, an antimetabole in which the Greek χ is clear) in English that cannot be said in Tana 'Ai ritual language.

Thus semantic parallelism guarantees that the cosmological axioms of the Wai Brama ceremonial system and religion are preserved in speech. The speech employed is highly elided. It is stripped of grammatical inflections and parts of speech. It lacks, in other words the syntax that allows, in ordinary, quotidian speech, for creativity and the expression of ideas never before articulated, counterfactuals, and the alternities by which the politics of communal life generate adaptations to changing circumstances. And there are few negatives and few imperatives in ritual speech.

While negative and imperative constructions are rare, they occasionally occur, usually as entreaties of spirits:

Deri lopa gliki hala,	[When I] sit do not lead me to error,
Gera lopa kolok hulir,	[When I] stand do not set me on a path to forgetting,

says a chanter on one occasion. On another, a chanter instructs spirits:

Deri lopa gliki hala,	[When I] sit do not lead me to error,
Gera lopa kolok hulir,	[When I] stand do let me retreat into forgetting,

Most of ritual speech is simple declaratives, highly elided.

Ritual language preserves cosmological axioms. Invention has no place in it, much less, creative composition on the part of individual chanters. Ritual language may be well or poorly executed in speech, but the assumption in Wai Brama is that it is the words of the ancestors, unchanged by chanters. It is whole and complete, and it is not composed of metaphors; listeners need not engage in interpretation. While recondite, its meanings are clear and unambiguous if they are understood at all. Its parallel form makes metaphor explicit; indeed, it reduces metaphoric freedom to an explicit minimum, leaving only precise metonymy. Its meanings are linguistically unidimensional. It contains few surprises, hence little information. It is thus *ritual* speech.

Performances of ritual speech are not subject to judgements on aesthetic grounds. Each chanter is as competent as the others. Each couplet spoken implies all other couplets, whether they are actually articulated on a given occasion or not – which, of course, they never are. Each couplet indexes every other. Hence, ritual speech is perfectly synecdochal – another way of saying that it is language stripped of the ambiguities of metaphor and reduced to inerrant metonymy.

Ritual language and the ritual speech in which it is manifested neither argues nor persuades; it is neither didactic nor expository. Above all, stripped of grammatical inflections for tense, number and agency, it says little about its grammatical subjects; it is in essence acausal, hence it does not predicate. Only in interpretation or translation into prose does it narrate history,[20] that is, the mythic histories of Wai Brama clans. Yet it is spoken, frequently but not necessarily in the presence of listeners (I hesitate to say audience). It is addressed as invocation to the noumenal presences in Wai Brama: *nitu* (spirits of the dead; ancestors), *guna déwa* (spirits of the springs and forest; the aboriginal spirits of Tana 'Ai) and *nian tana lero wulan* (the deity).

The ritual languages of Tana 'Ai and Sikka are substantially different from the day-to-day language of quotidian verbal communication. Ritual language is a formulaic poetical genre of Sara Tana 'Ai that is, while elided of grammatical inflections, nevertheless constrained to four words per line and is structured in couplets consisting of semantically paired words drawn from a stock of semantic dyads, many of which are the paired names of clan ancestors (Lewis 2013). Ritual language is so different from ordinary language that one is tempted to speculate that the neurological foundation of ritual speech may be different from that of ordinary speech. Speech in which words are ordered syntactically is largely (but not entirely) executed in the cortex of the human brain's left hemisphere. Some neurologists have recently suggested that the formulaic words of songs, prayers and expletives are stored in the right hemisphere and may be linked neurologically to the limbic system (Spinney 2007).

Ritual language is not narrative or story, although it indexes narratives. It evokes rather than narrates the stories it does not tell. These stories are myths, that is, narratives of origins, principally those of ancestors and clans.

From the perspective of its noumenal addressees, ritual speech is invocatory and invitational; it invites the spirits' attention and summons them into the presence of humans. For the spirits, ritual speech is oratorical. But for its living audience, it is ostension, a showing, a pointing out, an exhibition (if of nothing more than the chanters' skills) and ostensible, in both the sense of open to view and concealing real meaning behind a plausible (even meretricious) façade. In relation to the complex dramas of life, it is thus itself an element in a chiasmus.

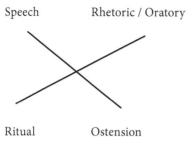

Speech   Rhetoric / Oratory

Ritual   Ostension

Cooking Rice for the Dead

Strecker has suggested that chiasmus may be found in dramas of life other than those of speech. In this there is potential for both gain and loss. The more general a concept, the less informative it is. But a general concept often equips us to see relations among many things more clearly than when we consider them more discretely. Such may be Strecker's idea of 'chiasmus phenomena'.

In the past, we have normally treated chiasmus as an element of rhetoric and as one of its devices, and rhetoric as employing oratory, the art of speaking in public eloquently or effectively. In Wai Brama, ritual speech is oratorical performance which involves a chanter and audience. That audience can be ancestral spirits, or spirits and men and women assembled together. Seldom is it addressed to the deity of the Ata Tana 'Ai. But such occasions are the most important in the ritual cycle of the domain. In general, ritual speech does not require a human audience since its efficacy lies not in the effects it creates in human listeners, but in consequent acts of spirits and the deity. Still, ritual speech can be heard – and listened to – by an audience. However that may be, ritual speech is a necessary component of all ritual.

Ritual also consists of acts which are not speech. These acts are sacrifices, which are acts of ostension. If we are to extend the concept of chiasmus to encompass acts other than speech and oratory, we must be confident that chiasmi can be found in acts of ostension and can be a device of ostension.

If we include in chiasmus events we may find outside of language such as ostensible decussations, inversions and reversals, then it may be useful to consider the rite of *hérin hugar*,[21] an inverted cooking of rice for the deceased, which takes place at the foot of the grave immediately after the inhumation of a corpse in Wai Brama.

A death in Wai Brama launches a sequence of three mortuary rites. The first is burial, which occurs as quickly after the death as possible, usually within hours. Each clan undertakes the third and final rites every few years for all its members who have died since the previous ritual. The rites of burial are sacrifices designed to prevent the newly released spirit from entering its mother's house, to which it is drawn.[22]

For *hérin hugar*, ritualists assemble rice and the accoutrements of cooking at the foot of the newly closed grave. Whereas rice is carefully cleaned before cooking for the living, a bit of soil may be added to the rice to be cooked for the dead. A ceramic cooking pot is upturned and placed on the ground. A dead taper is placed over the upturned pot or, more commonly nowadays, a gas cigarette lighter is flicked, backwards so that no flame is produced, above the pot. Water from a bamboo container and then rice are poured over the base of the upturned pot, thus running onto the ground. After a few moments, during which the rice for the dead 'cooks', the ritualist shatters the pot and bamboo water container, and slashes the basket in which the rice was brought to the grave site with his bush knife. He tosses the potsherds and tatters of the basket into the bush beyond the fence surrounding the house yard. Those in attendance then place offerings of tobacco and areca nut at the head of the grave, wash their hands, and retire to the house, thus ending the burial.

In Wai Brama, the dead inhabit a world that mirrors the world of the living. Everything in that world is the reverse, or an inversion, of things in the living world. Thus, if the newly deceased is to be given a meal, the procedure for cooking rice must be reversed: the fire is lit over the pot after it is placed on the hearth and does not burn, the pot is turned upside down, water is placed in (that is, outside) the pot before the rice is added, and vessels and utensils are destroyed so that they are whole for the dead; and all of this takes place at the border of the bush, the spirit's new (if temporary) home, rather than in the house.

Thus it seems that chiasmic phenomena are to be found in ritual in Wai Brama, but only in ritual's ostensible acts and not in speaking the language of ritual. Lest we are tempted to make too much of this, we should think of cooking for the dead as a chiasmus of a special kind, a liturgical chiasmus situated in the specific ritual context of a burial. Ritualists in that context are required to invert an ordinary sequence of actions but, as in ritual speech, they are not free to engage in the tropic playfulness of speech and action that occurs in everyday life.

If one asks about the rite at the foot of the grave, as I have done on the occasions of a number of burials, someone in Wai Brama will point out, usually with a grin or a giggle, that the cooking of rice is *hugar*, upside down, topsy-turvy and even – somewhat improprietously, given the circumstances

Figure 10.4 Chiasmic cooking of rice at the foot of the grave of Mo'an Rapa Ipir Wai Brama, the source of the domain of Tana Wai Brama, Munéwolon, 1979 (see Lewis 1988a: 275–80). (Photograph by E.D. Lewis)

in which it happens – humorous. I conclude from the cause attributed to Rénu's death and from their frank explanations of cooking for the dead that the people of Wai Brama fully appreciate the power and possibilities of chiasmus, and its dangers: the door to marvellous chaos and creativity which it opens must be kept firmly shut in dealings with the deity and spirits, as the boundary between the sacred and profane must be not be blurred.

CONCLUSION

Parallelism, I have argued, obviates chiasmus. Still, change creeps into ritual and into the verbal liturgy of ritual speech. Without violating the formulae dictated by semantic pairs, chanters can leave out bits of a history or an invocation. While missing couplets or episodes of a history may be indexed by what is said, they are not there; they are unsaid and may be forgotten in the next performance of the ritual or by the next generation of ritualists. Nonetheless, what is said preserves the cosmological axioms of the community's religion: the gendered cosmos, precedence in social relations, and the classifications by which the world is construed cognitively. All these are preserved by turning rhetoric into ritual. Rhetoric both creates and preserves culture.

The fatal sanction of chiasmus in ritual language, indeed the proscription of chiasmus in ritual speech and the fact that a proscription is needed, strongly suggest the power of creation and innovation inherent in the play of (and on) words in this rhetorical device. Ritual speech in Wai Brama is poetical, elegant, and expressive of the culture of the domain's people. But because of the information it encodes, it is not meant to be, and it cannot be, creative.

I would suggest that this negative instance, of a genre of oratory that is a-rhetorical, if not anti-rhetorical, argues strongly for the positive creativity of rhetoric. If, as Strecker and Tyler maintain, rhetoric structures culture and culture structures rhetoric (Strecker and Tyler 2009: 21), the abjuration of chiasmus in ritual language, the principal repository and medium of representation of Wai Brama expressive culture, denies a recursive relationship between culture and ritual. The words of Sara Tana 'Ai cast in the poiesis of ritual language become words set apart from the words of ordinary speech. They become sacred words, beyond time and change. If the relationship of their poiesis to culture were determinative or causal, the culture could not change. But, of course, culture does change. It changes in the daily to and fro of talk, negotiation, intentions, speakings and hearings conducted in ordinary speech, which provides ample territory for the techniques and devices of rhetoric. Thus, even within the parochial dynamics of the Wai Brama community, talk that changes things is in tension with the things unchangeable by speech. We find here insight into a particular ethnographic case and support for the Strecker and Tyler thesis.

This insight suggests another. In rituals in Wai Brama, the words of ritual speech are conceived (by the Ata Wai Brama themselves) to be the immutable words of the ancestors. Their recitation in performance, while thus informationless oratory, as an act, is the counterpart of sacrifice, a doing of something rather than a saying of something. Some time ago, I suggested that the acts that make up ostensible elements in Wai Brama ritual change over time from one performance or enactment to the next, and I proposed a mechanism by which such changes occur (Lewis 1989a). It may be that exigent speech and contingent sacrifice, the two components of a ritual enacted in a sacred space and time, actually serve as a means for accepting the changes brought about by rhetoric culture in the lives of the people and for incorporating those changes into 'culture'. One senses a mechanism of precedence (about which I have written at length) at work here. Moreover, in the tension between the unchangeable oratory and the mutable ostension of Wai Brama ritual, one suspects an interplay of rhetoric and culture, itself a chiasmus. But that is the subject of another essay.

For the people of Wai Brama, what it boils down to, with the same ambiguity in English as in Sara Tana 'Ai, is this: what the ancestors created, we preserve, so that what we create, the ancestors will sanction.

Notes

1. STA = Sara Tana 'Ai (the 'language' or 'way' of Tana 'Ai), the dialect of Sara Sikka (SS the language of Sikka) spoken in Tana Wai Brama; BI = Bahasa Indonesia, the national language of Indonesia derived from a dialect of Malay spoken on Sumatra and the archipelagic Malay of the Malayo-Indonesian islands. These abbreviations are used throughout. The inverted comma open to the left / ' / is a glottal stop, the presence or absence of which is phonemic in all Sikkanese dialects.
2. In STA, *gren mahé* is the 'celebration of the *mahé*', where *mahé* is the central sacrificial altar of the domain and the patch of forest in which the altar stands.
3. See Lewis 1996: 111–31, for a treatment of the temporal sequence in which invocation and sacrifice occurs in Tana 'Ai ritual.
4. Fox uses the words *oration* and *oratory* interchangeably. Performances in ritual language in Wai Brama are both oratorical and orations.
5. It is for this reason that one often finds a young man or even a boy performing the sacrifice of an animal. In every case, the sacrificer acts on behalf of a more senior person whose authority, in turn, can be traced in a sequence of delegations ultimately to the *tana pu'an* (SS 'source of the domain'), the ceremonial leader of the community.
6. See Lewis 1988a; Lewis 1988b: 246–81; Lewis 1989a: 175–98; Lewis 1989b: 490–501; Lewis 1996; and Lewis 2003: 27–51 on ritual and ritual language in Tana 'Ai. Lewis, Asch and Asch 1993 is a film about the *gren mahé* of Tana Wai Brama in 1980.
7. And their unexpected guest, Ms (later Professor) Janet Hoskins.
8. *Mo'an* (STA, SS) is an honorific of address and reference for men; *du'a* is the corresponding honorific for women.
9. George Steiner agrees, but calls this magical capacity *alternity*. 'We need a word which will designate the power, the compulsion of language to posit "otherness". ... Perhaps "alternity" will do: to define the "other than the case", the counter-factual propositions, images, shapes of will and evasion with which we charge out mental being and by means of which we build the changing, largely fictive milieu of our somatic and social existence. ... The dialectic of "alternity", the genius of language for planned counter-factuality, are *overwhelmingly positive and creative*' (emphasis added) (Steiner 1975: 222–23, 226; see also Lewis 1989a).
10. It is for this reason that ethnographers are justifiably interested in ritual and myth: it is in these systems of representation that the underlying reasons for the character of social relations in a community can be, if not observed, then at least reasonably inferred.

11. During the chanting, which lasted the whole of the second night of the *gren*, Timothy Asch filmed intermittently, but we left the Nagra tape recorder running continuously, except for reel and battery changes, while the Arriflex camera went on and off.

12. There is a complexity in this classification that can safely be ignored here: the compounds land–earth and sun–moon themselves are further distinguished by the recursive application of the fundamental classification of gender, such that land is masculine while earth is feminine and moon is feminine while sun is masculine, a formulation that looks suspiciously chiasmatic, but is not in its lexical rendition in ritual speech.

13. I should iterate that the recordings of chanting that night are long, and were almost, but not entirely, complete.

14. It is not often one finds pleonasm in a work as august as *Webster's*. Is not all speech expressive? We expect it to be so, thus even inexpressive speech expresses its own muddledness.

15. In a monographic treatment of the subject, the name of Richards would go here, along with a review of his contributions to the 'new rhetoric' of the twentieth century, especially Richards's *The Philosophy of Rhetoric* (1936).

16. A fuller citation is justified. Burke's 'eternal enigma' is being and non-being. In closing remarks on the relation between the permanent and the historic in his *Permanence and Change: An Anatomy of Purpose*, he makes the following somewhat doleful comment: 'We in cities rightly grow shrewd at appraising man-made institutions – but beyond these tiny concentration points of rhetoric and traffic, there lies the eternally unsolvable enigma, the preposterous fact that both existence and nothingness are equally unthinkable. Our speculations may run the whole gamut, from play, through reverence, even to an occasional shiver of cold metaphysical dread – for always the Eternal Enigma is there, right on the edges of our metropolitan bickerings, stretching outward to interstellar infinity and inward to the depths of the mind. And in this staggering disproportion between man and no-man, there is no place for purely human boasts of grandeur, or for forgetting that men build their cultures by huddling together, nervously loquacious, at the edge of an abyss' (Burke [1935] 1984: 272).

17. // to be read as 'paired semantically with'.

18. Larry McMurtry chose Whipple's antimetabole as an epigram for his novel, *Lonesome Dove*, which won the Pulitzer Prize for Fiction for 1986.

19. This idea is a powerful point of convergence between Tana 'Ai thought and Whipple's American West for a native Texan who has spent half his life living in and thinking about Flores.

20. And then only for the benefit of an anthropologist, who seeks meanings where, for his informants, there are only signs.

21. STA *hugar*, reversed, inverted, upside down; *hérin*, to cook.

22. The people of Tana 'Ai reckon descent through lines of mothers and daughters. Regardless of where they may reside, both women and men consider their mother's house to be their true home. For a fuller treatment of the mortuary cycle of the people of Wai Brama, including descriptions of the three mortuary rituals, see Lewis (1988a), Chapter XIII, 'The Life Cycle of the Spirit'.

References

Burke, Kenneth. 1968. *Language as Symbolic Action: Essays on Life, Literature, and Method.* Berkeley: University of California Press.

———. (1950) 1969. *A Rhetoric of Motives.* Berkeley: University of California Press.

———. (1935) 1984. *Permanence and Change.* Berkeley: University of California Press.

Cooper, Lane. 1932. *The Rhetoric of Aristotle.* Englewood Cliffs, NJ: Prentice-Hall.

Corbett, Edward P.J. (1965) 1971. *Classical Rhetoric for the Modern Student.* Second edition. New York: Oxford University Press.

Fox, James J. 1979. 'The Ceremonial System of Savu', in *The Imagination of Reality: Essays in Southeast Asian Coherence Systems,* ed. A.L. Becker and Aram A. Yengoyan. Norwood, NJ: Ablex Publishing Corporation.

Gove, Philip Babcock (ed.) 1971. *Webster's Third New International Dictionary of the English Language,* Unabridged. Springfield, MA: G & C Merriam Co.

Kennedy, George. 1997. *Comparative Rhetoric: An Historical and Cross-Cultural Introduction.* New York: Oxford University Press.

Lewis, E.D. 1988a. *People of the Source: The Social and Ceremonial Order of Tana Wai Brama on Flores.* Verhandelingen van het Koninklijk Instituut voor Taal-, Land- en Volkenkunde 135. Dordrecht, Holland and Providence, RI: Foris Publications.

———. 1988b. 'A Quest for the Source: The Ontogenesis of a Creation Myth of the Ata Tana 'Ai', in *To Speak in Pairs: Essays on the Ritual Languages of Eastern Indonesia,* ed. James J. Fox. Cambridge: Cambridge University Press.

———. 1989a. 'Why Did Sina Dance? Stochasm, Choice and Intentionality in the Ritual Life of the Ata Tana 'Ai of Eastern Flore', in *Creating Indonesian Culture,* ed. Paul Alexander. Sydney: Oceania Publications.

———. 1989b. 'Word and Act in the Curing Rituals of the Ata Tana 'Ai of Flores', *Bijdragen tot de Taal-, Land- en Volkenkunde* 145(4): 490–501.

———. 1996. 'Invocation, Sacrifice, and Precedence in the Gren Mahé Rites in Tana Wai Brama, Flores', in *For the Sake of Our Future: Sacrificing in Eastern Indonesia,* ed. Signe Howell. Leiden: Monographs of the Center for Non-Western Studies, Rijksuniversiteit te Leiden.

———. 2003. 'Ritual, Metaphor, and the Problem of Direct Exchange in a Tana Wai Brama Child Transfer', in *Framing Indonesian Realities: Essays in Symbolic Anthropology in Honour of Reimar Schefold,* eds Peter Nas, Gerard Persoon and Rivke Jaffe. Verhandelingen van het Koninklijk Instituut voor Taal-, Land- en Volkenkunde 209. Leiden: KITLV Press.

———. 2010. *The Stranger-Kings of Sikka.* Verhandelingen van het Koninklijk Instituut voor Taal-, Land- en Volkenkunde 257. Leiden: KITLV Press.

———. 2013. 'The Translation of the Said and Unsaid in Sikkanese Ritual Language', in *Astonishment and Evocation: The Spell of Culture in Art and Anthropology,* eds. Ivo Strecker and Markus Verne. New York: Berghahn Books.

———. (n.d.), Shot List (Visuals, Titles, Voice-Over Narration, and Sub-Titles) to *A Celebration of Origins.* Watertown, MA: Documentary Educational Resources, Inc., shot 90.

Lewis, E.D., Timothy Asch and Patsy Asch. 1993. *A Celebration of Origins: The Gren Mahé Rituals of Tana 'Ai.* Watertown, MA. Documentary Educational Resources, Inc., 16 mm film, 47 minutes, sound synch, colour.

Lewis, E.D. and Oscar Pareira Mandalangi. 2008. *Hikayat Kerajaan Sikka* [The Chronicles of the Rajadom of Sikka]. Maumere, Indonesia: Penerbit Ledalero.

Rappaport, Roy A. 1999. *Ritual and Religion in the Making of Humanity.* Cambridge: Cambridge University Press.

Richards, I. A. 1936. *The Philosophy of Rhetoric.* London: Oxford University Press.

Spinney, Laura. 2007. 'The Science of Swearing', *New Scientist* 2635/6: 52.

Steiner, George. 1975. *After Babel: Aspects of Language and Translation.* London: Oxford University Press.

———. 2001. *Grammars of Creation.* New Haven, CT: Yale University Press.

Strecker, Ivo and Stephen A. Tyler (eds). 2009. *Culture and Rhetoric.* New York: Berghahn Books.

Wallace, Anthony F.C. 1966. *Religion: An Anthropological View.* New York: Random House.

Whipple, T.K. 1943. *Study Out the Land: Essays by T.K. Whipple.* Berkeley: University of California Press.

CHAPTER 11

CHIASMUS, MYTHICAL CREATION AND H.C. ANDERSEN'S 'THE SHADOW'

Boris Wiseman, followed by a 'Response' from Lucien Scubla

■ ■ ■ ■ ■ ■ ■

MYTHICAL CREATION AND CHIASMUS

Whilst studying the myths told by various Amerindian societies, Lévi-Strauss noticed peculiar variations in the images they contained. For example, in one version of the story of Botoque (see *The Raw and the Cooked*, myths M7-M12) the hero, who has gone hunting for macaws, climbs a tree where he finds two eggs. He throws them to his brother-in-law who is waiting to catch them, but as they fall, they transform into stones that cut his brother-in-law's hands. In another version of this myth, told by a neighbouring population, Botoque climbs the ladder to the nest of macaws, and then lies to his brother-in-law, telling him that the nest is empty. His brother-in-law becomes impatient, so Botoque throws a stone at him (taken from his mouth, not the nest).

Lévi-Strauss's insight was to see that differences of this kind could be explained by a process of transformation. He came to articulate a theory of mythical creation whereby one myth is created by transforming elements borrowed from other myths, most often those told by neighbouring populations. He went on to develop one of the key twentieth-century theories of mythical invention, one in which logical substitutions and permutations, attributable to the unconscious combinatorial activity of the mind, give rise to a kind of constant kaleidoscopic rearrangement of mythical images. The four volumes of the *Mythologiques*, published between 1964 and 1971, follow this process of creation by transformation in minute detail from the furthest tip of southern Brazil to Oregon and the north-west coast of Canada.

Lévi-Strauss showed that the transformational process at work in the creation of Amerindian myths could be reduced to a relatively small number of rules or patterns, some of which resembled known musical structures (a fugue, a sonata, a rondo, etc.), while others required the articulation of a logic particular to mythical thought, but one closely linked to cognitive operations that Lévi-Strauss hypothesized were universal attributes of the way in which the human mind works. It was one of these patterns that Lévi-Strauss tried to grasp with his famous 'canonical formula', a formula which places chiastic inversion at the heart of mythical creation (Lévi-Strauss 1958b).[1] For Lucien Scubla, 'the formula is closely related to Lévi-Strauss's unaltered theoretical intuition, that of a morphodynamic process, inherent in mythical thought, engendering transformational cycles that display non-trivial loops' (Scubla 2001: 126). These 'non-trivial loops' and, more specifically, their affinity with chiastic reversal, are what will interest me here. Lévi-Strauss's canonical formula (CF) captures something of the very essence of the dynamism of chiastic inversion construed as a principle of aesthetic creation.[2] Recent studies, to which I will return, have explored the CF's applications in areas other than Amerindian mythology and have shown how to get beyond its seemingly austere formalism to tap into its explanatory potential. It is best thought of as what Tyler calls a 'thought picture' (this volume). Understanding the formula helps us to see the pattern when it recurs in a range of contexts, not just mythical. I treat it, though, as one among many possible mytho-poetic structures, and hence leave to one side the thorny question of the sense in which it is 'canonical'. It recurs in much the same way that the musical forms mentioned above recur in a range of musical and non-musical creations – François Truffaut's *Tirez sur le pianist*, for example, closely resembles a fugue. And in much the same way that mathematical and geometrical patterns – the Fibonacci sequence, for example – recur in music.

The standard version of the CF is usually expressed as follows:

$$fx(a) : fy(b) :: fx(b) : fa^{-1}(y)$$

The terms in the equation – 'a' and 'b' – are protagonists or 'agents'. In the Jivaro myths that Lévi-Strauss (1985) studies in *The Jealous Potter*, 'a' is a particular kind of bird, the Nighthawk – a solitary bird, known for its mournful cry. Each protagonist is associated with a 'function' (i.e. loosely speaking, a role or type of action). The Nighthawk, in Jivaro mythology, is associated with the function 'jealousy' (fx). The Nighthawk is a jealous bird or causes jealousy. There is another recurring protagonist in Jivaro mythology, a female character, who is term 'b' in this application of the CF. She is a potter. In the language of the CF, she supports the function 'potter'. Part of this way of seeing myth is derived from Vladimir Propp's influential *Morphology of the Folktale* which analyses the way in which the great variety of Russian folk tales are constructed out of a small number of recurring narrative situations and character types.

The CF is made up of four parts forming balanced pairs, and states an equivalence between the sets of relationships pertaining to each pair: $Fx(a)$: $Fy(b)$ on the one hand and $Fx(b)$: $Fa^{-1}(y)$ on the other. The moments of the CF describe a series of inversions that affect at once the attribution of functions to terms and the status of the terms and functions themselves. If one is to consider the formula as a whole, it is apparent that the terms switch place chiastically; in other words, they are redistributed to functions according to a cross-shaped pattern. However, as one tracks the transformations that link the four moments of the equation, one notices that in its final moment, one of the terms is replaced by its opposite ($a \rightarrow a\text{-}1$) and that it is simultaneously converted from a term into a function: $Fa^{-1}(y)$. This complicates the simple chiastic inversion the CF first seems to represent, and accounts for the distinctive double chiasm or 'double twist'[3] ('double torsion') that gives the CF much of its explanatory value. In the first half of the equation, the function fx (jealousy) is associated with the protagonist 'a' (Nighthawk) and the function fy (potter) with protagonist 'b' (woman). In the second half of the equation, it is the opposite. The function fx (jealousy) is first taken over by protagonist 'b' (woman) and then further twisted so as to give rise to an inverted Nighthawk function. In concrete terms, in the series of myths corresponding to the final moment of the equation (part 4), there is no mention of a Nighthawk. However, one finds in these myths another bird, the so-called Ovenbird, which occupies the same position as the Nighthawk, but whose every attribute is the opposite of those of the Nighthawk. Whereas the latter is a solitary, nocturnal bird, that lays its eggs directly on the ground and has morbid connotations, the former is a diurnal bird, that lives in harmony with its partner, constructs elaborate nests (out of clay) and is well known for its loquaciousness. The Ovenbird, in other words, is an inverted Nighthawk ($Nighthawk^{-1}$). Or rather, it converts the *term* Nighthawk into its inverted *function*, hence the double twist.[4] The CF is thus used in the *The Jealous Potter* to bring to light the underlying 'equation' around which the corpus of myths that Lévi-Strauss studies revolves. This equation, which one may also think of as a series of associations not unlike those that link images in Freudian dream-work, may be stated as follows: the function 'jealousy' (fx) of the Nighthawk (a) is to the function 'potter' (fy) of the woman (b) such as the function 'jealousy' (fx) of the woman (b) is to the inverted function Nighthawk (a^{-1}) of the potter

(y) [(Lévi-Strauss 1985: 79)]. This is the concealed 'proposition' organizing the surface narrative, the analogue of what psychoanalytic theories would see as the disavowed wish each dream expresses. It has no such status here, however. Far from expressing an unconscious wish, one is invited to see it as something like a logical tool for producing equivalences, whose manipulation is one of the means whereby the categories that underpin a given culture's belief-systems are supposed to be explained or generated.

In what follows, I will try to use the CF, without applying it systematically, to explore mythical resonances in H.C. Andersen's tale 'The Shadow' (1847). Before doing so, however, I would like to make three remarks about the relationship between mythical thought, the CF and chiasmus.

(1) As presented by Lévi-Strauss, the CF is not present in any particular myth, but rather constitutes a hidden armature upon which a series of myths are constructed. Each social group gives a new content to the formula within its particular historical and social context. Such a model splits mythical narratives into at least two levels of organization, that of the explicit story and that of the concealed armature (system of categories) underpinning it. The relationship between the two has often been presented by analogy with Saussure's distinction between the level of 'langue' and that of 'parole', which is another way of creating a textual unconscious (here, assimilated to intertextuality – the unconscious of one myth is another myth). This is no doubt valid, but the CF owes at least as much to Jakobson's understanding of the specificity of the poetic use of language, his famous theory of the 'poetic function' (Jakobson 1960). We know that this theory informed Lévi-Strauss's own theory of totemism (Lévi-Strauss 2008: 717) and the same basic model appears to have been subsequently transposed to the domain of myth, although Lévi-Strauss does not, to my knowledge, explicitly recognize the fact. Jakobson's theory of the poetic function is based on a blurring of the two linguistic operations that underpin ordinary communication: the *selection* of words from sets of semantic cognates (child, kid, toddler, etc.) and their combination into a *sequence* forming an utterance. As with Jakobson's 'poetic function', with myth there is 'a projection of the principle of equivalence from the axis of selection into the axis of combination' (Jakobson 1960: 358). In other words, an underlying equivalence – or equation – determines the sequence that makes up either the poetic phrase or the mythical narrative. In Jakobson's theory of the poetic use of language, what is being equated are sounds, whose similarity or dissimilarity determine, from below as it were, the poet's choice of words, as in Poe's: 'While I nodded, nearly *napping*, suddenly there came a *tapping*, As of someone gently *rapping*' (ibid.: 367–68). As Jakobson puts it 'The equation is used to build a sequence' (ibid.: 358). The nature of the 'equation' in poetry

is complex. It draws on more than mere phonetic resemblances. It includes rhythmic and syntactical considerations too, and many other features affecting the duration or modulation of sounds or sound patterns. The key point is the interconnection between sound and sense (absent in non-poetic uses of language). With Lévi-Strauss's CF, the equation connects different kinds of elements – an almost limitless list of images extracted from a social group's sensorium (animal species, plants, noises of various kinds, natural phenomena, etc.) which are turned into the terms and functions of a mytho-poetic equation. Here too, underlying equivalences determine the sequence which makes up the narrative. What is particularly significant in the present context is that the process whereby myth makers pass from the first level of mythical organization (the equation underlying a myth) to the second level (its instantiation in a narrative) involves a chiasm. Here the 'equation that determines the sequence' also determines that the sequence is twisted and even twisted twice. It is as if Levi-Strauss's model of mythical genesis constituted a kind of generalization of one very specific example of the poetic function, illustrated by the juxtaposition of two words in the first verse of the last stanza of Poe's famous poem *The Raven*: 'And the Raven, never flitting, still is sitting, *still is sitting*'. As Jacobson points out (1960: 372) it is because 'raven' and 'never' are inverted mirror images of one another (n-v-r → r-v-n) that one interprets their juxtaposition as a semantically meaningful one ('never', in turn, recalls the Raven's grim refrain 'nevermore' which evokes, by paronomasia, the lost Lenore). The phonetic reversal that links the two words grounds their semantic interplay. In its chiastic functioning, this simple example, used by Jakobson, provides a parallel of sorts for the more general principle illustrated by the CF: that of a formal equation producing meaning, and doing so by means of a kind of twisting of form. Chiastic reversal, in Lévi-Strauss's model of mythical genesis, is essentially what connects a narrative's explicit content to the equation underpinning it – it is constitutive of the chain of mythical transformations. The CF describes the evolutions of a germinal cell for which Poe's association of words provides a parallel of sorts. Its stages of development form a series of complicated loops that, together, form a cycle. As we shall later see, the final moment of the cycle – $fa^{-1}(y)$ – constitutes a kind of recapitulative involution, an inversion within an inversion. In short, what the CF tells us is that inverted symmetries (and inverted symmetries within inverted symmetries) are central to the dynamics whereby mytho-poetic thought, in whatever its guises, creates new myths out of old ones.

(2) The equation that underpins the CF has the form 'A' is to 'B' such as 'C' is to 'D' (A : B : : C : D). In other words, it has the form of what Aristotle called analogical metaphors (*Poetics*, 21, A1). And perhaps it is from analogy and

metaphor that it obtains its chiasticity, and hence its productivity – its capacity to generate new semantic worlds out of old ones.[5] Aristotle's famous example, given in the *Poetics*, is that of the 'dusk of life', whose meaning he derives from the implicit equation: youth is to old age such as dawn is to dusk. What is most relevant in the context of this argument is not so much the substitution of a metaphoric sense in place of a literal one, crucial though this is to an understanding of metaphors and their creative/disruptive powers. It is an almost incidental side effect of the use of analogical metaphors, a feature of the way in which they relate to one another (as opposed to the phenomenal world or to experience). As he conveniently puts it, they are often susceptible of reciprocal exchange. 'If the cup is the shield of Dionysus, then it is fitting for the shield to be called the cup of Ares'. Mythical transformations – the 'non-trivial loops' described by the CF – are in many ways extensions of this principle of reciprocal exchange, which dictates that the role of the two parts of a metaphor switch place: literal sense becomes figurative and figurative becomes literal. If the cup in the first part of the above example is literal and the shield its metaphorical substitute, the opposite is true in the second example. Nothing predestines a particular term to fulfil a literal or a figurative sense. They are defined as such in relation to one another, and can often be switched round. The struggle of the long-distance runner may provide a metaphor for life, just as the journey of life may be a metaphor for the struggle of the long-distance runner. In *The Story of Lynx*, Lévi-Strauss analyses a series of myths about the origins of wind and fog which revolve around a series of implicit associations. The first group of myths in the series equates the vaporized water of fog to a cloak worn by the sky or to a second skin. In the second, seemingly unrelated group of myths, it is the clothes and ornaments worn by human beings that are equated to astronomical phenomena – ornaments are to the skin what rainbows are to the sky, this group of myths suggests. The series of mythical transformations is obtained by a reciprocal exchange of the kind described above. The basic equation underlying this particular series of myths is: vapour : sky :: ornaments : skin. The myth's ability to generate new variations lies in part in the reversibility of the metaphorical equations that give rise to it, as well as to the possibility of connecting one set of metaphors to others, hence the layered nature of mythical codes.

(3) In concrete terms, the chiastic structure of the CF expresses the fact that the first and last myths in many of the transformational sequences studied by Lévi-Strauss are often symmetrically inverted versions of one another. The Bororo reference myth M1, with which the *Mythologiques* series starts, is a myth about the origin of rainwater that inverts a neighbouring Gé myth about the origin of fire. The equation that underpins this particular sequence is: $fire = water^{-1}$.

Significantly, the empirical evidence suggests that chiastic inversion occurs specifically when a myth crosses a cultural boundary (Lévi-Strauss 1973: 223). In other words, the process of inversion is inherently linked to the assimilation and appropriation by one social group of a mythical corpus borrowed from another social group. This confirms the affinity, noted by others in this volume, of the figure of chiasmus to liminality (we have already seen above that chiastic inversion is intimately connected to the process whereby a myth emerges from a set of structures that are essentially unconscious). Here, chiasmus appears as the privileged figure of the cultural encounter. In the Lévi-Straussian model, the point of contact between self and other is also the point upon which the mythical chiasms turn. Chiasmus, in this respect, is presented as a figure of regeneration. In the course of the process of dissemination, myths that are dislocated from their culture of origin lose some of their coherence. They tend to fall prey to an entropic principle, whose effects increase the closer one gets to the borderline between cultures, a place of mixing and merging. Lévi-Strauss's intuition, formalized by the CF, is that when a myth passes a certain threshold of coherence, instead of disintegrating entirely, it inverts, thus becoming something new and regaining its lost coherence. Chiasmus is a means by which myths (and maybe other kinds of creations) are reborn from their ashes. Lévi-Strauss illustrates his point by means of an analogy that may have been borrowed from Marx, that of the camera obscura. Marx (see *The German Ideology*) uses it to describe the inversion operated by ideology, which always presents, he claims, an upside down image of human beings and their relations. Lévi-Strauss's model of myth projects Marx's analogy from the vertical axes that connects infrastructures to superstructures onto the horizontal axes that connects one culture to its neighbours, in the process turning the analogy into a general principle of intercultural communication:

> The process is similar to that which occurs in optics. When an image is projected through a sufficiently large aperture it may be seen clearly. As one reduces the size of the aperture, the image progressively distorts and becomes difficult to perceive. Nevertheless, when the opening is reduced to no more than a point, which is when *communication* is on the verge of being interrupted, the image inverts and regains its clarity. (Lévi-Strauss 1973: 223; my translation)

A MYTHICAL MATRIX

In a pioneering study later taken up by Lucien Scubla (2001), Elli Köngäs Maranda and Pierre Maranda (1971) make a valuable connection between the structure of the CF and the key intuition at the origin of the structural theory of myth, namely that myths 'provide a logical model capable of overcoming a contradiction' (Lévi-Strauss 1958b: 264). In his seminal article on 'The Structure of Myths' (Lévi-Strauss 1958b), Lévi-Strauss had interpreted the references to agriculture and war in Zuni origin myths as a means of encoding the opposition between life and death. However, unlike life and death, it is possible to intercalate a third term between agriculture and war, namely hunting. Hunting is a form of killing, like war, but a form of killing that provides sustenance, like agriculture. Hunting is a mediating term, at once similar and different to the terms between which it has been inserted. In line with this problem-solving model of mythical invention, the Marandas proposed that the CF similarly describes the process whereby a problem or contradiction is first posed and then resolved. The equation first postulates the existence of two agents, 'a' and 'b', who are opposed to one another and who support antagonist functions: fx and fy. It then describes an intermediary stage, to which I will return, the equation's key third moment, and finally, in its last part, it resolves the initial conflict. This resolution is neither a simple victory – the reversal of the relation between 'a' and 'b' – nor a synthesis, in the manner of Hegelian dialectics, but rather the 'double twist' already evoked in what precedes.

Scubla's gloss on this interpretation of the CF is worth citing in full, as it relates the CF to elemental mythical scenarios that are no doubt important to mythical creation across a large number of different cultures. As we shall see below, his model also seems to fit well H.C. Andersen's 'The Shadow':

> In many tales a is a negative character (the traitor, the seducer, etc.) who epitomizes Evil, represented by the function fx, while b is the hero, the righter of wrongs and defender of Good, represented by the function fy. Hence the opposition fx(a) : fy(b), the first side of the canonical formula, which simply expresses the conflict of antithetical values exemplified respectively by a and b. Then, the hero plays the role of mediator inasmuch as he turns the negative value with which the evil character is endowed against the latter, but only by assuming it himself for a time in the process, the outcome of which is the defeat of the adversary and the triumph of Good over Evil. Hence the presence of the expression fx(b) at the beginning of the second side of the formula, indicating that the hero b is taking charge of the counter-value x in his fight against a, and also the specific structure of the final component $fa^{-1}(y)$, expressing the idea that the triumph of Good cannot be reduced to an elimination of Evil, in other words that $fa^{-1}(y) > fx(b)$. (Scubla 2001: 138)

In Scubla's translation of the CF, its third moment, the moment when the agent of Good briefly takes on the function previously associated with his antagonist, corresponds not so much to a moment of mediation (as Maranda and Maranda conceive it) but to a moment of contagion and undifferentiation (mixing). In Scubla's version, the formula starts with opposition (A/B), brings about mediation or mixture (M) and finally resolves this situation by means of a twist that is productive of new differences (X). Hence his own simplified presentation of the canonical formula: A/B → M→ X, which captures the basic pattern of foundation myths which 'describe the passage from the undifferentiated world of primeval times to the highly differentiated world of the present time through the mediation of a singular event' (Scubla 2001: 193). The final part of the formula, $fa^{-1}(y)$, then becomes '[the] stage on which the mediation [or mixing] process is reversed' (ibid.: 140). The denial of symmetry is crucial to the dynamism of the CF as a generative principle. The formula is not:

$Fx(a) : fy(b) :: fx(b) : fy(a)$.

This version of the CF, evocative of Anthony Paul's balanced and orderly 'cross-shaped' chiasmus that avoids contradiction or the clash of meaning (this volume) constitutes an essentially sentimental version of the CF. It describes the simple victory of Good over Evil – the Evil doer becomes a doer of Good: $fx(a) → fy(a)$. By contrast, the double twist by which the formula actually concludes, suggests a complex transformation of the 'good' character, one that reminds us of the point made several times elsewhere in this volume, that the recurring terms of a chiasmus do not recur as the *same* terms. In Scubla's words: 'the final victory of Good (y) bestows on the latter a force it clearly did not yet have at the start of the conflict between a and b' (ibid.: 138). Hence not only is $fa^{-1}(y) > fx(b)$ but $fa^{-1}(y) > fy(b)$. Scubla further explains this as follows: 'the exaltation of Good is closely connected to the annihilation of its adversary: a becoming a^{-1}. So that the final expression of the canonical formula, $fa^{-1}(y)$, would then mean that the apotheosis of Good (y) can only be achieved on the corpse (a^{-1}) of an evildoer' (ibid.: 138). To which one should add that the conversion $a → a^{-1}$ implies an incorporation of the evildoer into the hero, evocative of certain theories of cannibalism. Scubla sums up the key intuition towards which the preceding interpretations of the CF converge. What the CF captures is 'the idea of a *generative conflict*, the idea that every structure is born from the conflict between two antagonists who also attract one another' (Scubla 1998: 11). Every chiasmus, one might add, is at once structure and process, a form – X – whose parts can be grasped synchronically, and a process whose moments require a sequential understanding.

H.C. Andersen as Mytho-Poet

A number of the insights into morphogenetic[6] processes derived from the above discussions of the CF and its chiastic features may be used to read Andersen's tale, 'The Shadow' (1847). The tale may be summarized as follows: Whilst on vacation in a hot country, a learned man loses his shadow. Having sent it in jest to investigate his mysterious neighbour's apartment, he wakes up to find that his shadow has truly gone. For many years the learned man lives with this curious lack, until one evening, as he is sitting in his parlour, there comes a knock on his door. He opens it to discover an exceedingly thin but well dressed man who turns out to be none other than his fugitive shadow, now almost human. The learned man discovers how his shadow transformed into human form in the dwelling place of Poetry (the mysterious apartment he had sent his shadow to investigate). Sometime later, the learned man and his shadow agree to go on a journey together to a distant kingdom, but this time it is the learned man who will play the role of the shadow's shadow. Once arrived at the kingdom, the shadow meets the king's daughter whom he seduces. When the shadow tells the learned man that he plans to marry the princess, the learned man threatens to reveal the shadow's true identity. But no one believes him any longer. Under the guise of mercifully putting him out of his misery, the shadow has his old master executed and marries the princess, thus ensuring that he will soon himself become king.

'The Shadow' tells a typically Hegelian story, that of the slave turning the table on his master. One of its culminating points occurs when the emancipated shadow turns to his former master, now his own shadow, and accuses him of impersonating a human being. His perverse statement of the very opposite of what is true captures verbally the shadow's sadistic subjugation of the learned man.

The relationship between learned man and shadow is chiastic through and through. These characters are conceived from the start as inverted mirror images of one another (they are not merely doppelgangers). This is revealed discreetly, for example, in a seemingly anodyne piece of dialogue. Having invited the learned man to accompany him on a trip, the shadow asks for the learned man never to reveal the shadow's true identity. The learned man accepts and adds: 'I promise, and a man is true to his word', to which the shadow replies 'A word is true to its shadow', the narrator adding: 'And of course that was the way it had to talk' (Anderson 2005: 227).

Other details confirm that a structure of inversion binds the two central protagonists together, such as the compromise that the learned man and the shadow arrive at regarding the terms of address they use with one another. The shadow refuses to be addressed with the familiar 'du' form but accepts

to use 'du' when he himself addresses the learned man. This has been interpreted as a fictional reworking of an episode from Andersen's life. But it is
also a natural consequence of the rooting of the tale in the inversion: master/
slave → slave/master. Like all the other aspects of the relationship between
these two characters, the way in which they address one another also map
onto a figure of chiastic inversion.

	addresses using	is addressed using
shadow (oppressor)	du	dem
learned man (kind)	dem	du

This basic generative cell dictates the curious relationship that the central
characters entertain with the alternation of day and night. One may easily
understand why the presence/absence of the sun may become an important
feature of a tale in which one of the central characters is a shadow. It is used
here, however, in a special way, one that ties this story to a recurring motif
well known to Andersen scholars (Massengale 1993), that of two mutually
exclusive words (the drama in Andersen's tales often results from characters'
inability to cross the boundary between two such worlds). The excessively
bright midday sun makes the shadow shrink, while the softer light of the
moon or candles extends the shadow, giving it supernatural proportions. In
the scene in which it gains its independence, it 'stretches', anthropomorphic-
ally, all the way to the neighbour's balcony. The opposite is true of his master,
as the shadow notes: 'In the moonlight I was almost more distinct than you
were' (Andersen 2005: 229). Later on in the story, master and shadow walk
together 'side by side, in front or in back, depending on where the sun stood'
(ibid.: 230). The sun ensures that they endlessly switch positions without
ever being together in the same place. When the one appears, the other must
disappear.

It is of course in the series of transformations in the identities of the
characters that the chiastic and perhaps mythical imaginary governing this
story is most clearly apparent. The first part of the story in effect explains
how a shadow takes on human form while the second how a human being
is transformed into a shadow – first symbolically, by becoming his shadow's
shadow (a slave), then literally, when he is put to death. It is at this level that
the relationship of the tale to the specific structures of the canonical formula is most apparent, albeit a somewhat modified, perhaps even dislocated
canonical formula.

First of all, the story fits the three moments of the canonical formula as
analysed by Scubla and summed up in his simplifying diagram A/B → M →X,
already cited above. It follows the same basic pattern whereby an opposition

or conflict between characters (master and shadow) is first mediated by one of the characters who assumes for himself the value associated with his opponent and then goes on to defeat that opponent (see above). How is this?

Moment 1: The 'conflict of antithetical values' (i.e. that which is symbolized in the CF by the opposition between fx(a) and fy(b), the first half of formula) is not, here, initially, an overt combat but a political fight, one might say – a fight to have one's identity recognized by the Other. The shadow's desire, at first, is to be valued on an equal footing with a human being. His struggle is psychological as much as physical, and in this respect Andersen's tale marks its distances with mythical structures and enters a more literary universe (see Scubla's 'Response' on this evolution). Despite this, in another respect, the beginning of Andersen's tale remains close to the structure of foundation myths that Scubla's template describes. This is arguably one of its originalities for, like myth, it accounts for the origin of conflict by showing the 'passage from the undifferentiated world [of primeval times] to the highly differentiated world of the present'. Indeed, the moment when the story first steps into fantasy, when the shadow splits from his master, is the moment when doubles – a man and his shadow – become opposites. Observing his shadow projected onto his neighbour's house, the learned man jokingly invites it to go in and find out who lives there. He nods to his shadow and the shadow nods back, as may be expected. Then 'the stranger turned, and his shadow turned too' (ibid.: 225), each disappearing into a *different* world, respectively, the learned man's house and what we will later discover is the dwelling place of Poetry (the mysterious and luminous house across the road). The moment when master and shadow simultaneously stand up and turn looks like a moment of undifferentiated repetition, but repetition conceals differentiation – Self becomes Other.

As is the case with foundation myths, this original act of differentiation sets the story and mytho-poetic thought in motion by creating opposition and conflict. It starts the series of canonical 'loops' whose role is to resolve the contradiction that gave rise to them (more on this contradiction below). From this moment onwards, we enter a sequence of a type that is reminiscent, although not exactly, of the CF. For the formula is reversed; the story is not that of the triumph of Good over Evil but Evil over Good. Accordingly, with Andersen, it is the Evil character, not the Good one, that occupies the key role of the mediating figure (he is the hero of the story).

Moment 2: The mixing associated with the third term of the CF and the second moment of Scubla's simplified rendition of it, consists in an exchange of functions: fx(a) → fx(b). It occurs in Andersen's tale when the shadow first returns. By now, the shadow has started to take on a recognizably human form – in other words, he has started to take over the function 'human' of the learned man. In the process, he has also taken on his knowledge and understanding, since the metamorphoses operated in the dwelling of Poetry gives the shadow Faust-like omniscience – 'I've seen everything, and I know', says the transformed shadow (Andersen 2005: 230). The role of both characters is to name the world. However, unlike the learned man, who reveals 'the true the good and the beautiful', as we are told on more than one occasion (e.g. on p. 230) the shadow reveals 'what an ignoble world it is' (ibid.: 229).

Instead of a hero taking on the negative attributes of an evil-doer in order to conquer him, we have the opposite: an (anti-)hero converting a positive attribute (knowledge) to his advantage (the shadow uses his knowledge of other peoples' guilty secrets as a means of acquiring power and wealth). This 'mixing' of functions, which is a sign of the proximity of Andersen's tale to mythical modes of creation, here results in a transformation in the physical appearance of the character who supports it. When the shadow returns as the exceedingly thin being that the learned man at first does not recognize, he is part-shadow, part-human.

Moment 3: It is more difficult to say in what way Andersen's tale operates a form of closure similar to the double twist of the canonical formula, $fa^{-1}(y)$.[7] The king's daughter is the means by which the shadow carries out his main task: the symbolic inversion that is the killing of the learned man, which is also the condition of his own apotheosis (he goes on to marry the princess and rule with her over the kingdom). But this is no more than chiastic reversal, although one in which, as Scubla points out (see his 'Response' below), the perpetrator of the evil deed acquires an enhanced status in comparison to the figure he had to eliminate to acquire it.

To see the double twist, one needs to return, here, to the problem-solving model of myth-making which Maranda and Maranda argue lies behind the CF. The particular problem that 'The Shadow' takes up is inherited from Plato. It is that of the nature of images. The question preoccupied Plato throughout much of his life and he approached it in different works from different angles. For example, in one of the great middle period dialogues, the *Phaedo*, the question of the image is linked to metaphysical problems, in particular that of the relationship between the world of Forms and that of things (in the later *Sophist* it is linked to a problem that was to open the way for the discipline of logic, that of the status of false statements). Plato's formulations set the scene for a certain conception of phenomenal reality that was to shape much of subsequent Western thought, through the Middle Ages, the Renaissance and up to Modernity. He essentially construed the relationship between the world of Forms (or Ideas) and perceptible reality by means of an analogy between original and copy. In this scheme, phenomenal reality itself is relegated to the rank of a mere image or appearance.

The relationship between shadow and learned man is of a similar kind. Andersen's tale takes place in a world that is reminiscent of Plato's cave, one in which reality is endlessly divisible into ever more subtle grades of appearances. We are in the same un-decidable universe in which projections of seemingly real things hide further projections (thus, when the shadow splits away from his master, another, smaller shadow starts to grow in his place). In the Platonic scheme, the images made by artists are the lowest kinds of copies, endowed with the least degree of reality. He calls them 'semblances' or 'phantasma'. They occupy a rank beneath those other kinds of copies (indeed copies of copies, since reality is itself an image) which are manufactured objects, such as a bed or a table. At least these keep the proportions of the original which they seek to replicate, Plato argues, whereas the sculptor, for example, must distort the top of a very large statue so that it does not look too small at a distance. The work of art thus occupies the lowest rank in a descending scale.

Andersen's cast of characters have been let loose to explore the familiar terrain of the image, marked out by Plato. They have donned Platonic clothes, those of the eikon (likeness) the phantasm and their various models. But as one might expect from a maker of semblances such as Andersen, the story he tells takes a deliberately contrary view of things, and it is here that we encounter again the canonical formula. One might think of the shadow's story as the story of the revenge of the signifier over the signified. The above Platonic scheme institutes an order in which representations of things (signifiers) are always engendered by and come after the things they signify. The mathematician René Thom captures this principle very well: 'In the interaction of signified and signifier it is plain that, swept along by the universal flow, the signified emits, engenders the signifier in an uninterrupted, ramifying growth' (cited in Lévi-Strauss 1987: 216). In the world of 'The Shadow', however, the opposite is true.

Let us look again at the terms and functions in Andersen's story. We have seen that the shadow, as he comes to occupy the position of the mediator fx(b) assumes for himself the function of the learned man, which is essentially to name the world, although he inverts that function since what he names is that which is Evil, whereas the learned man names 'the true, the good and the beautiful'. Both characters are what one might call 'predicators', but the learned man fails in this domain, whereas the shadow is successful. It is what he asserts to be true about the world that is believed and indeed is what allows him to dominate others. His ascendency over the learned man starts when he insists that everyone call the learned man 'shadow', whereas the learned man's own threat to reveal that the shadow is masquerading amounts to nothing. There is a figure in Andersen's story who may be said to embody – quite literally – the function 'naming'; it is the allegorized figure of Poetry. And it is from Poetry (i.e. the signifier) that the shadow is born, as his nakedness discreetly indicates. In other words, Andersen's tale does not convert a term into an inverted function, as is the case in the closing sequence of the CF, but an inverted function into a term – allegorized Poetry, who in turn gives birth to a double, the shadow, who may thus be said to more generally represent fiction. Poetry's progeny is a curiously ambiguous figure. When he first knocks on his former master's door, it is only his smart clothes and fashionable accessories that make him seem human: 'The shadow was dressed all in black, made from the finest black cloth, with patent leather boots, and a top hat that could be snapped closed so only the crown and brim remained. ... The shadow was exceptionally well dressed, and that was exactly what made him a human being' (Andersen 2005: 227). The clothes only thinly conceal the shadow's lingering and disturbing alterity, the void beneath the clothes that relegates the shadow to the realm of mere appearances and assimilate him to a sort of dislocated signifier in want of a signified. In *The Sophist*, Plato asks about the image: how can there be something which seems real without being real? When the shadow first returns he is the very embodiment of this contradiction. But rather than be damned by it, as it were, he turns it into his strength. For here, unlike in Plato's scheme, it is the image or phantasm – in modern terms, the signifier – that has the last word. The twists and turns of the canonical formula are here the means of a mythopoetic reminder, one similar to that made by René Thom in the second part of the citation started above. Having stated the general rule that the signified engenders the signifier in an uninterrupted ramifying growth, he goes on to remark: 'But the signifier re-creates the signified every time we interpret the sign. And, as exemplified by biological forms, the signifier (the offspring) can become the signified (the parent); all it takes is a single generation' (cited in Lévi-Strauss 1987: 216).

'The Shadow', one may conclude, functions in the manner of an Amerindian myth in as much as it contains a system of images that stand in lieu of concepts, which can be used to solve a problem or paradox, although the term 'solve' is perhaps misleading. The images deployed by mythical thought allow the transposition or displacement of the terms of a problem into another set of terms, here fictional, which can themselves be manipulated. It is a sort of tool for analogical transposition. The story of the learned man and his shadow is a tool of this kind, or at least it is *also* a tool of this kind, one that allows us to put to the test a whole series of unquestioned assumptions about the genealogical relationship between reality and appearance, model and image, signifier and signified, as well as the many other systems of thought that these genealogies hold in place.

At the time of writing an early draft of this essay, I sent it to Lucien Scubla, asking him for his comments. What I received in return turned out to constitute a far more substantive response than one might expect on such occasions. The relevance of his remarks to the topic under discussion here, and the interest that they present in particular for H.C. Andersen scholars, convinced me that they should be published here in extenso. *I would like to thank Lucien Scubla for his remarks.*

Response by Lucien Scubla – 27 July 2010

'H.C. Andersen and the Canonical Formula'

I have just read the Andersen tale and the study you have made of it. Two things struck me whilst reading the story: the fact that its narrative armature is rooted in mythical and ritual sources and that these have been elaborated upon according to more modern literary canons. To my mind, this situates Andersen's story somewhere in-between the fairy tale and the novel.

This story, which ends in a marriage with a princess, is clearly constructed according to the model of what Marie Delcourt, in her book on Oedipus, calls 'the legend of the conqueror'. In it, a hero wants to accede to the throne, but must first overcome obstacles, which includes the murder of a figure preventing him from fulfilling his ambition. The Andersen tale is a variant of this scenario.

The specificity of Andersen's version is best grasped by means of a comparison with two or three Classical examples. In the Roman ritual of the 'King of Nemi', which Frazer took as a guiding thread for his celebrated study of sacred kingship (*The Golden Bough*), the new king must always kill his predecessor. The same is true, despite many differences between them, in the two versions of the legend of the Ring of Gyges respectively told by Plato and Herodotus. In the reformulations of Greek myths by Classical tragedians, Oedipus kills a man who is both the ruling king and his father. In Andersen's tale, to accede to the throne, the shadow must kill what one might think of as his 'symbolic father'.

In each case, we encounter the same conflict, leading to the same kind of outcome. The old king is supplanted by a young king, the father by his son, the man by his shadow.

What is new about the Andersen tale is how that outcome is reached. The actions of the hero are no longer determined by ritual obligations nor are they the result of an inescapable destiny – they arise from the hero's exercise of his free will. Throughout the tale, the shadow demonstrates that he is calculating and cunning. He lies to his master by laying claim to an omniscient understanding that he is unable to prove when challenged by the princess. He is forced to deceive her and then to falsely claim that the learned man has gone mad. His duplicity is summed up by the grief that he expresses at the death that he himself has caused. Far from being constrained by ritual prescriptions or the forces of destiny, it is he who tricks everyone and pulls the strings behind the scenes. It is in this respect that H.C. Andersen's tale departs from the ritual and mythical sources on which it draws to elaborate new narrative structures of the kind belonging to the novel. The materials are the same as those used by Classical authors but they have been disassociated from their traditional ritual functions. One of the classical attributes of the king is 'to see without being seen'. Whether he likes it or not, the sacred king must not be scrutinized by others. He must live secluded in his palace and is often concealed by a screen when he receives visitors. This is part of the 'burden of kingship' that Frazer described so well. In Andersen's tale, the shadow uses his guile to enter the private worlds of human beings and steel their secrets for his own benefit. The shadow is not a sacred figure but an impostor.

It is interesting that as myths, legends and fairytales evolve away from their common ritual sources, they also distance themselves from reality by incorporating fantastical elements. In the ritual of Nemi and Herodotus' version of the legend of Gyges, there are no magical features. In Plato's version of the Ring of Gyges, it is the discovery of a ring which renders its carrier invisible that gives Gyges the idea of killing the king and taking his place. In Andersen's story, fiction wins over reality in every sense. In this respect, as you say in your own way, the tale, which ends with the triumph of the shadow, tells the story of the apotheosis of Poetry, i.e. of fiction. The learned man represents the real world, which he must try to describe as accurately as possible, albeit by bringing to light a hidden reality concealed beyond the world of appearances. The shadow represents Poetry, which is to say fiction, i.e. the colourful display of illusions, fantastical and imaginary worlds. Reality and fiction clash, as do science and poetry, and it is the latter that is victorious, at least within the fictional world of Andersen's fairytale …

If this analysis is correct, does the recourse to the canonical formula help us consolidate or add to it? Several reasons suggest one should advance cautiously.

First of all, what we are dealing with here is not a myth, but a fairytale that has distanced itself from its mythical sources. It is true that Lévi-Strauss himself first of all applied his formula to a ritual (the *naven* ritual), not a myth. But that does not detract from my point if one admits, alongside Hocart and the Cambridge ritualists, that myth itself derives from ritual and that they therefore share similar structures. The structures found in fairytales are not always traceable to ritual sources.

Indeed, you yourself indicate that Andersen's tale is best discussed not so much in terms of the standard version of the canonical formula, but a weakened version of it, which you do not fully explicate. It seems to me that that version is the Mosko version, itself slightly modified: fx(a) : fy(b) : : fx(b) : fy'(a). I have substituted y' > y to indicate that, after the final reversal, the shadow (a) does more than take the place of the learned man, he comes to occupy a higher position than him. Expressed in Hegelian terms, one might say that in becoming his master's master, the slave has acquired a higher rank than his master originally had.

Furthermore, the canonical formula, as you remind us, ends with the closure of a loop.[8] In this fairly tale, this does not happen. It presents a simple chiastic reversal. The situation at the end of the story does not bring us back to the beginning; it is diametrically opposed to it.

Also, in your preliminary remarks on analogy, you underline the principle of reversibility. If A : B : : C : D, then C : D : : A : B, and vice versa. This may be true when A, B, C and D are numbers. I am not convinced it is always the case when they are not. The example you give

vapour : sky : : ornaments : skin

does not seem easily reversible to me. In French at least, the inverted formula has an odd ring to it. What does express perfect reciprocity, is the Mosko formula, i.e. the canonical formula minus its double twist[9] (the formula reduced to a sort of chiasmus):

fx(a) : fy(b) : : fx(b) : fy(a)

a formula in which functions (x,y) exchange their arguments (a,b), in the same way that two clans exchange wives, according to the model of restricted exchange (Kariera system). In mathematics, this formal corresponds to a Klein group.

Notes

1. See also: Maranda and Maranda 1971; Racine 1995 (section on 'mirror symmetries'); Scubla 1998 (in particular pp. 78–81 and 177–78); and Scubla 2001.

2. The argument that follows focuses on the question of mytho-poetic genesis. It tries to grasp a recurring feature in a creative syntax. However, the questions it addresses have counterparts in pragmatics and rejoin the terrain of mnemonics. Chiastic patterns are also important because they help in the recollection and transmission of complex narratives. Biblical scholarship has shown, for example, that chiastic sequences play an important part in the constitution of narrative units. This use of chiasmus is particularly important in oral traditions. Edwina Palmer (2000: 81)

has recently argued that the chiastic reversals that one finds in the word play that is typical of ancient Japanese Fudoki poetry is a vestige of a pre-literate oral heritage. Palmer associates these reversals with practices of synonymic substitutions, which are common in such poetry. One is reminded, here, of Saussure's still unproven but influential theory that Latin Saturnian verse and Vedic hymns contain concealed anagrams of key words (hypograms). These examples also relate to oral traditions, and it may not be a coincidence that a writer so chiastic in his literary imagination as H.C. Andersen had one foot in oral tradition (his first tales were reworkings of popular stories he heard in the workhouses of Odense, Denmark). Each of these examples point towards a more general and widespread 'anagrammatic function' underpinning poetic invention as such, of which chiastic reversal may be seen to be a special case.

3. Hence the title of Maranda's (2001) edited volume on the CF: *The Double Twist*. See also the special issue of *L'Homme* (1995, Vol. 35) devoted to the CF.

4. Could the double twist of the CF be a reminiscence of gift theory? The rights and duties that bind the parties involved in gift exchange are also symmetrical but contrary. And if gifts must be returned – you must give to me, as I give to you – it is in part because the failure to do so threatens to invert the value of the gift, to turn it into poison ($a \to b \to b \to a^{-1}$). According to this reading, the force of the gift resides in the reversibility of its social value.

5. Luc Racine has shown (1995) that although the CF contains an analogy it cannot be *reduced* to an analogy.

6. Its concern is 'the genesis of form'. Its sources lie in the study of the creation of biological forms. See, for example, the pioneering work of Scottish naturalist, D'Arcy Wentworth Thompson, whose significance for the foundation of structural anthropology has been acknowledged by Claude Lévi-Strauss. For a presentation of morphogenetics, see Petitot-Cocorda 1985.

7. My focus here is on the story itself, rather than its connections to other texts, which would no doubt offer other possibilities and enable one to place the story in a transformational group. Victor Stoichiṭă (1997) has usefully brought to light a recurring medieval motif, that of a shadow that witnesses the crime committed by its owner. Here, the shadow is a personification of guilt and often drives its owner to commit suicide. Could the shadow's crime in Andersen's tale be seen as an inverted suicide and thus be connected by transformation to the mythical schemas identified by Stoichiṭă? No doubt yet other possibilities would be provided by a close scrutiny of the relationship between Andersen's text and one of its acknowledged sources, Adelbert von Chamisso's *Peter Schlemihl*.

8. I usually express this canonical closure, this looping of a loop, in simplified form, by means of two complementary formulas, one dynamic, the other static. In other words I represent it as a dynamic process (a transformational series) : A/B --> M --> X --> [A'/B'] in which a structural relation is maintained (the invariable component of the transformation) A : B : : M : X : : [A' : B']. I sometimes illustrate this with respect to the first two volumes of Lévi-Strauss's *Mythologiques*, which analyse a process raw/cooked --> honey --> tabacco --> [nature/culture] and a relation raw : cooked : : honey : tobacco : : [nature : culture]. Indeed, tobacco smoke reestablished the difference between nature and culture that honey had blurred (since the former represents the ascending movement towards the spiritual – i.e. culture – and that

the latter is a paradoxical foodstuff, ready for human consumption, but prepared, i.e. cooked, by nature, as it were).

9. The double twist consists in transforming fy(a) into $fa^{-1}(y)$, which implies two operations: the inversion of the term (a) and the exchange of values between functions and terms – a becomes a^{-1} and, by virtue of a sort of supplementary chiasm, fy(a) becomes fa(y). As J. Morava has shown, the simplified version of the canonical formula (Mosko version) corresponds to a Klein group in mathematics; whereas Lévi-Strauss's canonical formula proper takes us into the realm of quaternion groups.

References

Andersen, Hans Christian. 2005. 'The Shadow', in H.C. Andersen, *Fairy Tales*, trans. Tiina Nunnally. London: Penguin, pp. 223–35.

Jakobson, Roman. 1960. 'Linguistics and Poetics', in Thomas A. Sebeok (ed.), *Style in Language*. Massachussets: MIT, pp. 350–77.

Lévi-Strauss, Claude. 1958a. 'La Geste D'asdiwal', *Annuaire de l'Ecole pratique des hautes études. Section des sciences religieuses (1958-1959)*: 3–43.

———. 1958b. *Anthropologie structurale*. Paris: Plon.

———. 1973. *Anthropologie structurale deux*. Paris: Plon.

———. 1985. *La Potière jalouse*. Paris: Plon.

———. 1986. *The Raw and the Cooked*, trans. John and Doreen Weightman. Harmondsworth: Penguin.

———. 1987. *The View From Afar*, trans. Joachim Neugroschel and Phoebe Hoss. London: Penguin.

———. 2008. *Œuvres*. Paris: Gallimard, Editions de la Pléiade.

Maranda, Pierre (ed.). 2001. *The Double Twist: From Ethnography to Morphodynamics*. Toronto: University of Toronto Press.

Maranda, Elli Köngäs, and Pierre Maranda. 1971. *Structural Models in Folklore and Transformational Essays*. The Hague: Mouton.

Massengale, James. 1993. 'A Divided World: A Structural Technique in Andersen's Original Tales', in Johan de Mylius, Aage Jørgensen and Viggo Hjørnager Pedersen (eds), *Andersen og Verden*. Odense: Udgivet of H.C. Andersen-Centret, pp. 262–75.

Palmer, Edwina. 2000. 'The "Womë-No" Poem of "Harima Fudoki" And Risudal Orality in Ancient Japan', *Bulletin of the School of Oriental and African Studies* 63(1): 81–89.

Petitot-Cocorda, Jean. 1985. *Morphogenèse du sens*. Paris: PUF.

Propp, Vladimir. 1968. *Morphology of the folktale*, trans. Laurence Scott. 2nd edition. Austin/London: University of Texas Press.

Racine, Luc. 1995. 'La formule canonique du mythe: analogie et cassifications sociales', *L'Homme* 135: 25–33.

Scubla, Lucien. 1998. *Lire Lévi-Strauss: le déploiement d'une intuition*. Paris: Odile Jacob.

———. 2001. 'Hesiod, the Three Functions, and the Canonical Formula of Myth', in Pierre Maranda (ed.), *The Double Twist: From Ethnography to Morphodynamics*. Toronto: University of Toronto Press, pp. 123–55.

Stoichiță, Victor. 1997. *A Short History of the Shadow*. London: Reaktion.

NOTES ON CONTRIBUTORS

■ ■ ■ ■ ■ ■ ■

Ben Bollig is Fellow and Tutor in Spanish at St Catherine's College, University of Oxford. He published *Néstor Perlongher: The Poetic Search for an Argentine Marginal Voice* with University of Wales Press in 2008 and *Modern Argentine Poetry: Displacement, Exile, Migration* in 2011. Alongside Dr Cornelia Graebner of Lancaster University, he coordinates the Poetics of Resistance research group. A volume of essays by its members was published by Peter Lang in 2011, entitled *Resistance and Emancipation: Cultural and Poetic Practices* (eds Bollig and Arturo Casas). His translations of the poetry of Cristian Aliaga appeared in a bilingual volume, *La causa clínica/The Clinical Cause* (Manchester Spanish and Portuguese Studies, 2011) and his other translations of poetry from Spanish have been published in various journals. He is an occasional contributor to *Guardian Weekly* and *El extremo sur de la Patagonia: Confines*, and has been an editor since 2003 of the *Journal of Latin American Cultural Studies*.

Robert Hariman is a professor of rhetoric and public culture in the Department of Communication Studies at Northwestern University, where currently he serves as chair of the department. He is the author of *Political Style: The Artistry of Power* (University of Chicago Press, 1995) and *No Caption Needed: Iconic Photographs, Public Culture, and Liberal Democracy* (University of Chicago Press, 2007), which is co-authored with John Louis Lucaites. He also has published several edited volumes and numerous journal articles in various disciplines, and his work has been translated into French and Chinese. He and co-author John Lucaites post regularly at www.nocaptionneeded.com, their blog on photojournalism, politics and culture.

E. Douglas Lewis (Ph.D., Australian National University), a native of Texas and educated at Rice and Brown universities, began his research on the peoples of Sikka on the island of Flores in eastern Indonesia in 1977. He has lectured on anthropology in universities in Australia and the United States and is currently Adjunct Professor of RMIT University, Melbourne, Australia, in the School of Global, Urban and Social Studies. His main subjects were kinship, alliance and social organization, the anthropology of religion, and the evolution and neurobiology of consciousness, language and mind. He is author of numerous essays and articles, mainly on the peoples of the Regency of Sikka on Flores. Among his books are *People of the Source: The Social and Ceremonial Order of Tana Wai Brama on Flores* (1988) and *Hikayat Kerajaan Sikka* [The Chronicles of the Rajadom of Sikka] (2008). He co-produced, with Timothy and Patsy Asch, *A Celebration of Origins* (1994), a film about ritual in the Tana 'Ai region of Sikka. His most recent book is *The Stranger-Kings of Sikka* (Leiden, KITLV Press, 2010).

Anthony Paul was born in North Wales and read English at New College, Oxford. He lectured on translation studies and English literature at the University of Amsterdam from 1972 to 2002. He is the author of *The Torture of the Mind: Macbeth, Tragedy and Chiasmus* (Amsterdam, 1992), several works of fiction, translations, including a collection of poems by the Frisian poet Obe Postma, *What the Poet Must Know* (2004), contributions to symposia on literary translation and Shakespeare, and much literary journalism. He contributed to *Culture and Rhetoric* (2009) and is co-editor with Boris Wiseman of the present volume. His most recent novel *More than a Dream* was published in 2013.

Philippe-Joseph Salazar was educated at Lycée Lyautey (Casablanca) and Louis-le-Grand (Paris), and is a graduate from École normale supérieure and the Sorbonne where he studied philosophy, anthropology and critical theory under Emmanuel Levinas and Roland Barthes. He is a sometime director in rhetoric and democracy at the Collège international de philosophie in Paris, founded by Jacques Derrida, and a distinguished professor of rhetoric and humane letters at the University of Cape Town, South Africa. Laureate in 2009 of the Harry Oppenheimer award, Africa's premier research prize, in recognition of his pioneering work in rhetoric studies.

Lucien Scubla is researcher in anthropology at CREA, Ecole polytechnique, Paris.

Ivo Strecker is Professor Emeritus of Cultural Anthropology at the Johannes Gutenberg University of Mainz, Germany. For over forty years he has done ethnographic research with the Hamar of southern Ethiopia, and in the course of time he has developed a growing interest in the relationship between rhetoric and culture. Together with Jean Lydall he has published *The Hamar of Southern Ethiopia* (1979). Further publications include *The Social Practice of Symbolization* (1988); *The Perils of Face* (edited with Jean Lydall, 2006); *Culture and Rhetoric* (edited with Stephen Tyler, 2009); and *Ethnographic Chiasmus* (2010).

Isabelle Thomas-Fogiel has been a professor at University Paris 1, Panthéon-Sorbonne, France, since 1997. She was invited professor, University of Montreal, Canada (2007–8) and is currently a Full Professor at the University of Ottawa. She has written about the philosophy of art, continental philosophy (German Idealism) and postmodernism. She is the author of five books: *Le concept et le lieu, figures de la relation entre art et philosophie* (Paris 2008); *Référence et autoréférence, étude sur le thème de la mort de la philosophie dans la pensée contemporaine* (Paris 2006; American translation, New York 2009); *Fichte, réflexion et argumentation* (Paris 2004); *Critique de la représentation* (Paris 2000); *Présentation de la doctrine de la science de Fichte* (Paris 1999).

Stephen Tyler is Herbert S. Autrey Professor of Anthropology (Emeritus) at Rice University, Houston, Texas. He received his Ph.D. in Anthropology at Stanford University after doing field work among the Koyas, a Dravidian-speaking tribe in Andhra Pradesh, India. Among his previous publications are: *Koya: An Outline Grammar. Gommu Dialect* (University of California Publications in Linguistics, vol. 54, 1968); *India: An Anthropological Perspective* (Pacific Palisades, California, 1973); *The Said and the Unsaid: Mind, Meaning and Culture* (New York 1978).

Alain Vanier, MD, Ph.D., is a member of Espace Analytique, an independent Lacanian group. He is professor, director of graduate studies and of the Centre de Recherches Psychanalyse, Médecine et Société (CRPMS) at University Paris Diderot, Paris. He is the author of books, such as *Lacan* (New York 2000), and many articles, including recently 'Fear, Paranoia and Politics', *The Psychoanalytic Review* 97(2); and 'The Object between Mother and Child: From Winnicott to Lacan', in *Between Winnicott and Lacan: A Clinical Engagement*, Lewis A. Kirshner ed. (New York and London 2011).

Phillip John Usher received his Ph.D. from Harvard University and is currently Assistant Professor of French and Comparative Literature at Barnard College, Columbia University. He is the author of *Errance et Cohérence: Essai sur la littérature transfrontalière à la Renaissance* (Paris 2010) and of an English translation of Ronsard's *La Franciade* (New York 2010). He is currently working on the relationship between epic and the sister arts in the French Renaissance.

Boris Wiseman is Associate Professor of French and Francophone Studies at Copenhagen University. He is the author of *Lévi-Strauss Anthropology and Aesthetics* (CUP 2007) and has edited two collections of essays on Lévi-Strauss, a special issue of *Les Temps modernes* (2004) and the *Cambridge Companion to Lévi-Strauss* (2009). He has co-edited, with Adriana Bontea, a special issue of the journal *Paragraph* 2011 (34.2) on the works of French philosopher Claude Imbert, *Claude Imbert in Perspective: Creation, Cognition and Modern Experience*; and with Anthony Paul this book *Chiasmus and Culture*. He has an interest in aesthetics and the senses, and is currently working on the visual capture of movement in nineteenth-century France.

Index

■ ■ ■ ■ ■ ■ ■